This edition first published in 2004 by Motorbooks International, an imprint of MBI Publishing Company, Galtier Plaza, Suite 200, 380 Jackson Street, St. Paul, MN 55101-3885 USA

Motorbooks International titles are also available at discounts in bulk quantity for industrial or sales-promotional use. For details write to Special Sales Manager at Motorbooks International Wholesalers & Distributors, Galtier Plaza, Suite 200, 380 Jackson Street, St. Paul, MN 55101-3885 USA.

ISBN 0-7603-1823-9

Edited by Dennis Pernu
Layout by Brenda Canales
Cover photograph by Peter Vincent

Printed in the United States of America

# The Ultimate HOT ROD Dictionary

# The Ultimate HOT ROD Dictionary

## A-BOMBS to ZOOMIES

**JEFF BREITENSTEIN**

*Illustrated by Troy Paiva*

**MOTORBOOKS**
INTERNATIONAL

# *Acknowledgments*

I n a way, I consider this book a body of information *by* the entire rodding community and *for* the entire rodding community. I'll be the first to admit that there are many people who know more about this subject than I do, and I've had the great pleasure of interviewing some of them in my information-gathering process. A number of these individuals border on celebrity or even legend status, but all treated me with genuine down-to-earth respect. It was a pretty cool thing.

So many people have graciously helped me with this book's creation that it's difficult to know where to begin. Perhaps the greatest contribution came from the project's illustrator, Troy Paiva. Without Troy's substantial talent and commitment, this book would never have been realized. In addition to Troy and his incredible artwork, a number of friends and new acquaintances really stood out by generously sharing their time, knowledge, and resources. My appreciation especially goes out to Ilene Roth, Moldy Marvin, and Bert Grimm of the Ed Roth estate, Jeanette Page, Jim "Butch" Sherry, Lou and Shiner McClenahan, Paul Flynn, Richard LeJuerrne, Fred Hartwell, Mike Lebenbaum, Keith "Big Daddy" Loomis, Tom Hanna, Tony Miller, Chris McCoy, Art Himsl, Dennis Prater, Greg Sharp, Dave Hartley, Rick Dore, Bob Ballew, Rodney Woolnough, Steve Mickens, Kirk Taylor, Mike Sanders, Rich Elliot, Paul Haun, Greg Taylor, Peter Vincent for the cover photo, and my MBI editor, Dennis Pernu.

Additional specialized information was thoughtfully provided by Gary Glasgow, Gordon Reynolds, Mike Durhan, Don Allen, Dean Hudson, Jim and Randy Salter, John Moses, Brett Barris, David Simon, John Peters, Gary Morales, Keith Weesner, Mike Mercado, Tim Oswald, Eric Dove, Rob St. Germain, Cliff Sheldon, Red Hamilton, and Maeva Bencich.

Just as important were the contributions of my family and many friends, who offered the encouragement and moral support needed to get me started and to keep me working when the going got tough. It's a wonder what a few kind words or a warm meal can do to inspire and motivate. Thanks so much to Ray and Dorothy Breitenstein, Steve Breitenstein, Gaby Stupp, Marian Choy, Joanne Lehmkuhl, Frank and Charlene Campos, Julie Paiva, "Johnny Raunch" McCrea, Marcia and Jerry Phillips, Cliff, Sylvia, Samantha and Natalie Jepsen, Chuck Linne, Heather Ireland, the troops at DHL (Sherri Milburn, Winston McDade, Mike Guele, Roberto Arteaga, Maria Tiongson, Louie Verano, and Mike Villanueva), Dr. "Cwittie" Hunter, Vic and Barbara Basuino, Ken Merrill, "Baby Rey" Bitter, Marcie Olivera, Steve and Lynda Basuino, Diann Cantwel, Charlie Campos, Bub and Liz Hartwell, Nora Tusin, Pat and Debbie Ickes, Delia Chi, Scott and Sharon Hagberg, Annie Gaw, and the guy who instigated this whole darn thing, my English 100 teacher, Jeff Goldthorpe.

Thank you all!

# *Introduction*

This whole thing started out as a relatively simple college term paper. Let's just say I'd been away from school for quite a few years and was taking a beginning English course at a local community college. For a final semester paper, our teacher loosened his normally rigid assignment parameters, setting us free to write about "anything to do with language." The idea came to me immediately. Why not write about the unique language of rods, customs, and drag racing, a topic that I had a genuine interest in? And, as an added bonus, I wouldn't have to do *any* new research, since I'd been busy with that task for the greater part of my life. I'd be beatin' and cheatin' the system in fine style.

In my paper I expounded at length on the rod and custom vernacular's cultural implications (blah, blah, blah), in the process getting an "A" on the paper and in the class. Everybody was happy, everything was cool. But, of course, that wasn't the end of the story.

As a sort of detached, insignificant (grade-wise anyway) addendum to the paper, I put together a little glossary of my own in a traditional dictionary format. I didn't get too far, maybe 40 entries, mostly because it wasn't really a required part of the assignment. In a preliminary draft, however, I had randomly lumped together several hundred slang terms and expressions. Seeing this original list kinda set Mr. Teacher to trippin'. I guess it must have really impressed him because he strongly encouraged me to "do something" with the material . . . and *that* is precisely how this book was born.

The concept of a "hot rod language" glossary is far from new. It's been realized many times in the past. Glossaries of rod and/or custom slang have often been included as supplements to books, on record album jackets, as parts of magazine articles, and even in conjunction with museum displays. While some have been well crafted and quite accurate, others have appeared haphazard in both style and content (obviously written by non-enthusiasts). Automotive journalism luminaries Pat Ganahl, Dean Batchelor, and Gray Baskerville have all done true justice to the subject. The earliest example that I've come across was published in the November 1948 issue of *Hot Rod,* during that magazine's first year of publication. Titled "Racing Jargon," the roughly one-page feature was broken down into categories: Engine, General; Engine Components & Accessories; Engine Rebuilding; Frame and Body; Miscellaneous Car Terms; and General Terms. It's interesting to note that overt slang is most often conspicuously absent from very early rodding publications, most likely because such a strong emphasis was placed on legitimizing the hobby at that time.

I found inspiration in these efforts and yet somehow always felt as though much more could and should be done with the subject. The most complete glossary that I'd encountered featured a "mere" 128 entries, while the smallest contained only 20 terms. Much more fascinating and colorful material lay waiting to be explored and documented. I found myself wondering why no one had attempted a truly comprehensive work on the topic. I became aware of a full-scope dictionary devoted to surfer slang, a dictionary of hip-hop terminology, and even a "hippie dictionary." Why hadn't anyone taken on the language of rodders? Maybe more experienced authors had a better understanding of how much time and effort a project like this would involve. As previously mentioned, I considered myself reasonably well versed on the subject before I began. It wasn't long before I was appropriately humbled. As I launched into actual research and writing, a world full of additional material and details came to light. From the perspective of this literary beginner, it's been truly a monumental undertaking . . . often challenging, sometimes frustrating, but always interesting and fulfilling.

The project's been a real treasure hunt from the outset. Hot rodding terms and expressions "are where you find them," as the saying goes. My greatest source of research has come in the form of magazine articles and books. I have access to an extensive collection of early hot rodding and customizing periodicals dating well back into the 1950s (thanks Fred and Augie!). Someday I hope to find time to read them all cover to cover, though I may have to wait for retirement on that one. With the more recent explosion of interest in hot rod and custom car heritage, modern magazine articles and books have become outstanding sources, as well. Naturally, the Internet has been an invaluable tool, and interviews with respected experts and "old timers" have contributed to the cause tremendously.

One of the first challenges that I faced with this project was establishing parameters. It's sometimes been a little tough to figure out where to draw the line—what is a truly unique colloquialism and what is more a part of mainstream speech? Some material clearly fits into both categories. In these cases, I asked myself, "Is this term or expression more often used by rodders than it is by the general public?" If the answer was yes, I typically included it, but I also sought to include any "mainstream" expressions that have an even slightly different meaning when used by hot rodders. In these situations, definitions are provided only for meanings that represent irregular or unique slang. To put this another way, a term like "driver" would not be defined as "any individual who drives a car," but rather only in the subculture-specific version of "a rod or custom car that sees extensive highway use."

I've also made a conscious decision to include only terms and expressions that are clearly automotive or "car culture" related. Of course, the term "car culture" is itself open to interpretation. Some might consider rockabilly music or retro clothing styles to be directly and unequivocally related to car culture. To my mind, however, these various cultures are not mutually inclusive—one does not necessarily need the other to exist. Though often related, they are at their essences different. In fact, practitioners of today's popular retro- and/or rat-rod movements (those most closely associated with tie-in cultures) echo this sentiment. As the modern yet ultratraditional *Hop Up* magazine's motto clearly states: "It's about the Iron."

While some culture-specific dictionaries include biographies of significant and relevant individuals as entries, for several reasons I've chosen not to follow this practice. My feeling is that people's names shouldn't be considered a part of a general language base. To express this argument another way, if a reader were to look up an important historical character like Abraham Lincoln in *Webster's Unabridged*, he'd surely be disappointed by Mr. Lincoln's absence. From a more practical standpoint, however, hot rodding's rich and colorful history has produced so many essential and historical characters that it would be very difficult to make decisions regarding inclusion or exclusion. Further, I have, in my own personal collection, two excellent and thorough books devoted exclusively to the brief biographies of hot rodding's most significant figures. In short, it's been done before.

Note: This expressed, I must clarify the exceptions within this work that prove the rule. In some instances, rodders' or customizers' names have come to take on truly expanded meanings. This is the case with both Kenneth "Von Dutch" Howard and Wally Parks. To that end, the dictionary's "Von Dutch" and "Wally" entries include definitions of non-personal meanings, as well as short bios of the actual individuals to help provide background and context.

I'd also like to explain my reasons for including materials that some readers may find vulgar or offensive. Dispersed throughout this work are a number of terms and expressions that either constitute outright profanity or suggest racist or sexist attitudes. To begin with, I would like to state that these do not necessarily represent my own personal views or opinions. My mission has been that of an objective lexicographer, with *objective* being the key word. I've really strived to work without brand, style, or character bias. Even the book's quotations are generally close interpretations of things that I have actually heard said through the years. I believe that rather than censoring or repressing any content, it is better to present the material in the most honest, complete, and accurate way possible, allowing the reader to make his or her own decisions about usage.

During the course of the writing process, it gradually occurred to me that it might be more interesting to expand somewhat beyond the curt, skeletal definitions typically offered by dictionaries. I often found myself asking, "So what? Why is this thing important? How is it significant?" In response to my own questions, I've tried to add a strong measure of historical content, cultural implications, and general trivia to the definitions. If the origins and/or time frames of expressions could be reasonably determined, I've attempted to include this information, as well. It's my consideration that these additions will provide the reader with a broader and more complete and interesting experience.

A final note: Despite my sincere efforts, this is obviously not a "complete" end-all reference work on the hot rod language. To create such would, of course, be a practical impossibility. Further, I strongly suspect that with such a high volume of information, it's a pretty safe bet that I've slipped up someplace. If this is the case, I apologize to the reader in advance. Whenever possible, I've tried to confirm or corroborate information through multiple sources, but even this doesn't always guarantee correctness. I have done the best job possible with the information available to me at the time of writing.

# A

**A**, see A-BONE

**A-body 1.** *n.* Official corporate designation for a series of General Motors intermediate-sized automobiles produced during the 1960s and 1970s MUSCLE CAR era. PERFORMANCE models sharing the GM A-BODY platform include the Chevrolet Chevelle SS, Pontiac GTO (see GOAT), Oldsmobile 442, and Buick Gran Sport and GS. **2.** *n.* Chrysler Corporation's designation for its series of compact models produced during the 1960s and 1970s MUSCLE CAR era. Significant FACTORY PERFORMANCE models based on the Chrysler A-BODY platform include the RACE HEMI-equipped Plymouth Barracuda (see HEMICUDA) and Dodge Dart DRAG cars of 1968, Dart GTS and Swinger models, Plymouth Duster 340, and Dodge Demon 340.

A-body[1]
1970 BUICK GSX

**A-bomb** *n.* Any Model A Ford (see A-bone) that has been extensively modified for improved performance. A HOT ROD Model A.

**A-bone** *n.* Any Model A Ford. Produced from 1928 through 1931, the ubiquitous and adaptable Model A has maintained perennial favor as a foundation for high-performance and HOT ROD modification. Model A's were produced in two general series, with 1928 and 1929 models being very similar and the substantially restyled 1930 models being carried over to 1931 with only minor changes. Because of this, it is common for hot rodders to use the expressions "'28–'29 A" or "'30–'31 A." Note that Ford Motor Company's first production vehicle, introduced in 1903, was also designated Model A, but given its very early period of manufacture and relatively low production numbers the type had virtually no relevance in hot rodding.

**acid-dipped** *adj.* Dipped in a liquid acid solution to reduce metal thickness and, as a consequence, weight. Generally relates to steel, FACTORY-produced auto bodies used in mid-1960s DRAG racing applications (prior to the proliferation of custom and AFTERMARKET fiberglass [see 'GLASS] and carbon fiber replica bodies).

**Aero Warrior** (AIR-oh) *n.* Any aerodynamically enhanced PERFORMANCE model produced exclusively for STOCK CAR racing or STOCK CAR racing homologation during the AERO WARS period. Examples of AERO WARRIORS include the 1969 Dodge Charger 500 and Dodge Charger Daytona, the 1969 Ford Torino Talladega (see DROOP-SNOOT) and Mercury Cyclone Spoiler II (see DROOP-SNOOT), and the 1970 Plymouth Superbird (see 'BIRD).

Aero Warrior
1969 DODGE
CHARGER DAYTONA

**Aero Wars** (AIR-oh) *n.* The intense STOCK CAR racing rivalry between Ford Motor Company and Chrysler Corporation during the 1969 and

1970 NASCAR seasons, resulting in the creation of limited-edition aerodynamically enhanced racing and production vehicles (AERO WARRIORS). The type culminated with the radical Dodge Charger Daytona of 1969 and Plymouth Superbird of 1970 (see 'BIRD), each featuring a dramatically extended nosepiece and tall airfoil mounted above its rear DECK LID. In the interests of driver safety (through overall speed reduction) and increased competitiveness from non-represented manufacturers, the AERO WARRIOR cars were effectively outlawed by NASCAR beginning with the 1971 season.

**aftermarket** *adj.* Relating to any non-OEM automotive part or component. A replacement part manufactured and marketed by any producer other than an original automobile manufacturer. In its hot rodding context, the term AFTERMARKET is most often used to describe performance-enhancing speed equipment.

**air dam** *n.* GROUND EFFECTS device similar to a CHIN SPOILER but extending closer the ground and usually featuring a more vertical, blunt inclination.

**airstripper** *n.* Early-1950s term for any purpose-built, maximum-performance DRAG racing vehicle (see AIRSTRIP RACING).

**airstrip racing** *n.* Early-1950s term for organized DRAG racing. Term derived from the fact that many early DRAG meets were held on abandoned or out-of-service airport landing strips.

**Alcohol's for drinking, gasoline's for washing parts, and nitromethane's for racing.** Expression of preference for NITRO racing fuel over methanol or gasoline for its quality of producing absolute maximum performance.

**alky** (AL-kee) *n.* Any methyl alcohol (Methanol) racing fuel. Alcohol yields tremendous performance benefits over gasoline by burning more coolly, thereby providing a much denser fuel mixture and allowing for substantially higher compression ratios (see SQUEEZE). While methanol was used in circle-track racing applications from the early part of the twentieth century, HOT RODDERS were commonly running the fuel on the DRY LAKES by the 1940s. When organized DRAG racing was first popularized during the early 1950s, the new sport adopted the use of methanol. With the exception of the FUEL BAN years, alcohol-burning competition classes have figured prominently in DRAG racing history.

**all engine** *adj.* Relating to any very small, lightweight vehicle powered by an exceptionally large (physical size and/or displacement) engine. Traditionally used to describe a vehicle that is substantially to ridiculously overpowered for its size and weight.

**all motor** *adj.* Relating to any PERFORMANCE vehicle or PERFORMANCE engine operating in a fully NATURALLY ASPIRATED state (as differentiated from one employing a POWER ADDER like a supercharger [see BLOWER], turbocharger [see TURBO], or nitrous oxide injection [see NITROUS]). The term ALL MOTOR often carries with it a tone of pride or superiority, implying that the use of a POWER ADDER is somehow superficial or even constitutes a type of "cheating." The term has experienced its strongest popularity at the turn of the twenty-first century.

**AMBR** (pronounced as separate letters) *n.* The America's Most Beautiful ROADSTER award as presented each year at the *Grand National Roadster Show* (see OAKLAND ROADSTER SHOW). The AMBR title was first awarded in 1950 to bodyman and RODDER Bill NieKamp for his extensively modified 1929 Ford ROADSTER (no AMBR award was given at OAKLAND's inaugural 1949 event). NieKamp's Model A (see A-BONE) featured a shortened and CHANNELED body, 1927 Essex frame RAILS, full BELLY PAN, custom three-piece hood, custom aluminum TRACK NOSE, hopped-up 1942 Mercury FLATHEAD V8, blue leather upholstery, and ocean-blue paint. Besides winning OAKLAND's BIG TROPHY, NieKamp's ROADSTER managed an outstanding 142 miles per hour at EL MIRAGE.

BILL NIEKAMP'S
**AMBR**-WINNING ROADSTER

**angel hair** (also **angel's hair**) *n.* White, cotton-like material used to enhance the appearance of a HOT ROD or CUSTOM CAR's interior space or the overall look of an automotive show display. Available in sheet form, ANGEL HAIR is sometimes employed as an automotive headliner, rear package tray covering, and dashboard appliqué. In a typical car show presentation, it is fluffed and spread liberally around the base of a vehicle to imply that the subject is floating in a sea or cloud of ethereal mist. ANGEL HAIR is also sometimes spread around the full circumference of rear tires in an imitation of rubber-burning smoke. Since achieving its greatest popularity during the early-1960s, ANGEL HAIR has most often been perceived as being in poor taste by HOT RODDERS and CUSTOMIZERS.

**angle channel**, see WEDGE CHANNEL

**angle chop**, see WEDGE CHOP

**ankle-burners**, see FLAMETHROWERS

**A-pillar** *n.* An integral body member or structural post supporting a vehicle's top at a point where it meets the windshield.

**asphalt eater** *n.* Any exceptionally FAST or QUICK vehicle. Term most popular during the 1950s and 1960s.

**ass end**, see REAREND

**ass-end gears** *n.* Any automotive rear axle's final-drive ratio gear set (see REAREND).

Auburn dash panel[1]

**Auburn dash panel 1.** *n.* (also **Auburn dash**) Any dashboard instrument panel as originally installed on 1931 through 1933 Auburn automobiles. The classic AUBURN DASH PANEL featured a simple-but-elegant, generally rectangular style accommodating five gauges in a straight inline configuration. A large central speedometer was flanked on each side by two smaller instruments (water temperature, fuel level, amperes, and oil pressure). Beginning in the late 1930s, AUBURN DASH PANELS were commonly swapped into contemporary HOP UPS/HOT RODS as a relatively inexpensive and attractive means of attaining comprehensive instrumentation. The STOCK dashboards of HOT ROD type vehicles (most often 1920s and 1930s vintage Fords) were necessarily modified by the dropping or extending of their lower edges to accomodate the larger Auburn panels. As an alternative, entirely custom dashes were sometimes also created. The AUBURN DASH PANEL's popularity peaked during the 1940s and declined following the early 1950s. During the 1990s and into the twenty-first century, original AUBURN DASH PANELS have proven highly desirable additions to traditionally styled RETRO RODS. **2.** *n.* Any complete 1931 through 1933 Auburn dashboard (including full-width sheet metal panel and instrument cluster) as modified and adapted to a hot rodding application.

**auto** *n.* Any automotive automatic transmission.

**A-V8** (pronounced as separate letters) *n.* Any Model A Ford (see A-BONE) equipped with a V8 engine. Model A's were FACTORY-produced with FLATHEAD four-cylinders exclusively, making any V8 substitution a matter of custom fabrication. Though 1932 and later model Ford ROADSTERS were commonly raced in early DRY LAKES competition, 1928 and 1929 A-V8s were especially preferred for their lighter weight and smaller frontal area. The A-V8 term was most often used during hot rodding's formative years (1930s through 1950s) to describe the then-popular FLATHEAD Ford V8-into-Model A chassis conversion.

**AWB**
1965 DODGE FUNNY CAR

**AWB** (usually written, not spoken) *n.* Altered WHEELBASE. Automotive modification serving to shift axle/spindle centerline positions (and, as a consequence, wheels) farther forward than would be normal in a regular production vehicle. AWB modifications were most commonly performed to full-bodied DRAG racing SEDANS of the mid-1960s to enhance WEIGHT TRANSFER characteristics and thus traction.

**Awful Awful** *n.* Any AA-series FUEL ALTERED DRAG racing vehicle. The letters AA (the obvious inspiration for the AWFUL AWFUL nickname) represented the fastest of the 1960s through early-1970s Altered racing classes. While a single "A" class designation denoted the most potent engine displacement to overall car weight ratio permitted, the addition of a second "A" allowed for the inclusion of a supercharger (see BLOWER) in the package.

# B

**babbitt pounder** (also **babbitt beater**) *n.* Derogatory, generally 1950s-era term for any Chevrolet inline six-cylinder engine using bearings of a type by then considered archaic. The type's BABBITT POUNDER name was derived from its unique sound, a consequence of the low-pressure, oiling system employed to accommodate those bearings. Commonly used in early automotive engines, these "babbitt-type" bearings were made by pouring molten "babbitt" (a malleable metallic compound) onto crankshaft and connecting-rod journal surfaces, then machining the resulting bearings to precise tolerances, a process that differed significantly from the one used to manufacture modern insert-type bearings. At the height of the term's popularity, the Chevrolet SIX was a reasonably popular PERFORMANCE alternative to the FLATHEAD Ford V8.

**baby Hemi** *n.* Any EARLY HEMI engine produced by Chrysler Corporation's Dodge and DeSoto divisions (Plymouth never offered an EARLY HEMI, relying instead on a less-expensive polyspherical HEAD design). The type's BABY HEMI name is derived from its relatively small physical size and internal displacement when compared with Chrysler's other HEMI offerings. While somewhat overshadowed by their larger Chrysler division counterparts, the Dodge and DeSoto EARLY HEMIS were each produced in high-performance variations and were considerably popular in racing and hot rodding applications.

**baby moons** *n.* Chrome hubcap type featuring a completely smooth, brightmetal convex surface and relatively small size (BABY MOONS cover only the center portion of a steel wheel). The term and style both experienced their greatest popularity during the 1950s and 1960s.

the **back door** *n.* The finish line or BIG END timing TRAPS of any DRAGSTRIP.

**back half 1.** *n.* The rear half of any vehicle's chassis structure along with any immediately related body components, which may include the rear portion of an automotive frame, differential (see REAREND), rear suspension components, fuel tank, sheetmetal trunk floor and wheelwells, rear tires, and wheels. In order to maximize any production vehicle's DRAG racing potential, its BACK HALF must be significantly reconstructed to provide added durability and improve its traction properties. **2.** *v.* To significantly modify any STOCK vehicle by reconfiguring its rear-half components for improved DRAG racing performance. Such modifications generally include narrowing the rear frame structure to provide clearance for exceptionally large rear tires and wheels; installing a durable, high-performance REAREND (also narrowed for tire/wheel clearance); modifying or replacing the STOCK fuel tank; installing WHEEL TUBS to provide adequate tire/wheel clearance; and replacing STOCK suspension components with a high-performance system (sometimes including WHEELIE BARS). Example: "If you're really serious about going FAST, you're eventually gonna have to BACK HALF the car."

**back it up** *v.* In DRAG or LAND-SPEED RACING, to follow up a record-setting (either ET or speed) PASS or RUN with a similar performance to make the record official.

**backlight** *n.* Any automotive rear-window glass. Originally a manufacturer's or industry term, BACKLIGHT is often used by RODDERS and CUSTOMIZERS who are especially conscious of automotive aesthetic and design principles.

**back-pedal** *v.* To partially release or reduce throttle during the course of a DRAG RACE, generally to either avoid breaking out (see BREAK OUT) or to gain traction.

**bagged** *adj.* Equipped with a custom airbag suspension system. Airbags (or alternately airsprings) replace or augment conventional automotive suspension springs to improve ride quality and provide an easily adjustable RIDE HEIGHT. Constructed of rubber and high-strength fabric, airbags create an actual type of spring when inflated with air. By releasing air from a system's bags, a vehicle may be instantaneously dropped to give an exceptionally low, visually appealing STANCE. When a more practical, roadworthy RIDE HEIGHT is desired, air is added to the springs to raise the vehicle in a matter of seconds. For convenience and versatility, most systems include an onboard air compressor and storage tank. Airbags have experienced strong popularity in STREET ROD, CUSTOM CAR, and various STREET MACHINE applications during the late-1990s and at the turn of twenty-first century. The airbag principle was adapted from its use in semitrucks, luxury cars, and industrial equipment.

**Bakersfield**, see MARCH MEET

**balanced** *adj.* Relating to any automotive engine or engine subassembly that has been painstakingly brought into precise weight tolerances to improve its overall, and especially high-RPM, performance.

**baldy caps** (also **baldies**) *n.* General term for any AFTERMARKET hubcap type with a smooth, unadorned convex surface. Most often used in reference to BABY MOON hubcaps.

**balls** *n.* Power. Horsepower or torque as produced by any engine.

**baloneys 1.** *n.* Any automotive tires, but especially the large rear tires of a HOT ROD or DRAG racing vehicle. **2.** *n.* Any appreciably worn-out or "bald" automotive tires.

**bang a blower** *v.* To experience a moderate-to-strong fuel backfire within a supercharged engine's BLOWER case and intake manifold. Although not as destructive as a true BLOWER EXPLOSION, to BANG A BLOWER can nevertheless cause significant damage to the BLOWER, INTAKE, and related components.

**'banger** (also **banger**) *n.* An abbreviation of the term FOUR BANGER. May refer to virtually any four-cylinder automotive engine but is most often used to describe the FOURS produced during the 1920s and 1930s (the first engines to be commonly PERFORMANCE-modified by HOT RODDERS).

**banjo rearend 1.** (also **banjo**) *n.* Early REAREND type featuring an overall shape (including integral torque tube) resembling an actual banjo. In its hot rodding context, the term BANJO REAREND most often refers to a Ford product produced from the 1928 through 1948 model years. Commonly featured on HOT RODS into the 1960s era. **2.** *n.* Any modern REAREND of a front-loading (Hotchkiss) design. In this usage, the banjo reference describes the housing's round center section in conjunction with one of the unit's two axle tubes. [Rare]

**banjo steering wheel** (also **banjo wheel**) **1.** *n.* Unique steering wheel type available on various Ford passenger cars during the 1936 through 1939 model years. Its distinctive styling incorporates three groups of five narrow spokes, reminiscent of a banjo's five strings. Commonly featured on the HOP UPS and HOT RODS of the late 1930s and 1940s. **2.** *n.* Any non-Ford or AFTERMARKET steering wheel incorporating the basic design elements found in the original Ford BANJO WHEEL.

1939 FORD
banjo steering wheel[1]

**banzai run** (BAWN-zai) *n.* Any all-out competition DRAG racing PASS applying the most aggressive fuel mixture, engine/chassis tuning, and driving style possible. Most commonly used during the 1960s.

**barefoot pedal**, see SURFER PEDAL

**bark the tires** *v.* To break traction in an abrupt but loud manner either by accelerating from a standing start or as an upshift SCRATCH. Term derived from the resulting sound, similar to that of a dog's bark.

**barn car** (also **barnster**) *n.* Any vehicle that has been stored away for a long period of time in a rural barn or similar structure. Often features a somewhat rough and patinated overall appearance, but nonetheless remains in an appreciably complete, original, and unmolested condition. Auto restorers, collectors, and HOT RODDERS generally consider a BARN CAR to be a very desirable find.

**barn-door aerodynamics** *n.* Any exceptionally poor automotive aerodynamics, but most often used to describe the large, broad frontal areas typical to many early production vehicles. A major detriment in LAND-SPEED RACING and high-speed DRAG racing applications.

**barrel** (also **barrel ass** or **barrel along**), see HAUL

**bash** *n.* Any DRAG RACE. Most often used during the 1960s in its MATCH BASH context.

**basket case** *n.* Any vehicle or major vehicle system that has been completely disassembled for the purposes of renovation or restoration. The term BASKET CASE typically refers to a project that has sat idle for a long period of time and is in the process of changing ownership, with various small parts being collected together in a "basket" for transportation.

**bathtub** *n.* Early expression for any PHAETON model automobile (later, generally supplanted by the alternative slang term TUB). Name derived from vehicle's likeness to an actual bathtub when its top is lowered or removed altogether.

**BBC** (usually written, not spoken) *n.* Any BIG-BLOCK CHEVY engine (see RAT).

**bbl** (usually written, not spoken) *n.* Abbreviation for the term "barrel" as commonly used in reference to the venturis within an automotive carburetor (see CARB). Abbreviation is also employed by the oil and petroleum industries to represent the volumetric unit of one barrel (42 U.S. gallons).

B-body[2]
1994 IMPALA SS

**B-body 1.** *n.* Chrysler Corporation's designation for its series of intermediate-sized automobiles produced throughout the 1960s and 1970s MUSCLE CAR era. Significant PERFORMANCE models sharing the Chrysler B-BODY platform include the Plymouth MAX WEDGE-powered Savoy and Belvedere SEDANS, Plymouth GTX (see X), Plymouth Road Runner (see BIRD), Plymouth Superbird (see 'BIRD), Dodge MAX WEDGE-powered Dart and 330 SEDANS, Dodge Coronet R/T, Dodge Super Bee (see BEE), and Dodge Charger Daytona. **2.** *n.* Official corporate designation for a series of General Motors full-sized models produced from the early 1960s to the mid-1990s. Although GM created many PERFORMANCE-oriented B-bodies during the 1960s through 1970s MUSCLE CAR era (based on the Pontiac Catalina [see CAT], Pontiac Grand Prix [see GP], Chevrolet Impala [see IMPY], Chevrolet Bel Air, Chevrolet Biscayne [see BISCUIT], etc.), the B-BODY term, in its General Motors context, is most often used to describe the popular full-sized Chevrolets of the 1990s. As a final encore to its high-performance, rear-drive V8 SEDAN production, Chevrolet released the Impala SS for the 1994 through 1996 model years. Powered by a potent 260-BHP, 350-CID LT1 engine, the mid-1990s Impala SS recaptured the essential character of the first Impala SS produced in 1961.

the **Beach** *n.* Lions Associated Dragstrip. Located in Wilmington, California, Lions, or LADS as it was alternately referred to, remained an extremely popular drag racing venue from its 1955 inception until its closing in 1972. Always innovative, Lions pioneered the Jr. Fuel class, ET bracket racing, and a hanging-light precursor to the Christmas Tree starting system. Lions managers included such notables as Mickey Thompson, C. J. "Pappy" Hart, and Steve Evans. The track's Beach name was derived from Wilmington's close proximity to the city of Long Beach.

the **Beach**
Lions Dragstrip logo

**beam axle** (also **beam** or **I-beam**) *n.* Any automotive front axle featuring the cross-sectional shape of an I-beam. Most early American production automobiles featured beam axle-based front suspensions until the type was eclipsed by smoother-riding independent frontends, generally during the 1930s and 1940s. Historically, the beam axle has been the standard foundation of the hot rod front suspension, and although largely replaced by the tube axle since the 1960s, it is still preferred in many hot rodding applications for its traditional appearance (especially when it is drilled for lightening and/or features a significant drop).

**beans** *n.* Power. Horsepower or torque as produced by any engine.

**beast** *n.* Any exceptionally powerful, quick, or fast vehicle. Term experienced its greatest popularity during the 1950s.

**beat** (also **beat-down**), see chopped

**beater** *n.* Any old, substantially dilapidated vehicle. At the turn of the twenty-first century, enthusiasts have commonly and popularly used the term by to describe rat rod-type vehicles.

**beauty rings** *n.* Any brightmetal automotive wheel trim rings. Appearance enhancing beauty rings affix to the outside rim of each wheel and are most often used in conjunction with some form of hubcaps (caps 'n' rings).

**Bee** *n.* Any Dodge Super Bee model performance car. Closely related to its Plymouth Road Runner (see Bird) counterpart, the Super Bee was introduced for the 1968 model year as a low-budget, stripped-down muscle car. From 1968 through 1970, Super Bees were based on the intermediate Coronet model, but for 1971 the Bee shared sheetmetal with the Dodge Charger. As with the Road Runner, a warmed-up version of the 383-cid V8 was standard power for the Super Bee, but available motors ranged to the renowned 426-cid street Hemi. Never achieving the same popularity as the Road Runner, the Super Bee was discontinued following the 1971 model year.

**beehive**
OIL FILTER CANISTER

**beehive** (also **beehive oil filter**) *n.* Any AFTERMARKET finned-aluminum oil filter canister as significantly popularized during the 1940s and 1950s. The type features a generally cylindrical shape with rows of horizontal cooling fins, creating a beehive-like appearance. Remotely mounted (most often to a vehicle's firewall), BEEHIVE canisters were traditionally favored for their appearance as well as function, and have been more recently fitted to the RETRO RODS and RAT RODS of the 1990s and early twenty-first century.

**Beep-Beep horn** *n.* Distinctive automotive horn featured as standard equipment on all Plymouth Road Runner models (see BIRD). As a unique marketing gimmick, the Road Runner's BEEP-BEEP HORN actually imitated the sound made by the popular Warner Brothers cartoon character. From 1969 through 1980, BEEP-BEEP HORNS were painted a light lavender color and featured a special "Voice of road runner" decal.

**Bellflower cruiser** (also **Bellflower Boulevard cruiser or Bellflower custom**) *n.* CUSTOM CAR type appreciably developed during the 1960s in and around the Southern California community of Bellflower. As the popularity of traditional Anglo-culture CUSTOM CARS dramatically waned through the 1960s, localized CUSTOMIZERS perpetuated the type with their unique adaptation to the classic style. Typical BELLFLOWER CRUISER characteristics included 1950s- or 1960s-era, full-size domestic automobile platform; mild custom body modifications; elaborate custom paint schemes; radically lowered body through suspension modifications; Astro Supreme chrome FIVE-SPOKES or Buick Skylark wire wheels (see SKYLARK WIRES); narrow-band whitewall tires; and BELLFLOWER TIPS.

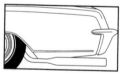

**Bellflower tip**

**Bellflower tips** *n.* Exhaust tip type initially popularized as a feature of the 1960s-era BELLFLOWER CRUISER CUSTOM CAR. In the classic BELLFLOWER TIP installation, an exhaust tailpipe exits the vehicle's underside immediately behind the rear wheel, then curves rearward, tracing a straight line beneath the rear quarter panel until terminating at the rear bumper. The final, straight segment of a BELLFLOWER TIP is flared to a larger diameter, chrome plated, and finished in a PENCIL TIP.

**bells** *n.* Any grouping or series of exhaust pipes with tips flared in the shape of bells.

**belly button** *n.* Sometimes used by RODDERS to describe Chevrolet's SMALL-BLOCK V8 engine (see MOUSE). The SBC's exceptional popularity has led some to disparage it as ordinary, mundane, or uninteresting. The BELLY BUTTON reference suggests that the engine is so common that, like a navel, "everybody has one."

**belly pan** *n.* Sheetmetal body panel, custom fabricated to tightly conform to the underside of a racing vehicle. Often used to streamline a vehicle's chassis area in LAND-SPEED RACING applications.

**belly tank** (also **belly tanker** or **tank**) *n*. LAND-SPEED RACING vehicle with body constructed from a World War II fighter aircraft auxiliary fuel tank. Though the 165-gallon tanks carried under P-51 Mustang and P-47 Thunderbolt fighters saw some limited use, by far the most popular was the P-38 Lightning's 315-gallon tank. The first BELLY TANK STREAMLINER (the type was later reclassified as a LAKESTER) was created by HOT RODDERS Bill Burke and Don Francisco in 1946. Powered by a 1934 FLATHEAD Ford V8, the front-engined car set a 131-mile-per-hour record on EL MIRAGE dry lake. A succession of imitators followed, with TANKS achieving outstanding performance levels throughout the 1950s and beyond.

**belly tank** LAKESTER

**beltline** *n*. On any vehicle, the horizontal division between the main body structure and the smaller glass or GREENHOUSE area covering the passenger compartment.

**bench race** *v*. To discuss HOT RODS, DRAG racing, or motorsports in a relaxed, social context or manner. Derived from the concept that the participants are sitting on an actual bench at an arbitrary location away from any vehicles. Example: "We'll have to get together and BENCH RACE over a couple of beers."

**bend the throttle** *v*. To aggressively run an engine or vehicle at full throttle.

**bent eight** *n*. Early expression for any eight-cylinder engine in a "V" configuration (see V8). Typically used during or prior to the 1950s mass-proliferation of the V8 engine.

**bhp** (usually written, not spoken) *n*. Brake horsepower. The common measurement of an engine's power output, brake horsepower is registered on an engine dynamometer. Integral to the dynamometer, a "brake" instrument resists the rotational energy of a running engine's output shaft, thereby measuring power levels.

**big arm** *adj*. Traditional HOT RODDER term relating to any relatively long engine STROKE.

**big-block** *n*. Any V8 engine featuring a relatively large physical size and internal displacement (generally between 350 and 450 CID). The term BIG-BLOCK is most often used to differentiate between various engine series produced by a single manufacturer. For example, Chrysler Corporation's LA Series engines produced in 273- through 360-CID forms are generally referred to as SMALL-BLOCKS, while Chrysler's B and RB Series engines produced in 350- through 440-CID variations are considered BIG-BLOCKS.

**big cam** *n*. Any significantly high-performance camshaft (see CAM). Derived from the physically larger size of a PERFORMANCE CAM's lobes when compared to those of a corresponding low-performance model. Example: "He's just runnin' the usual GO-FAST GOODIES . . . INTAKE, HEADERS, CARB, BIG CAM . . . nothin' especially TRICK."

**big Chevy** *n.* Any BIG-BLOCK CHEVY engine (see RAT).

**big-cube** *adj.* Relating to any exceptionally large displacement engine.

the **big end** *n.* The finish line and adjacent area of any DRAGSTRIP. Example: "With the way the thing's geared, it's not much OFF THE LINE, but it comes on strong on the BIG END."

the **Big Go** *n.* The NHRA National Championship DRAG RACES, the premier annual NHRA-sanctioned DRAG racing meet. The first BIG GO was presented in Great Bend, Kansas, over the 1955 Labor Day weekend, and the Labor Day tradition persists to the present day. In the following years, the NATS were held at a variety of centrally located venues before finding a permanent home at the Indianapolis Raceway Park in 1961 (see INDY).

the **Big Go, West** *n.* The NHRA Winternationals, the organization's season-opening DRAG meet. The Winternationals have been held annually from 1961 to the present day at the Los Angeles County Fairgrounds (Pomona Raceway) in Pomona, California.

**big 'n' littles** *n.* Any very large rear tire/wheel combination and very small front tire/wheel combination as run together on the same HOT ROD, STREET MACHINE, or DRAG racing vehicle. BIG 'N' LITTLES have traditionally been popularized both for appearance and for practical DRAG RACE function. In DRAG racing, wide and tall rear tires provide greater traction, while narrow and relatively short front tires reduce rolling resistance and weight. The term BIG 'N' LITTLES may also relate to the short front tire/tall rear tire configuration as originally popularized in early dry lakes (see the LAKES) racing applications. Lakes racers valued tall rear RUBBER for its quality of raising overall final drive ratio; higher practical gearing served to produce greater TOP END speeds on the LAKES.

THE GRAND NATIONAL
ROADSTER SHOW'S
**Big Trophy**

the **Big Trophy** *n.* Single "perpetual" trophy as presented to each year's AMBR winner at the prestigious GRAND NATIONAL ROADSTER SHOW (see OAKLAND ROADSTER SHOW). Created for show promoter Al Slonaker by the Dodge Trophy Company, the 9-foot-tall trophy was the largest in the world when first awarded in 1950. The names of each year's AMBR winners are inscribed in plaques affixed to the BIG TROPHY's base.

**big-window 1.** *n.* Any 1956 Ford F-100 pickup truck (see EFFIE) featuring a large wraparound rear window, the most coveted of all F-100 models. **2.** *n.* Any vehicle featuring an exceptionally large rear BACKLIGHT. Term in this sense is generally used only when a given model was produced in both small- and large-window configurations. Chevrolet's "Task Force" series light trucks of 1955 through 1959 (also highly popular in street rodding applications) were all available as small and BIG-WINDOWS, with the BIG-WINDOW being a part of the upscale "deluxe" model option package. **3.** *adj.* Relating to any vehicle model featuring an exceptionally large rear BACKLIGHT.

**billboard stripes** (also **billboards**) *n.* Exceptionally large graphic stripe treatment, optionally available on high-performance Plymouth 'CUDAS during the 1971 model year. BILLBOARD STRIPES consist of broad white or black decals covering nearly the entire surface of each rear quarter panel. The forward portion of each stripe is tapered and terminates at the vehicle's numerical engine displacement (or in the case of 426 HEMI-equipped cars, simply the word HEMI) represented in the door area.

'CUDA **billboard stripe**

**billet** (BILL-et) **1.** *adj.* Relating to any automotive part or component that has been machined from a solid block, or "blank," of metal. In street rodding applications, BILLET components are generally aluminum, tend to possess a precise, ultramodern appearance, and are a principal element of the 1980s and 1990s HIGH-TECH HOT ROD or CUSTOM CAR style. BILLET parts may feature a low-sheen "brushed" finish or be polished to a high luster. **2.** *n.* A solid block, or "blank," of metal.

CUSTOM **billet**[1] WHEEL

**billet rod** *n.* Any HIGH-TECH-styled HOT ROD featuring an abundance of BILLET parts.

**billets** (also **billet wheels**) *n.* Any complete set of HIGH-TECH BILLET aluminum wheels as featured on a HOT ROD, CUSTOM CAR, or STREET MACHINE. Example: "Those 24-inch BILLETS really make the car."

**binders** *n.* Traditional HOT RODDER'S expression for any automotive brakes or braking system.

**Bird** *n.* Any Plymouth Road Runner model. Introduced for the 1968 model year, the original Road Runner was a low-priced, no-frills MUSCLE CAR based on the Chrysler intermediate B-BODY platform. Early Road Runners came with a high-performance version of the venerable Chrysler 383-CID V8 as standard equipment, while optionally available POWERPLANTS included the 440-CID SIX-BARREL and the legendary 426-CID STREET HEMI. From 1976 until its 1980 demise, the Road Runner was relegated to a model within the prosaic Volare series.

**'Bird 1.** *n.* Any Ford Thunderbird model (see T-BIRD). **2.** *n.* Any Pontiac Firebird PONY CAR. Produced from 1967 through 2002, the Firebird shared its General Motors F-BODY platform with the Chevrolet Camaro. Important Firebird and Firebird-based PERFORMANCE types include the Trans Am (see T/A), Formula, RAM AIR, and SD-455. **3.** *n.* Any Plymouth

**'Bird²**
1969 Firebird Ram Air
convertible

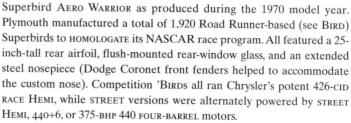

Superbird Aero Warrior as produced during the 1970 model year. Plymouth manufactured a total of 1,920 Road Runner-based (see Bird) Superbirds to homologate its NASCAR race program. All featured a 25-inch-tall rear airfoil, flush-mounted rear-window glass, and an extended steel nosepiece (Dodge Coronet front fenders helped to accommodate the custom nose). Competition 'Birds all ran Chrysler's potent 426-cid race Hemi, while street versions were alternately powered by street Hemi, 440+6, or 375-bhp 440 four-barrel motors.

**bird catcher,** see bug catcher

**biscuit**
1965 big-block Biscayne

**biscuit** *n.* Any Chevrolet Biscayne model. Replacing 1957's Two-Ten Series, the Biscayne was introduced as Chevrolet's mid-priced passenger car for the restyled 1958 model year. From 1959 through the 1972 end of its production run, the Biscayne was downgraded to Chevy's lowest priced full-size model. All Biscaynes included the signature elements of the true stripper type: conventional sedan (see post) design and bare-bones, no-frills light weight. When equipped with maximum-performance drivetrain options (e.g., W Series [see lumpy head] and later Mark IV [see rat] big-blocks), the humble Biscaynes represented a logical choice for full-size performance and racing applications.

**bite 1.** *n.* The straight-line, driven-wheel traction necessary in drag racing. **2.** *n.* Any automotive tire-to-road surface traction.

**blacky carbon** *n.* Gasoline. Term was most often used in drag racing applications during the 1950s and 1960s.

**blast,** see shot

**blat** *n.* Any classic throaty, rumbling exhaust sound. Often used in relation to flathead engines and/or glass-pack mufflers.

**blaze the tires,** see burn rubber

**blip the throttle** *v.* To apply a short, abrupt burst of throttle.

**block** *n.* Any automotive cylinder block, the essential foundation of all piston-type, internal-combustion engines. Most often made of cast iron, a cylinder block is a large, angular "block" significantly including the engine's cylinders (a series of long holes cast and machined into the block), supporting journals for the crankshaft (see crank) and often the camshaft (see cam), passages for motor oil and (usually) coolant, and various mounting surfaces for additional parts and components.

**blockhuggers** *n.* Type of exhaust headers configured to fit very closely to the sides of a cylinder block (see block). Commonly used in street rodding applications where the combination of a narrow, early-model chassis and a large, late-model V8 engine require a tight-fitting exhaust system.

**blow apart** *v.* To completely disassemble an automobile or major automotive system. Term is frequently used to describe one of the final stages in a labor-intensive custom or restoration project; after all major construction and/or fabrication work has been completed, the restorer or CUSTOMIZER will often BLOW APART the vehicle to facilitate the painting and final finishing of all components prior to the project's ultimate reassembly.

**blow** someone's **doors off** (also **blow** someone **off** or **blow off** someone) *v.* To soundly beat an opponent in a DRAG RACE. From the fantastic concept that a faster vehicle may pass a slower one with such velocity that the slower vehicle's doors will be "blown off" in the resulting turbulence or vacuum.

**blower** *n.* Any automotive positive-displacement supercharger. A supercharger is a mechanical pump serving to force greater volumes of air/fuel mixture into a running engine, thereby improving overall engine efficiency and increasing power output. Although several supercharger types have historically been utilized in hot rodding applications, the Roots style has virtually dominated the field since the 1960s. Named for the Roots brothers, who pioneered the use of air-moving pumps in industrial applications, the Roots "blower" concept was originally used in the late 1800s to ventilate mine shafts. During the late 1950s, HOT RODDERS began to commonly adapt GMC (later Detroit Diesel) Roots-type BLOWERs to their V8 engines. Initially produced to complement two-cycle diesel engines, GMC (or JIMMY) BLOWERS have been manufactured in a variety of sizes; 4-71, 6-71, and 8-71 models were the most popular for hot rodding and DRAG racing, until they were significantly displaced by fully AFTERMARKET units.

6-71 GMC **blower**
TOPPED WITH
HILBORN INJECTORS

**blower explosion** *n.* Any major or catastrophic explosion of fuel within a supercharged engine's BLOWER case. BLOWER EXPLOSIONS most often occur in FUEL racing applications and always result in major mechanical failure. To improve spectator and participant safety and reduce potential damage to the vehicle, modern race-style BLOWER MOTORS generally feature several precautionary systems: manifold "pop-off valves" or "burst panels" serve to release pressure in many cases, while straps and/or full "blankets" restrain parts should a supercharger be blown loose from its motor.

**blower motor** *n.* Any supercharged engine.

**blown 1.** *adj.* Supercharged (see BLOWER). **2.** *adj.* Completely destroyed or thoroughly damaged by a major mechanical failure. **3.** *adj.* Extensively modified for improved performance (generally describing an engine). [Rare]

**blow off the tires** *v.* During the course of a DRAG RACE, to overpower a vehicle's driven wheels in a sudden and severe loss of traction and thus seriously compromise acceleration, generally resulting in a race loss. Most often used in reference to high-horsepower "pro-class" DRAG vehicles.

**blow** someone **out of the water** (also **blow** someone **into the weeds** or **blow** someone **back into the weeds**) *v.* To soundly beat an opponent in a DRAG RACE. To win a race by a very large margin.

**blow-proof bellhousing**, see SCATTERSHIELD

**blue crescent** *n.* Any Boss 429 high-performance engine produced by Ford Motor Company during the 1969 and 1970 model years. Derived from Ford's BLUE OVAL logo and the company's description of the engine's combustion chamber shape.

blue dot IN
1950 PONTIAC TAILLIGHT

**blue dots** (also **blue dot taillights**) *n.* Small, faceted blue glass "dots" that create an overall purple glow when installed into the lenses of OEM-type red taillights. BLUE DOTS experienced moderate popularity from the 1940s through the late 1950s in a variety of HOT ROD and CUSTOM CAR applications. Historically, BLUE DOTS have been illegal when fitted to street-driven vehicles, and because of strict law enforcement their use was effectively suspended by the early 1960s. As with other early automotive trends, however, usage has been revived in more recent years, with lax law enforcement fueling even stronger popularity than in the 1940s and 1950s. BLUE DOTS may be purchased individually and installed into existing STOCK taillights, or as complete replacement lenses with dots already fitted.

FORD'S **blue oval**[1] LOGO

**blue oval 1.** *n.* Ford's traditional logo featuring the company name in script within a BLUE OVAL field. **2.** *adj.* Relating to any Ford Motor Company product. Example: "I still appreciate seeing an early Ford STREET ROD with BLUE OVAL power."

**blueprinted** *adj.* Relating to any engine or engine assembly that has been painstakingly brought into extremely precise tolerances for the purposes of improving its longevity and/or performance.

**boat anchor** *n.* Any dense, heavy automotive component (cylinder block [see BLOCK], cylinder-head casting [see HEADS], axle assembly, etc.) perceived as being worthless in its originally intended application. May be used to describe a part that has been damaged through use or one that is thought to be inherently inefficient by original design. Term implies that component's only reasonable use would be as a metal weight. Example: "It kicked a ROD right through the side of the BLOCK. Looks like you've got a nice BOAT ANCHOR on your hands."

**boattail Riviera** (also **boattail Riv** or **boattail Rivi**) *n.* Any Buick Riviera (see RIV) produced during the 1971 through 1973 model years.

This third-generation Riviera displayed a complete redesign from previous models, with unique styling features focused on a dramatically sweeping BELTLINE (mirrored in deeply sculptured side panels) and a highly distinctive boattail rear roof and window treatment. While the BOATTAIL RIVIERA has achieved moderate popularity as a foundation for CUSTOM CAR and LOWRIDER modification, its controversial boattail design is often perceived to be aesthetically incompatible with such a large, expansive automobile. BOATTAIL RIVS were all powered by variations of Buick's 455-CID BIG-BLOCK engine.

1972 **boattail Riviera**

**bobbed** *adj.* Relating to any automotive component that has been shortened or abbreviated for lightening or aesthetic purposes, but most often referring to a "cut-down" auto body panel.

**bob job 1.** *n.* Any HOT ROD modified in the BOBTAIL style. **2.** (also **bobbed job**) *n.* Any traditional (generally 1934 or earlier-bodied) HOT ROD featuring BOBBED fenders.

**bobbed** REAR FENDER ON 1932 FORD COUPE

**bobtail** (also **bobtailed**) *adj.* Relating to a vehicle (most often a pre-1930s bodied HOT ROD) with the rearmost portion of its body (pickup bed, TURTLE DECK, etc.) removed for weight savings and/or aesthetics. May also relate to a vehicle with its rear-body portion retained but radically shortened or abbreviated in some manner. Example: "Back in the day, BOBTAIL ROADSTERS were nearly as common as those with full bodies."

**body in white** *n.* Any pristine but significantly bare automobile body as delivered fresh from its original FACTORY manufacture. Sometimes secured for use as the foundation for a competition vehicle buildup.

**body-off** *adj.* Relating to any vehicle renovation or modification project that involves the removal of the body from its frame, a very thorough and painstaking procedure. Example: "If I could find myself another decent TRI-POWER GOAT, I'd definitely give it the BODY-OFF treatment this time around."

**body rot** *n.* Any auto body corrosion or rust. Metal oxidation through exposure to air and moisture. A frequent and often daunting challenge when working with VINTAGE TIN.

**bog 1.** *n.* A momentary lack of response to an open-throttle condition, as experienced by an engine or vehicle. A condition of faltering or stumbling under acceleration that most often occurs when a throttle is abruptly and aggressively opened from an idle or low-RPM engine state. **2.** (also **bog down**) *v.* To experience a hesitation or faltering in any open-throttle situation. **3.** *n.* Australian HOT RODDER term for any polyester-based auto body filler.

**boil the hides** (also **boil 'em** or **boil 'em off**), see BURN RUBBER

**'bolt**, see STOVEBOLT

**'Bolt**, see THUNDERBOLT

**bolt on** (also **bolt in**) *n.* Any high-performance part or component that may be easily bolted to a vehicle. Strongly implies an ease of installation, dismissing more complex or skill-oriented practices like engine disassembly, welding, and custom fabrication.

**bolt-on** *adj.* Relating to any high-performance part or component that may be easily bolted to a vehicle.

1939 CHEVROLET **bomb**

**bomb** *n.* LOWRIDER type representing a modern interpretation of an early and traditional CUSTOM CAR style. BOMB LOWRIDERS are always based on early-era production vehicles (generally pre-1955) and in many respects are appreciably restored to their original FACTORY condition. The most distinctive element of the BOMB style is its profusion of vintage OEM and AFTERMARKET accessories. Additions often include bumper guards, fender markers, windshield sun visors, fog lights, headlight visors or shields, fender skirts, CONNIE KITS, spotlights (see SPOTS), dash-mounted traffic light viewers, and rear-window blinds. Further CUSTOM modifications typically come in the form of a drastically lowered RIDE HEIGHT (often with the use of hydraulic suspension) and small-diameter AFTERMARKET wire wheels. This "add on" school of customizing is a fundamental departure from the traditional Anglo CUSTOM CAR style which tends instead to remove trim and accessories. BOMBS often feature precisely restored engine compartments, with six-cylinder engines modified only with SPLIT MANIFOLDS and dual exhaust systems. The most desirable BOMB foundations are Chevrolet passenger cars produced from 1937 through 1954, but any vehicles of similar vintage are considered acceptable. BOMB-style trucks are also common with the preferred models being the Chevrolet and GMC light trucks produced from 1947 through early 1955 (1954 GMC). The BOMB LOWRIDER style has enjoyed strong popularity from the 1970s through the turn of the twenty-first century.

**Bondo** (BON-doe) *n.* Any polyester-based auto body filler. The extreme popularity of the Bondo brand has led to its name being used in a generic manner.

**Bondo bucket** (also **Bondo bum**, **Bondo barge**, or **Bondo buggy**) (BON-doe) *n.* Derogatory term for an auto body that has been repaired with excessive amounts of BONDO body filler.

**bones 1.** *n.* Original wood substructure supporting sheetmetal body panels on most mid-1930s and earlier vintage vehicles. **2.** *n.* Any bare automotive frame rails or frame assembly.

'bones, see WISHBONES

bone stock *adj.* Strictly and absolutely unmodified from an original state as produced by an automobile manufacturer.

boneyard *n.* Any automobile wrecking yard or commercial dismantler. Traditionally, BONEYARDS were a popular source for parts and components needed to build a HOT ROD or CUSTOM CAR.

bonnet air cleaner *n.* Any AFTERMARKET air cleaner featuring an overall cylindrical shape and external sides curving gently inward to meet a slightly recessed, flat top. A BONNET AIR CLEANER may have smooth, solid outer sides (admitting air only from an underside opening) or incorporate louvers across its outer surface for the introduction of air. Most often used to describe the small, chrome-plated air cleaners popularly used on high-performance, multi-TWO-BARREL induction systems of the 1950s.

Bonneville (BAWN-uh-ville) *n.* Bonneville Speedway on the Bonneville Salt Flats of western Utah, often referred to as "the world's fastest racing course." While numerous speed records had been previously set on the FLATS, true HOT RODDERS first ran BONNEVILLE as an experimental test meet in the summer of 1949. The meet's success marked the beginning of an unbroken series of LAND-SPEED RACING events that continues to the present day.

Bonneville chop (BAWN-uh-ville) *n.* Any extreme closed-car (generally relates to early model COUPES) chop treatment (see CHOPPED) performed on a LAND-SPEED RACING vehicle for the purpose of high-speed streamlining. A BONNEVILLE CHOP leaves side and rear windows as mere slits and generally features severely "laid back" A-PILLARS. Windshields are often cut somewhat into the vehicle's roof area to improve driver visibility.

Bonneville chop ON
1934 FORD COUPE

Bonneville Speed Week, see SPEED WEEK

Bonney (also Bonnie or Bonny), see BONNEVILLE

book, see HAUL

boots *n.* Early HOT RODDER's expression for any automotive tires. Term most popular during the late 1940s and 1950s.

bore *n.* The measured diameter of an engine's cylinders.

bored (also bored out) *adj.* Increased in diameter through a machining process (said of an engine's cylinders or, more generally, of a cylinder block [see BLOCK]). Cylinder blocks are BORED to either true their cylinders or to purposefully increase engine displacement.

1970 Mustang **Boss²** 302

**Boss 1.** (also **Boss motor** or **Boss engine**) *n.* Any Boss-series PERFORMANCE engine produced by the Ford Motor Company from 1969 through 1971. BOSS ENGINES represented the highest level of contemporary development within a given FoMoCo engine series and, in the case of the Boss 302 and Boss 429, were sold to the public as a means to HOMOLOGATE Ford's racing programs. BOSS MOTORS were produced in three distinct types: **a.** The Boss 302 (302 CID and based on Ford's 90-degree engine series) was the high-revving response to Chevrolet's 1968 dominance of the SCCA Trans-Am road-racing series (see Z). Produced during the 1969 and 1970 model years, BOSS 302 engines were equipped with free-breathing, canted-valve HEADS to provide excellent TOP END performance. The Boss 302 was significantly underrated at 290 BHP. **b.** The Boss 429 (429 CID and based on Ford's 385 engine series) was also produced during 1969 and 1970 and featured highly exotic aluminum HEADS with "crescent" combustion chambers (see BLUE CRESCENT). Initially created for NASCAR competition, the Boss 429's detuned STREET version was rated at 375 BHP. **c.** The Boss 351 (351 CID and based on Ford's 335 engine series) represented the final Boss iteration, appearing only for the 1971 model year. Boss 351s featured canted-valve HEADS very similar to those used on the earlier Boss 302. Factory-rated at 330 BHP, the Boss 351 provided exceptional STREET performance and was considered the high point of 335-series engine design. **2.** *n.* Any FoMoCo production vehicle featuring a Boss-series engine. Boss 302s were released in Mustang SportsRoof (FASTBACK) and Mercury Cougar Eliminator models in both 1969 and 1970. Inspired by the Trans-Am racing series, Boss 302 models were treated to comprehensive handling and braking packages, making for excellent all-around vehicle performance. Larry Shinoda, formerly of Chevrolet and codesigner of the 1963 Sting Ray Corvette (see 'VETTE), named the Boss 302 and was appreciably responsible for the car's exciting appearance. Boss 429s were featured in Mustang SportsRoofs during 1969 and 1970, while just two racing Cougar Eliminators received the massive, TWISTED-HEMI engine in 1970. Boss 351s were featured in the newly redesigned 1971 Mustang exclusively.

**both ends of the record** *n.* Both the elapsed time and top speed records for any given DRAG racing class. Example: "He came away from the meet owning BOTH ENDS OF THE SS/SA RECORD with a 12.50 ET at 112.40 miles per hour."

**bottle fed** *adj.* Equipped with a nitrous oxide injection system (see NITROUS).

**bottle rocket** *n.* Any especially FAST or QUICK vehicle equipped with a nitrous oxide injection system (see NITROUS). The expression's bottle reference is derived from the steel canister that nitrous oxide is contained in prior to being introduced into a running engine, as well as from a popular form of generally illegal fireworks, typically launched from the opening of an empty beverage bottle.

**bottom end 1.** *n.* The lowermost portion or assembly of any automotive engine. Representing the fundamental core of an engine, the term generally refers to a cylinder block (see BLOCK), its main bearing assemblies, and its crankshaft (see CRANK). **2.** see LOW END.

**boulevard brawler** (also **boulevard burner**), see STREET SWEEPER

**bowtie 1.** *n.* Chevrolet's traditional logo, remotely resembling a man's bow tie. William Durant, the company's founder, claimed to have borrowed the design from a Paris hotel room's wallpaper pattern. (Durant's wife had a different account, explaining that the figure was discovered in a newspaper supplement.) **2.** *adj.* Relating to any Chevrolet product. **3.** *n.* Any vehicle produced by the Chevrolet division of General Motors.

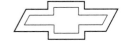

CHEVROLET'S **bowtie**[1] LOGO

**box 1.** *n.* Gearbox. Any automotive manual transmission. **2.** *v.* To modify a STOCK frame rail from an open "C" channel configuration (as viewed in cross-section) to a closed "box" shape for improved strength, rigidity, or sometimes appearance. **3.** *n.* Any automotive steering box.

**box car**, see SHOEBOX

**box skirts** *n.* Any of the generally rectangular-shaped FENDER SKIRTS commonly fitted to 1941 through 1948 model Ford production cars. The BOX SKIRT name distinguishes the type from the teardrop-shaped SKIRTS used in earlier model custom applications. BOX SKIRTS were often featured on 1940s through early-1950s era CUSTOM CARS

**B-pillar** *n.* On any SEDAN model automobile, the rigid structural body member or "post" connecting the roof and BELTLINE immediately behind the vehicle's front door.

**bracket racing** *n.* Any organized DRAG racing featuring a predetermined staggered start and a limitation to elapsed time (see ET). In BRACKET RACING, each competitor establishes an ET DIAL-IN based on his vehicle's previous performances. This numerical DIAL-IN is written on the vehicle's windows in white shoe polish. The difference between the two competing vehicles' DIAL-INS is translated to a handicap start, with the slower car (higher DIAL-IN number) signaled to leave first. Based exclusively on DIAL-INS, both vehicles should theoretically reach the finish line at the same time. Because each driver's REACTION TIME is measured separately from his or her ET (or DIAL-IN), that factor becomes crucial to the race's outcome. To win a bracket race, a driver must reach the finish line before his competitor without running QUICKER than his own DIAL-IN. If a racer records an ET lower than his DIAL-IN, it is referred to as a BREAKOUT and results in disqualification. If both vehicles BREAK OUT, the driver who fouls least is considered the winner and progresses to the next ROUND of competition. With the cost of HEADS-UP professional DRAG racing being prohibitive for most racers, BRACKET RACING affords virtually anyone the opportunity to compete based solely on skill and CONSISTENT vehicle performance. BRACKET RACING's popularity expanded dramatically during the 1970s and has remained strong into the early twenty-first century.

**brain bucket** *n.* Any safety helmet as used by a race-car driver.

**brakelight racing** *n.* When a driver lightly touches his brakes immediately prior to entering the BIG END timing TRAPS in any form of handicap or BRACKET RACING. A competitor that is clearly leading a race may attempt to slow his vehicle somewhat to avoid a BREAKOUT.

**brand X** *adj.* Relating to any automobile manufacturer's product that is so common as to be perceived as generic, ordinary, or mundane. Most often used in reference to Chevrolet's SMALL-BLOCK and BIG-BLOCK V8 engines due to their extreme popularity in all facets of hot rodding and motorsports. Also sometimes describes early Ford auto bodies (especially AFTERMARKET fiberglass [see 'GLASS] replicas) for their overwhelming prevalence in street rodding applications.

**break 'em loose** *v.* In any vehicle, to free-spin tires or BURN RUBBER as a result of overpowering the driven wheels.

**break out** *v.* While BRACKET RACING, to record a QUICKER elapsed time (see ET) than that established as a DIAL-IN. Barring other factors (a REDLIGHT start or crossing the track's centerline), a BREAKOUT results in a competitor's disqualification and race loss.

**breakout** *n.* The act of breaking out while competing in a bracket race.

**breathe** *v.* To introduce unburnt air/fuel mixture and/or to expel spent exhaust gasses in a relatively efficient, free-flowing manner (said of any engine or relevant engine component). An engine or engine part's capacity to BREATHE correlates directly with its ability to operate efficiently at high RPM and, as a consequence, produce greater levels of horsepower.

**brick 1.** *n.* Any HOT ROD, STREET MACHINE, or DRAG racing vehicle based on an especially un-aerodynamic 1950s- or sometimes 1960s-era production vehicle. Further suggests that such a vehicle is inordinately heavy. **2.** *n.* Traditional HOT RODDER's term for any exceptionally slow vehicle.

the **British Invasion** *n.* The tremendous influx of English-built vehicles into the ranks of the 1960s GASSER WARS. During the mid-1960s, the small 1933 through 1941 Willys COUPES (the body of choice beginning in the late 1950s) were significantly displaced by even smaller, lighter, and shorter-wheelbased Austin SEDANS and English Fords (Anglia two-door

SEDANS, Prefect four-door SEDANS, and Thames panel trucks). The term, in its DRAG racing context, is adapted from its more popular usage relating to a form of rock 'n' roll music of the same period.

**brodie** (also **brody**) (BROE-dee) *n*. The deliberate act of spinning tires or burning rubber in a rear-wheel-drive vehicle while negotiating a curve or corner. When engaged in a BRODIE, a vehicle is CROSSED-UP, with only its front wheels pointing in the true direction or travel. Sometimes performed in exceptionally tight circles solely for the purpose of entertainment or spectacle (see DONUT). The term originated with one Steve Brodie, who claimed to have jumped off the Brooklyn Bridge as a stunt in 1886. The expression subsequently came to describe any significant fall by an individual. Through the early part of the twentieth century its meaning was broadened to include all manner of reckless stunts, and by the 1950s, BRODIE had taken on its now-familiar automotive meaning.

**brodie knob** (also **brody knob**) (BROE-dee), see SUICIDE KNOB

**broil the hides**, see BURN RUBBER

**bubble-back Barracuda** *n*. Any Plymouth Barracuda PONY CAR produced during the 1964 1/2 through 1966 model years. While significantly based on the compact Valiant line, this first-generation Barracuda featured a highly unique FASTBACK roof with a large bubble-like wraparound rear window. BUBBLE-BACK BARRACUDAS could be FACTORY-ordered with a Formula S PERFORMANCE package, including various suspension upgrades and a warmed-up 273-CID V8. Not satisfied with SMALL-BLOCK power, some racers (including STOCK CAR standout "King" Richard Petty and the legendary team of Ronnie Sox and Buddy Martin) shoehorned the powerful 426 RACE HEMI into the early Barracuda and competed in various experimental STOCK DRAG classes. During this same period, Bob Riggle's mid-engined *Hemi Under Glass* Barracuda wowed audiences with outrageous exhibition wheelstand passes (see WHEELSTANDER).

**bubble hood**, see TEARDROP HOOD

**bubble skirts** *n*. Any AFTERMARKET or custom FENDER SKIRTS of a relatively large size and bulbous shape. Popularized in late-1950s through early-1960s CUSTOM CAR applications, the outward-bulging convex shape of BUBBLE SKIRTS was perceived by some to "visually lower" a vehicle.

**bubble top 1.** *n*. Any of several HARDTOP model automobiles produced during the late 1950s through early 1960s that featured a bubble-like GREENHOUSE with a windshield and BACKLIGHT cut high into the roof, and delicate, gracefully curving A-PILLARS and C-PILLARS. From a PERFORMANCE standpoint, the most renowned BUBBLE TOP types were the

348-CID- and 409-CID-powered (see LUMPY HEAD) Chevrolet Impala and Bel Air Sport COUPES of the 1959 through 1962 model years. BUBBLE TOP CHEVYS achieved great PERFORMANCE success both on the street and in sanctioned DRAGSTRIP competition. Chevrolet's SWOOPY, glass-dome roof was shared among GM sister divisions, with each producing its own respective PERFORMANCE models during this period. Notable also within the BUBBLE TOP genre were the elegant Ford Galaxie Starliner COUPES of 1960 and 1961. With their potent FE Series BIG-BLOCK motors, the Starliners were strong performers, especially in NASCAR competition. **2.** *n.* Exotic custom HOT ROD type produced generally during the early 1960s. The typical BUBBLE TOP featured a futuristic, handcrafted body and a large, clear "bubble" in place of a conventional glass GREENHOUSE or ROADSTER soft top. Ed "Big Daddy" Roth's *Beatnik Bandit* (1961), Bill Cushenbery's *Silhouette* (1963), and Dean Jeffries' *Mantaray* (1964) are celebrated examples of this type.

THE *SILHOUETTE*
**bubble top²**

**bubble-top** *adj.* Relating to any BUBBLE TOP-type production HARDTOP model automobile.

a **buck** *n.* One-hundred miles per hour. Example: "With those gears it'll run a BUCK-twenty all day long."

**bucket 1.** see T-BUCKET **2.** *n.* Any early-model ROADSTER body structure of the type commonly featured in T-BUCKET HOT ROD or STREET ROD construction.

**bucket seats** (also **buckets**) *n.* Any vehicle seat designed specifically for use by one passenger (as distinguished from a bench seat, which spans the width of a vehicle). Dates to the early part of the twentieth century, as evidenced by its use in 1910s-era Model T (see T-BONE) advertising.

**bucket-T**, see T-BUCKET

**budget muscle car** *n.* Any no-frills STRIPPER model MUSCLE CAR emphasizing high-performance along with a relatively low initial purchase price. Often feature bench seats, column-shift automatic transmission, standard-equipment wheels, and rubber mats in place of interior carpeting. While closely related to the JUNIOR MUSCLE CAR, the BUDGET MUSCLE CAR is differentiated by its maintained commitment to exceptional performance. Notable examples include the first-generation Plymouth Road Runner (see BIRD), Dodge Super Bee (see BEE), and Ford's 1969 Fairlane Cobra with its 428 Cobra Jet (see CJ) power.

**Buford** (also **Bu'**) (BUE-ferd) *n.* Any complete automobile or automotive component produced by the Buick division of General Motors.

**Buford**
1950 BUICK STREET ROD

**bug** *n.* Early hot rodder's expression for any vehicle stripped to its bare essentials for the purpose of improved performance. Most recognized use came with Dick Kraft's *The Bug*, an early-1950s RAIL JOB and one of the first purpose-built DRAGSTERS.

**bug catcher 1.** *n.* Type of high-performance fuel-injection HAT commonly featured in supercharged (see BLOWER) racing applications and produced by Enderle Fuel Injection. Characterized by their somewhat triangular shape, three large throttle-actuating butterfly valves, and, oftentimes, three distinct ribs on their uppermost surface. Originally popularized in various 1960s-era DRAG racing applications, Enderle's popular BUG CATCHERS were later joined by larger versions dubbed BIRD CATCHER and BUZZARD CATCHER, respectively. **2.** *n.* Any high-performance fuel-injection unit configured in the general style of an Enderle BUG CATCHER.

ENDERLE **bug catcher**[1]

**buggy springs** *n.* Archaic automotive suspension system consisting of a single set of transversely mounted leaf springs. Commonly featured as original equipment on early-twentieth-century automobiles, this traditional suspension remains popular in many vintage (especially Ford-based) HOT ROD applications. Term relates to the type's usage on pre-automobile horse-drawn buggies.

**Buick wires** (also **Buick Skylark wires**), see SKYLARK WIRES

**build-up** (also **buildup**) *n.* Generally a 1950s-era expression for any engine extensively modified for improved performance.

**built** *adj.* Extensively modified for improved performance. Example: "That SMALL-BLOCK he's runnin' is seriously BUILT. I've seen him crack high-twelves on street tires."

**built to buzz** *adj.* Relating to any high-performance engine designed and constructed to operate at an exceptionally high RPM level. Example: "Those little 302 CHEVYS were definitely BUILT TO BUZZ."

**built to the hilt** *adj.* Modified for absolute maximum performance. Term may relate to any complete vehicle or vehicle component, but is most often used to describe a high-performance engine.

**Bulletbird** *n.* Any Ford Thunderbird produced from 1961 through 1963 model years. This nickname for these third-generation T-BIRDS is derived from their aggressive bullet-like profile. Standard power came in the form of a 390-CID FE Series V8 producing 300 BHP. During 1962 and 1963, a special "M-code" 390 was optionally available, featuring a three-Holley TWO-BARREL induction system and 340 BHP. A unique "Sports ROADSTER" package was offered with the BULLETBIRD for the 1962 and 1963 model years and featured a removable fiberglass (see 'GLASS)

**Bulletbird**
1962 THUNDERBIRD
SPORTS ROADSTER

tonneau with integral driver and passenger headrests. When installed, a tonneau covers a standard convertible's back-seat area, effectively creating a stylish two-passenger ROADSTER. The model's convertible top is operable with or without the tonneau in place. All Sport ROADSTERS came equipped with exotic chrome Kelsey-Hayes (see KELSEYS) wire wheels that were available as an extra-cost option on all 1962 through 1964 T-BIRDS regardless of configuration.

**bullet-nose Stude**
THE *FRANKENSTUDE* STUDEBAKER

**bullet-nose Stude** (STEW-dee) *n.* Any of the uniquely styled passenger cars produced by the Studebaker Corporation during the 1950 and 1951 model years. While largely based on Studebaker's standard 1947 POSTWAR platform, these models were distinguished by their radical FRONTEND, an exotic signature element in the form of a central and protruding chrome bullet ornament. Recognized for their unusual and distinctive appearance, BULLET-NOSE STUDES are sometimes modified in a STREET MACHINE or CUSTOM CAR style. The most sophisticated and renowned of all BULLET-NOSE STUDE customs was conceived by designer Thom Taylor and created by builder Greg Fleury during the 1990s. Dubbed *Frankenstude,* this complex showpiece was substantially custom-fabricated but featured a conglomeration of 1947 through 1951 OEM Studebaker body panels.

**bulletproof** *adj.* Extremely durable and resilient. May relate to any automotive component, but especially those mechanical parts taxed in severe-duty racing applications.

**bullets[1]** ON
1958 CHEVROLET

**bullets 1.** (also **bullet taillights**) *n.* Any of the highly distinctive taillight lenses provided as original equipment on 1959 production model Cadillacs. Since their introduction, CADILLAC BULLETS have been adapted to a multitude of CUSTOM CAR applications. **2.** *n.* Any AFTERMARKET CUSTOM CAR accessories or adornments featuring a pronounced BULLET shape. In CUSTOM CAR applications, may variously describe hubcap centers, license plate bolts, dashboard knobs, valve stem caps, steering wheel centers, lug nuts, and windshield wiper replacement caps.

**bumblebee stripe 1.** *n.* Distinctive stripe featured on Dodge high-performance vehicles from 1968 through 1970 model years. (BUMBLEBEE STRIPES were closely associated with Dodge's Scat Pack PERFORMANCE program.) Although produced in a number of variations, Dodge BUMBLEBEE STRIPES consisted of a single (or sometimes double) broad band completely circling a vehicle's rearmost body panels. **2.** *n.* Painted stripe featured on Chevrolet Camaro models during the 1967 and 1968 model years. The Camaro's BUMBLEBEE STRIPE comprised a single broad band outlined with pinstripes and circled the immediate leading portion of the vehicle's bodywork.

**bumblebee stripe[1]** ON
1968 DODGE SUPER BEE

**bump** *n.* For a given DRAG racing class or situation, an ET number that is considered viable to qualify for actual racing ROUNDS.

**bumped** *adj.* In DRAG racing, relating to any driver or vehicle eliminated from an event's competition by not posting a sufficient elapsed time (see ET) during qualifying.

**bumper bullets**, see DAGMARS

**bumper tits** (also **bumper nipples**) *n.* Any bullet-shaped automotive bumper ornaments or guards as significantly popularized during the 1950s (see DAGMARS). The "tits" name refers to the vulgar but popular slang term for a woman's breasts (itself a derivative of the word *teat*).

**bumpstick** *n.* Any automotive camshaft (see CAM). Derived from a camshaft's long, stick-like shape and series of raised lobes or "bumps" to actuate valve movement.

**burndown** *n.* The act of deliberately delaying the staging of one's own vehicle at the outset of a high-powered professional class DRAG RACE. BURNDOWNS build drama and tension and are often undertaken in attempts to overheat an opponent's running engine.

**burnout** *n.* In any vehicle, the practice of intentionally burning rubber, generally performed from a standing start or a very low speed. In organized DRAG racing, the BURNOUT plays an important practical role. As a pre-race ritual, tread-free SLICKS are burned through a shallow water pit, resulting in much hotter, softer, and stickier tires with greatly enhanced traction properties. Long, loud, smokey BURNOUTS have long played a significant role in the drama and spectacle of DRAG racing. Example: "I still say that 'Jungle Jim' was the all-time BURNOUT king."

**burn out** *v.* To perform a BURNOUT.

**burnout contest** *n.* Competition to determine which competitor can perform the longest, smokiest, most intense BURNOUT. An impromptu BURNOUT CONTEST may occur between legitimate DRAG racing opponents to enhance the spectator appeal of their normal pre-race routine. Formal, organized BURNOUT CONTESTS are also sometimes held at MUSCLE CAR or STREET MACHINE gatherings, with participants burning down treaded, street-legal tires.

**burn rubber** *v.* To overpower a vehicle's driven wheels to such an extent that the tires lose traction with the road surface and spin freely. As the tires spin, friction and heat build, burning rubber away from the tire's surface in the form of smoke and small molten solids.

**burn the tires** (also **burn the tires off**), see BURN RUBBER

**bust 'em loose**, see BREAK 'EM LOOSE

**butt** *n.* Early (generally pre-1960s) expression for any automotive differential (see REAREND).

**butterfly mags** (also **butterfly wheels** or **butterfly-spoke mags**) *n.* Any American Racing Equipment 200-S MAG WHEELS (see DAISY MAGS). Describes a spoke shape reminiscent of a butterfly's wings.

butterfly steering wheel

**butterfly steering wheel** *n.* Unique steering device as commonly employed on DRAGSTERS from the 1950s to present. Replacing a conventional round steering wheel, a BUTTERFLY STEERING WHEEL consists of individual hand grips fixed to a pair of deeply splayed handles. While impractical for normal driving conditions, a BUTTERFLY STEERING WHEEL offers the advantages of compactness and responsiveness in straight-line DRAG applications.

**buttons 1.** *n.* Any automatic transmission shifting mechanism that allows the driver to initiate gear changes by pressing designated selector BUTTONS. Several American manufacturers featured button shifting as original equipment during the 1950s and 1960s, with button groupings affixed to either a vehicle's dashboard or steering wheel hub. While novel, button-type shifters were widely noted for their poor efficiency and jamming, leading all major manufacturers to abandon the type by 1965. Push button shifters were featured on Chrysler Corporation products from 1956 through 1964, including many early-1960s MOPAR PERFORMANCE and MUSCLE CARS. **2.** *n.* Any small, simple hubcaps covering only the central portion of a vintage steel automotive wheel.

button tuft IN
T-BUCKET ROADSTER

**button tuft** *n.* Automotive upholstery type featuring a deeply padded underlay and a covering material divided into rectangular or diamond-shaped sections by the regular placement of small retaining buttons. Popular in 1960s and early-1970s STREET ROD applications, BUTTON TUFT mimics a style of OEM upholstery commonly applied to early-twentieth-century production vehicles.

**buzz** (also **buzz up**) *v.* To REV an engine to an exceptionally high RPM level.

**buzzard catcher**, see BUG CATCHER

**B-ville** (also **B'ville**) (BEE-ville), see BONNEVILLE

# C

**C1**, **C2**, **C3**, **C4**, **C5**, and **C6** *n.* The six Chevrolet Corvette (see 'VETTE) series. Corvette models are separated into chronological "generations" with each exhibiting dramatic styling and/or technological innovations over the previous. These respective 'VETTE generations are expressed as C1 through C6 Corvettes (C1 from 1953 to 1962, C2 from 1963 to 1967, C3 from 1968 to 1982, C4 from 1984 to 1996, C5 from 1997 to 2004, and the C6, introduced for the 2005 model year). No 1983-designated Corvette was ever released for public sale, as the 1984 C4 model immediately followed the 1982 production run.

**C5**
2003 Z06 CORVETTE

**cabin job** *n.* Any SLINGSHOT DRAGSTER as produced during the mid- to late 1950s and featuring a fully enclosed driver's compartment or "cabin." Significant examples include Ed Cortopassi's custom fiberglass-bodied (see 'GLASS) *Glass Slipper* and the highly competitive Dode Martin/Jim Nelson *Masters Dragliner*.

**cabin job**
THE *MASTERS DRAGLINER*

**cabover**, see COE

**cabriolet** (also **cabrio**, **cabby**, or **cab**) (CAB-ree-oh-lay) *n.* Any of the open-car models, generally of a 1930s or earlier vintage, that featured seating for two persons and shared much in common with contemporary ROADSTER models. What fundamentally distinguishes the types from one another, however, is the cabriolet's roll-up glass windows and body-integral windshield posts. Because of these differences, the CABRIOLET is sometimes referred to as either a "convertible COUPE" or "ROADSTER with roll-up windows." Although moderately popular as a HOT ROD foundation, the CABRIOLET has never achieved the same acceptance as the COUPE or ROADSTER due to its relatively limited production; more formal, rigid bodylines; aerodynamics (the CABRIOLET's windshield structure could not be fully removed as could a ROADSTER's for racing); and slightly heavier weight.

**Caddy** (also **Cad**) **1.** *n.* Any complete automobile produced by the Cadillac division of General Motors. Noted for its elegance and prestige, the Cadillac marque has long provided both inspiration and raw material to automotive CUSTOMIZERs. Since the 1930s, OEM Cadillac styling cues have been adapted to myriad non-CADDY production vehicles, while Cadillac vehicles themselves have a significant history as CUSTOM CAR foundations. The exotic Cadillac models of the late 1940s through the 1950s, in particular, have experienced strong popularity in a variety of CUSTOM and STREET MACHINE applications. **2.** *n.* Any Cadillac-manufactured engine. In its engine context, the term CADDY was most commonly used during the 1950s to describe the revolutionary OHV Cadillac V8s introduced in 1949 (see KETTERING V8). Contemporary HOT RODS, CUSTOM CARS, and

**Caddy[1]**
1959 CADILLAC-BASED
CUSTOM CAR

STREET MACHINES of all conceivable types were modified by the inclusion of CADDY V8 power.

**Cadillac bullets** (also **Caddy bullets**), see BULLETS (Definition 1)

**California rake** *n.* Traditional term for any pronounced vehicle body and chassis RAKE marked by a low FRONTEND and a relatively high rear-body position. Initially popularized during the 1950s to describe the then-unique STANCE applied to California-based HOT RODS.

**calliope stacks** (ca-LYE-ah-pee) *n.* Any high-performance fuel-injection VELOCITY STACKS consisting of a grouping of long, vertical, metallic tubes. First popularized during the 1960s, a variety of CALLIOPE STACK types have experienced strong favor in racing applications up to the present day. Name derived from similarity in appearance to calliope musical instruments. Closely associated with circuses and vintage riverboats, which consist of numerous cylindrical steam whistles (each toned in a different note) played in the manner of an organ.

**call shotgun** (also **call shot**) *v.* To verbally lay claim to the front passenger-seat riding position in an automobile (see RIDE SHOTGUN).

**cam** *n.* Any automotive camshaft, the mechanical device governing the movement of an engine's intake and exhaust valves. High-performance CAMS are especially significant to HOT RODDERS, as their specific configurations (or GRINDS) in large part determine an engine's performance characteristics.

**camel humps** (also **camel hump heads**) *n.* Original-equipment SMALL-BLOCK Chevrolet V8 (see MOUSE) cylinder heads (see HEADS) as produced in assorted styles from the 1961 through 1968 model years. Available in SEDAN and Corvette (see 'VETTE) applications, the free-flowing, large-valve CAMEL HUMPS were considered highly desirable during their period of manufacture. Named for their unique, twin-hump casting marks.

**camgrinder** *n.* Any individual or corporation engaged in the production or manufacture of custom, generally high-performance camshafts (see CAM).

the **camgrinder wars** *n.* Closely associated with the 1960s GASSER WARS, the CAMGRINDER WARS pitted major camshaft (see CAM) manufacturers against one another. Noted CAM manufacturers like Engle Racing CAMS, Iskenderian Racing CAMS, Crane Engineering Company, and Howard's Racing CAMS fueled intense rivalries with inflammatory national print advertisements that boasted of the manufacturers' racing successes while challenging the similar claims of others. The antagonistic exchanges ultimately served to sell more product to the general hot rodding public.

**Camino** *n.* Any Chevrolet El Camino hybrid pickup truck/passenger car. El Caminos were produced during the 1959 and 1960 model years (based on CHEVY's full-size line) and again from 1964 through 1982 (based on the intermediate Chevelle series). Many of the same high-performance and MUSCLE CAR options found in Chevrolet's passenger cars were made available to the El Camino throughout their production runs. El Caminos have long experienced strong popularity as the foundations for STREET MACHINE modification.

Camino
1959 CHEVROLET EL CAMINO

**cammer 1.** *n.* Ultimate-performance 427-CID SOHC V8 engine produced by Ford Motor Company from 1965 through 1968. The CAMMER is highly unique for its exotic aluminum HEADS featuring HEMI combustion chambers and a single-overhead CAM configuration (one camshaft in each HEAD). Ford's ultrapowerful CAMMER (factory-rated at 615 BHP with single FOUR-BARREL induction) was developed expressly to challenge the superiority of Chrysler's 426-CID RACE HEMI engine design. While SOHC engines were never FACTORY-installed in any Ford vehicles but available only on an OVER-THE-COUNTER basis, FoMoCo contracted to have a handful of CAMMER-powered DRAG RACE vehicles produced during the 1965 and 1966 seasons. SOHC-powered Mercury Comet HARDTOPS and Ford Mustang FASTBACKS dominated A/FX-class DRAG competition during that period with solid 10-second ETs. CAMMER motors also experienced substantial success as the POWERPLANTS of BLOWN FUEL DRAGSTERS from the mid- to late 1960s. **2.** *n.* Any engine featuring a single- or double-overhead camshaft configuration.

**the can** *n.* In DRAG racing, traditional expression for any 100 percent nitromethane (see NITRO) fuel load.

**cancer** (also **body cancer**), see BODY ROT

**candy apple** (also **candy**) **1.** *n.* Extremely deep, rich paint type achieved by applying multiple layers of translucent, tinted paint over an opaque reflective base coat that is traditionally gold or silver. This opulent paint treatment gained strong popularity during the 1950s with the work of renowned CUSTOM CAR builder Joe Bailon. Beginning with his famed *Miss Elegance* 1941 Chevrolet COUPE, Bailon created a series of highly notable CUSTOMS, each highlighted by his celebrated CANDY APPLE red paint schemes. Name derived from its similarity in appearance to a candied apple confection. **2.** *adj.* Relating to any CANDY APPLE-type paint as used in an automotive application.

**canted headlights** (also **canted quads**) *n.* Any QUAD HEADLIGHT treatment (two headlights on each side) configured in a diagonal manner. General Motors, Ford Motor Company, and Chrysler Corporation manufactured vehicles with then-exotic CANTED HEADLIGHT arrangements during the late 1950s and early 1960s. Custom QUAD

canted headlights ON
1961 CHRYSLER 300G

HEADLIGHT conversions of the same period often featured a canted layout as well.

**cantilever top** (also **cantilevered top** or **cantilever roof**) (CAN-tuh-leave-er) *n.* Vehicle roof type wherein a solid top is anchored only at its rearmost end and projects virtually unsupported over the open space of the vehicle's interior. A windshield, if employed at all, is structurally independent and offers no roof support whatsoever. Because of their inherent structural weaknesses, cantilever-topped RODS are generally limited only to show-circuit duty. CANTILEVER TOPS enjoyed brief popularity during the early to mid-1960s on exotic custom SHOW-style HOT RODS. Examples of vehicles employing CANTILEVER TOPS include: Carl Casper's 1965 AMBR-winning *Ghost* ROADSTER and the Darryl Starbird-designed *Li'l Coffin* SEDAN (the multiple-show-winning *Li'l Coffin* was the subject of a popular 1/24th scale Monogram model kit and a 1/64th scale Hot Wheels diecast toy car).

**cantilever top** ON THE *LI'L COFFIN* CUSTOM ROD

**caps** *n.* Any automotive hubcaps.

**caps 'n' rings** *n.* Hubcaps and BEAUTY RINGS used together on the same application. The traditional CAPS 'N' RINGS HOT ROD wheel treatment experienced its strongest popularity during the 1940s and 1950s but has regained favor with the RETRO ROD/RAT ROD movements of the 1990s and early twenty-first century.

**carb** *n.* Any automotive carburetor, a mechanical device employed to mix fuel with air prior to introduction into a running internal-combustion engine.

**car club 1.** *n.* Any formally organized social club whose activities are focused on HOT RODS, STREET MACHINES, and/or CUSTOM CARS. While such organizations existed at least as early as the 1930s, they experienced their greatest popularity from the 1950s through the mid-1960s period (an April 1957 *Life* magazine article cited an astounding 15,000 active CAR CLUBS in the United States). Early CAR CLUBS often pooled their talents and resources to create club-sponsored competition vehicles and to promote good public relations with a variety of civic and community-oriented projects. During the 1950s, clubs also commonly directed their energies toward the establishment of legal, sanctioned DRAGSTRIPS in their respective areas. To express their pride and unity, club members wore coveralls, shirts, and jackets emblazoned with their clubs' names. Additionally, members' vehicles were often distinguished by cast-aluminum CLUB PLAQUES affixed, most often, to their rear bumpers. Following a long period of minimal activity, traditional-style CAR CLUBS have once again achieved strong popularity during the 1990s and early twenty-first century. An integral part of the RETRO ROD/RAT ROD movements, modern CAR CLUBS feature names like Lucky Devils, Road Zombies, Autoholics, Shifters, Deacons, and Auto Butchers. **2.** *n.* Any CAR CLUB dedicated to and focused on LOWRIDERS.

Unlike their Anglo-culture ROD and CUSTOM counterparts, LOWRIDER-oriented CAR CLUBS have maintained a strong and consistent presence from the 1960s through to the early twenty-first century. Clubs like the Imperials, Groupe, and Lifestyle have played an important role in the development of lowriding and in broader Chicano culture.

**car hopping**, see HOPPING

**carry the wheels** (also **carry the frontend**) *v.* In any vehicle, to perform or experience a WHEELSTAND.

**Carson top 1.** *n.* Any sleek, non-folding custom convertible top as produced at the Carson Top shop in Los Angeles, California. The typical CARSON TOP featured a CHOPPED height, white or light-colored fabric covering, and heavy padding for aesthetic purposes. The first CARSON TOPS were created during the mid-1930s, but the type achieved its greatest popularity with the FAT-FENDERED CUSTOM style of the late 1930s to early 1950s. **2.** *n.* Any custom top featuring the essential look and characteristics of a true CARSON TOP.

Carson top[1] ON 1941 BUICK CUSTOM

**CAR*toons*** *n.* Comic-book styled automotive humor magazine produced from 1959 through 1991. *CAR*TOONS was initially released by Trend Books on a quarterly basis and later by Petersen Publishing as a bimonthly. Classic *CAR*TOONS feature series included *Unk and Them Varmints* (1964 through 1975) and artist George Trosley's *Krass and Bernie* (1973 through 1991).

**Cat** *n.* Any Pontiac Catalina model. From 1959 through 1963, the Catalina represented Pontiac's ultimate performance vehicle, and as the smallest, lightest full-size model produced during this period was the natural choice in high-performance and racing applications. Catalinas equipped with powerful Super Duty 389-CID, and later maximum-performance Super Duty 421-CID engines, were a dominant force both on NASCAR's superspeedways and on the nation's DRAGSTRIPS. As early as 1960, Pontiac began producing lightweight aluminum body panels for the Catalina to further enhance the model's DRAG performance. At first available only on an OVER-THE-COUNTER basis (with consumers having to fit parts to their own vehicles), the lightweight program arrived on Pontiac's assembly line for the 1962 model year. During both 1962 and 1963, lightweight SuperDuty Catalinas were FACTORY-produced expressly for DRAG racing, employing Super Duty 421-CID engines and the extensive use of aluminum components. For early 1963, Pontiac took the effort still further, creating a limited number of SWISS-CHEESE CATALINAS. In 1963, General Motors established a strict ban on all FACTORY-sponsored racing activity, effectively ending the Catalina's competition career. From 1964 through 1967, the Catalina carried on as Pontiac's full-size PERFORMANCE vehicle in the form of the personal-luxury Catalina-based 2+2.

catch rubber, see GET RUBBER

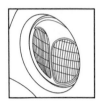

cat eye HEADLIGHT SHIELD

cat eyes (also cat's eyes or cat-eye shields) *n.* AFTERMARKET headlight shields featuring a distinctive appearance similar to a cat's eyes. Often applied to traditionally styled CUSTOM CARS, CAT EYES are light-gauge brightmetal caps affixed to the external surfaces of common sealed-beam headlights. The CAT EYE's narrow central dividing band flows upward and spreads into a dual arch pattern, partially covering the light's upper area. While ostensibly serving to protect the headlights' surfaces, CAT EYES are employed more for their distinctive styling than their practical function.

caught napping (also caught sleeping) *adj.* Relating to a relatively bad REACTION TIME at the outset of a DRAG RACE.

C-body *n.* Official Chrysler Corporation designation for its series of full-size models produced throughout the 1960s and 1970s MUSCLE CAR era. Significant examples include 1970s Chrysler/Hurst 300-H models and the Plymouth Sport Fury GTs of 1970 and 1971. The limited-edition 300-H was specially modified by Hurst Performance and featured a fiberglass (see 'GLASS) hood with functional air scoop (see RAM AIR), 'GLASS DECK and rear SPOILER, leather BUCKET SEATS, heavy-duty suspension, and a 375-BHP 440-CID engine. Plymouth's similarly rare Sport Fury GT offered a unique "power bulge" hood in 1970, along with the same 375-BHP WEDGE 440 powering the 300-H. Optional for the Plymouth, however, was the renowned 440 SIX-BARREL and 390 BHP. For 1971, only the single-QUAD 440 (with its BHP slightly downgraded to 370) was available in the GT.

MID-1970S FORD C-cab
STREET ROD

C-cab *n.* Any HOT ROD, STREET ROD, or SHOW car based on a traditional C-CAB commercial vehicle body or facsimile thereof. The general C-CAB body style was employed by a broad range of manufacturers from the 1900s to the 1920s in both open and enclosed truck configurations. All C-CABS feature body-side cab openings cut in a deeply arched "C" shape. Early C-CABS generally include an arched roof above the cab area, providing additional passenger headroom while exaggerating the overall "C" styling effect. Due to the scarcity of complete early C-CAB vehicles, C-CAB RODS are often built from a mixture of vintage parts together with custom-fabricated body elements. C-CABS are sometimes created as replica-bodied variations of the popular FAD-T formula. The C-CAB HOT ROD type experienced its greatest popularity during the late 1960s and 1970s.

C'd *adj.* Relating to any automotive frame that has been reconfigured with a C-shaped arch directly above its rear axle assembly (see REAREND), creating the clearance necessary for the rear axle to be substantially raised (through suspension modifications) in relation to the overall chassis. This raising of the axle assembly, in turn, has the effect of lowering the rear portion of the vehicle.

**cfm** (pronounced as separate letters) *n.* Cubic feet per minute, the common measure or rating of an automotive carburetor's (see CARB) airflow capacity. The CFM abbreviation is always preceded by a numerical measurement.

**chameleon paint** *n.* Any exterior-finish paint as first popularized in late-1990s CUSTOM CAR and HOT ROD applications that appears to distinctly and dramatically change depending on the position from which the vehicle is viewed. Though similar in effect to PEARL paints, CHAMELEON PAINT color shifts are more pronounced, with complete body panels appearing as entirely different colors. The renowned House of Kolor specialty paint manufacturer has trademarked the "Kameleon" name to market its popular color-changing paint products.

**channeled** *adj.* Relating to a vehicle that is modified through extensive body alteration that involves completely removing the floor pan and reattaching it at a higher level within the body structure. The modified body is then lowered over and reaffixed to the vehicle's frame. The process serves to dramatically lower the vehicle's overall profile.

**channeled** 1932 FORD COUPE

**channel job 1.** *n.* Any complete vehicle that has been modified by having its body lowered through channeling (see CHANNELED). **2.** *n.* Any lowered body modification as accomplished through channeling (see CHANNELED).

**'charger** (also **charger**) *n.* Any supercharger (see BLOWER) or turbocharger (see TURBO).

**chase the long black line** *v.* To race on the BONNEVILLE Salt Flats. Derived from the straight black line painted across BONNEVILLE's flat expanse to designate its LAND-SPEED RACING course.

**cheater slicks** (also **cheaters**) *n.* Any DRAG racing tires featuring the overall construction of true DRAG SLICKS, but with a very marginal tread pattern so as to qualify for a street-legal status (see SLICKS). Both the tire style and the term experienced their strongest popularity from the late 1950s through the early 1960s.

**cheese grater grill** *n.* Automotive grill featured only on the 1971 Plymouth Barracuda and 'CUDA models. Flanked by four headlights (as opposed to the two featured on the previous and following model years), the elaborate grill design also featured five vertical bars dividing the assembly into six rectangular compartments. Name inspired by its similarity in appearance to the common kitchen appliance.

**'Chero** (CHAIR-oh) *n.* Any Ford Ranchero hybrid pickup truck/passenger car. The Ranchero experienced a number of significant design changes throughout its production life. From its 1957 introduction

through the 1959 model year, it was based on the then-full-size Fairlane passenger-car platform; from 1960 through 1966, it was downsized as a part of the compact Falcon line; from 1967 through 1976, it grew to mid-size Fairlane/Torino series proportions; and for the Ranchero's final years of 1978 and 1979, it was based on the luxurious Thunderbird/LTD line. Ford made high-performance options and equipment available to the Ranchero during much the model's manufacture run, and the cars have experienced moderate favor as a base for STREET MACHINE and CUSTOM CAR modification.

**cherry 1.** (also **cherry pie**) *adj.* Immaculate or perfect in appearance and function. Often used to describe pristine automotive parts or complete vehicles, the slang term CHERRY has traditionally been used in reference to both male and female virginity with implications extending to any pure unmolested state. **2.** *n.* Any vehicle, vehicle system, component, part, etc., that is in absolutely pristine condition. Example: "I'd love to get my hands on that guy's '55. The thing's an absolute CHERRY."

**cherry** something **out** *v.* To bring any vehicle (or vehicle system, component, etc.) into pristine, immaculate, or "perfect" condition.

**cherry picker 1.** *n.* Any hydraulically actuated hoist (generally semiportable) commonly used to remove or install automotive engines. **2.** *n.* Generally 1950s-era expression for any DRAG racer who deliberately CHOOSES OFF obviously slower vehicles so as to be assured of a win.

**Chevy** (also **Chev**) *n.* Any complete vehicle or vehicle component produced by the Chevrolet division of General Motors. Highly common CHEVY term has maintained strong and constant popularity throughout the HOT ROD era, coming to be virtually synonymous with the more formal "Chevrolet" designation. While still in use, the alternative term CHEV has significantly declined in favor since the 1950s and 1960s.

**chicken race** *n.* Contest of nerve or courage in which two participants race their vehicles directly toward one another. The "chicken" (traditional slang expression for a coward) is said to be the first to swerve away in avoidance of a head-on collision. Though on some level probably based in fact, the primarily 1950s-era legend of the CHICKEN RACE was most often propagated through questionable tabloid journalism, teen-oriented pulp novels, and juvenile delinquent HOT ROD films.

**chin spoiler** *n.* Any GROUND EFFECTS SPOILER mounted low and at the immediate leading edge of a vehicle (oftentimes beneath a front bumper). As with other OEM GROUND EFFECTS devices, CHIN SPOILERS presumably offer added high-speed stability, but more often serve only to enhance a vehicle's appearance. In some instances, CHIN SPOILERS also function to direct cooling air toward a vehicle's radiator. CHIN SPOILERS have been a relatively common addition to STOCK PERFORMANCE models from the late 1960s to present.

**chirp** (also **chirpie**) *n.* Any short, abrupt high-pitched sound produced by a vehicle's tires while breaking traction under hard acceleration. CHIRPS most often occur during gear changes. Example: "With a full-on POWERSHIFT, it'll get a fourth-gear CHIRP."

**Chizler** (also **Chizzler**) **1.** *n.* Any Chrysler Corporation-produced engine, but most often referring to the EARLY HEMI motors manufactured for the 1951 through 1958 model years. During the 1960s, Chris "The Greek" Karamesines campaigned a series of highly successful EARLY HEMI-powered RAIL DRAGSTERS, each named *Chizler*. **2.** *n.* Any Chrysler Corporation-produced automobile. [Rare]

**choose** (also **choose** someone **off** or **choose off** someone) *v.* To challenge another driver to a DRAG RACE. Most often relates to a spontaneous exchange in a street-racing environment or situation.

**chop job 1.** *n.* Any complete vehicle modified by chopping. (see CHOPPED) **2.** *n.* Any chopping modification as applied to a vehicle.

**chopped** *adj.* Relating to any vehicle that is modified through a radical body alteration that involves removing a horizontal cross-section from the entire GREENHOUSE area followed by the reattachment of the roof to the vehicle. Topless ROADSTERS or PHAETONS may be considered CHOPPED by having only their windshield height reduced. Traditionally a popular modification for improved racing aerodynamics, but more frequently is undertaken purely for aesthetic purposes.

chopped 1954 CHEVROLET
CUSTOM CAR

**chopped by a stocker** *adj.* Defeated (especially in a STREET RACE) by an unmodified or FACTORY-STOCK vehicle. During its greatest popularity in the 1940s and 1950s, the expression carried with it a strong tone of humiliation. Though American production vehicles gained steadily in performance throughout the 1950s, the term STOCKER wasn't commonly associated with true high-performance DRAG racing vehicles until the early 1960s.

**chopped down** *adj.* Generally 1950s-era description for any vehicle that has been modified through chopping (see CHOPPED).

**chopped flywheel** *n.* Any automotive flywheel that has been reduced in weight by having its surface machined or "turned." In some applications, a lightened flywheel may improve a vehicle's performance by allowing its engine to REV more quickly under load. The term, as well as the actual modification, experienced its greatest popularity during and prior to the 1950s.

chopped steering wheel

**chopped steering wheel** (also **chopped wheel**) *n.* Any automotive steering wheel modified by the removal of a section or sections of its outer rim. A popular feature on the radical, futuristic RODS and CUSTOMS of the early 1960s, CHOPPED STEERING WHEELS were intended to imitate the style found aboard jet aircraft or "rocket planes." Despite their obvious practical shortcomings, CHOPPED WHEELS have once again achieved a limited popularity in the retro HOT ROD and CUSTOM CAR movements of the late 1990s and early twenty-first century.

**chop-top** *adj.* Relating to any vehicle that has been CHOPPED. Example: "I'd take a CHOP-TOP COUPE over a HIGHBOY ROADSTER any day."

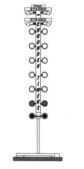

EARLY-1970S **Christmas Tree**

**Christmas Tree** *n.* Electronic light system employed to start most organized, sanctioned DRAG RACES from its 1963 introduction to the present day. CHRISTMAS TREE starting systems feature pre-STAGE and STAGE lights to guide drivers to their precise starting positions. When both racers are properly staged, preliminary amber lights flash, followed by a final green light to indicate the race's start. During the 1960s, a number of different light combinations and progressions were attempted, but in the early 1970s the NHRA officially established what is effectively a dual system. All race classes requiring handicap starting use a SPORTSMAN TREE, with each driver being signaled by a separate progression of amber bulbs lighting at .500-second intervals followed by the actual green "go" signal. DRAG racing's professional HEADS-UP classes rely instead on a PRO TREE flashing all amber lights simultaneously rather than in series. The green light on a PRO TREE typically follows its amber lights by .400 seconds. The PRO TREE was largely conceived with the spectator in mind; PRO TREE reaction times are more a product of a driver's reflexes, while the SPORTSMAN TREE allows the driver to skillfully anticipate the green signal. In both systems a REDLIGHT signals an early or foul start, immediately disqualifying the offending driver. Significantly, REDLIGHT starts are reduced with the PRO TREE. A similarity in appearance to an actual light-decorated Christmas tree is the obvious inspiration for the system's name.

**chrome dome** (also **chrome dome air cleaner**) *n.* Exceptionally large, bulbous chrome-plated air cleaner as FACTORY-featured on all Chrysler Corporation HEMI-equipped cars from the 1966 through 1968 model years with the exception of the 1968 Super Stock HEMI Darts and Barracudas (see HEMICUDA). Were also included on 1969 Dodge Charger R/T, 500, and Daytona models, which were not equipped with fresh-air hoods.

**chrome-reverse wheels** (also **chrome-reversed wheels** or **chrome-reverse rims**) *n.* Any steel automotive wheels modified by having their centers detached (from their outer rims), turned over, then reattached in a reversed position. The resulting wheels feature an attractive, deeper-than-stock positive offset and are further beautified by a chrome-plated finish. CHROME-REVERSE WHEELS are often run without hubcaps, but sometimes feature small center caps (generally of a smooth or BABY MOON style). Most popular during the early- to mid-1960s, CHROME-REVERSE RIMS lost favor with the mass proliferation of STREET-style MAG WHEELS.

**chunk**, see PUMPKIN

**cid** (also **ci**) (usually written, not spoken) *adj.* Cubic inch displacement, may be thought of as the volume of an engine's cylinders as swept by their pistons. An engine's displacement is calculated thusly: $\pi$ x cylinder radius$^2$ x engine STROKE x number of cylinders. A numerical designation most often precedes the CID abbreviation.

**CJ** (usually written, not spoken) **1.** *n.* Any Cobra Jet high-performance V8 engine produced by Ford Motor Company from 1968 through 1973. Variations were created in three distinct FoMoCo engine series: a. The FE Series 428-CID CJ from late 1968 through 1970; **b.** The 385 series 429-CID CJ from 1970 through 1971; and **c.** The 335 series 351-CID CJ from late 1971 through 1973. The 428 CJ and 429 CJ were each also produced as Super Cobra Jet (SCJ) engines, with additional PERFORMANCE and durability features incorporated in their design. Ford's Cobra Jet engines proved highly successful, providing exceptional performance in both STREET and STOCK-class DRAG racing applications. **2.** *n.* Any FoMoCo vehicle FACTORY-equipped with a Cobra Jet engine. PERFORMANCE-based models of Ford's Mustang (see 'STANG), Fairlane, and Torino, as well as Mercury's Cougar and Cyclone, all were furnished with Cobra Jet engines at various times in their production.

**clean 1.** *adj.* Relating an extremely smooth and uncluttered appearance. Common vehicle modifications undertaken to achieve a CLEAN look include shaving STOCK ornamentation and door handles, eliminating STOCK body seams, filling roof openings with custom sheetmetal (most early-model closed cars featured a large central gap in roof sheetmetal, typically covered with a flush and fixed canvas insert); and generally smoothing FACTORY bodylines. Term is often associated with the HIGH-TECH, BILLET, or MONOCHROMATIC movements of the 1980s and 1990s. **2.** *adj.* General term for superior (simple, effective, and aesthetically pleasing) engineering in automotive mechanics or fabrication. **3.** *adj.* Relating to a vehicle in excellent original condition, typically unaltered from its original FACTORY form.

**click it** (also **click it off**) *v.* To abort a complete PASS by fully lifting off of the throttle at any point during the course of a DRAG racing RUN. A racer may CLICK IT when experiencing a mechanical failure or control problem or during a TEST AND TUNE PASS where a complete RUN is not necessary.

**clip 1.** *n.* Any complete assembly or segment of a greater automotive chassis, but most often referring to a front chassis section including frame, suspension, and braking components (see FRONT CLIP). **2.** *v.* To replace any complete existing chassis section or portion (most often front) with a more modern, sophisticated, or generally improved assembly. Example: "I know it's a big job, but if you go ahead and CLIP the FRONTEND, you'll address all of those issues at one time."

**clone** *n.* Any vehicle constructed to be an exact or near-exact replica of a pre-existing machine. May replicate a rare or desirable production model or an individual, historically significant ROD, CUSTOM, or race car. The expression and building style were initially popularized during the 1980s and have maintained strong favor into the twenty-first century.

1930s-ERA **club plaque**[1]

**club plaque 1.** *n.* Any custom plaque bearing the name and, frequently, personalized logo of an individual ROD and/or CUSTOM CAR CLUB. (A standardized design is shared by all club members.) CLUB PLAQUES are generally cast in aluminum and, when finished, include polished areas and painted details. While sometimes produced in unusual shapes, CLUB PLAQUES are most often horizontal rectangles of approximately 5 x 9 inches. CLUB PLAQUES date to at least the late 1930s when SCTA affiliate clubs proclaimed their identities by affixing plaques to the rears of their vehicles. The CAR CLUB and CLUB PLAQUE traditions peaked during the 1950s and early 1960s but significantly waned through the following decades. With the RETRO ROD and nostalgia movements of the 1990s and early twenty-first century, traditional CLUB PLAQUE usage has, once again, returned to popularity. **2.** *n.* Any custom CLUB PLAQUE as employed by a LOWRIDER CAR CLUB. Although similar in principle to traditional HOT ROD and CUSTOM CAR plaques, LOWRIDER-style plaques (*placas* in Spanish) are typically larger than their hot rodding counterparts and feature intricate sandcast or laser-cut freestanding letters. Finished in either chrome or gold plating, LOWRIDER CLUB PLAQUES are most often mounted to a vehicle's rear package tray or immediately inside of its rear window.

**clutch off** *v.* Generally 1950s-era expression for popping the clutch at the outset of a DRAG RACE.

**C-monster,** see C-body

**cobwebbing** (also **cobweb painting** or **cobwebbed painting**) *n.* Custom automotive paint technique in which unthinned (or slightly thinned) acrylic paint is sprayed at very low air pressure to create a "stringy" cobweb-like effect. First established by famed painter Larry Watson in 1965 and experienced its greatest popularity during the remainder of the 1960s.

**COE** (pronounced as separate letters) *n.* Any vintage, heavy-duty truck of "cab-over-engine" design. During the mid- to late 1930s most American manufacturers radically reconfigured their heavy-truck cabs by moving the engine position rearward and placing the driver's compartment above, and generally forward of, the engine. The resulting models featured dramatically shortened and heightened blunt-nosed cab structures. In work applications, the cab-over-engine designoffered the advantages of a greater cargo-carrying area for a given WHEELBASE, better maneuverability, and improved driver visibility. Recognized for their highly unique bulbous style, COEs (most often 1940s and 1950s models) have achieved moderate popularity in street rodding applications during the 1990s and into the twenty-first century. Rodded COEs generally integrate original body panels with modern chassis and are sometimes reconfigured as contemporary-style extended cabs or crew cabs. Also commonly adapted to the role of car carrier, serving to transport conventional STREET RODS or even race cars over long distances.

1947 CHEVROLET **COE**
STREET ROD

**cog** (also **cogs**) **1.** *n.* Any automotive rear axle's final-drive ratio-gear set (see REAREND). **2.** *n.* Highly general term for any gear or gear set in a vehicle.

**cog collector** *n.* Any automotive manual transmission.

**Coke-bottle mags** *n.* Any American Racing Equipment 200-S MAG WHEELS (see DAISY MAGS). Derived from spoke shape resembling the classic glass Coca-Cola bottle design.

**Coke-bottle styling** *n.* Any automotive body styling bearing an overall resemblance to the traditional glass Coca-Cola bottle. When viewed in profile, vehicles exhibiting COKE-BOTTLE STYLING broaden subtly through the front fenders, narrow in the door area, then broaden, once again, to accentuate the rear quarter panels. Notable examples include the Pontiac GTOs (see GOAT) of 1966 and 1967, General Motors' F-BODY Chevrolet Camaro and Pontiac Firebird (see 'BIRD) of 1967 and 1968, and the second- and third-generation Dodge Chargers of 1968 through 1974.

**Coke-bottle styling**
1968 CAMARO
RALLY SPORT Z/28

**Connie kit** (also **Continental kit** or **Conti kit**) *n.* Any exterior spare-tire carrier as affixed to the rear of an automobile. A spare wheel and tire are retained within a hard-shell covering mounted to, or immediately in front of, a vehicle's rear bumper. The actual wheel cover is positioned nearly vertically but generally exhibits a slight forward cant. CONNIE KITS function to increase usable trunk space while adding an overall quality of style and elegance. Available on most domestic manufacturer's products from the mid- to late 1950s, CONNIE KITS also experienced moderate popularity in CUSTOM CAR applications during the same period. In more recent years, CONTINENTAL KITS have been more commonly fitted to LOWRIDER CUSTOMS. The type's name is derived from its usage on the exotic and influential Lincoln Continental luxury cars of 1940–1942 and 1946–1948.

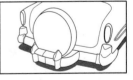

**Connie kit** ON
1954 CHEVROLET

**consistent** *adj.* Relating to any DRAG racing vehicle that records very similar ETs with each successive RUN or PASS. In BRACKET RACING especially, a CONSISTENT vehicle stands a much better chance of winning races.

**convert'** (con-VERT) *n.* Any convertible model automobile.

**cook**, see HAUL

**cop caps** *n.* Any very simple, elemental hubcaps of the type commonly featured on fleet police vehicles (see POVERTY CAPS).

**COPO Camaro** (COPO pronounced as separate letters or as COE-poe) *n.* Any limited-production, 1969 model Chevrolet Camaro featuring a FACTORY-installed (Central Office Production Order) high-performance 427-CID engine. (Chevrolet is rumored to have built a very small number of 427-powered 1968 COPO CAMAROS as well.) COPO CAMAROS with Chevrolet's L-72 cast-iron BLOCK 427, specifically, were capable of solid 12-second quarter-mile ETs in pure STOCK form. Note: Although different variations of the 427-CID engine were fitted to Camaros through the COPO program, the term is most often associated with the 425-BHP L-72.

**corked-up** (also **corked**) *adj.* Describes any automotive engine running through a full exhaust system including head pipes, mufflers, and sometimes resonators, catalytic converters, and/or tailpipes.

the **Corvette curse** *n.* Superstition rooted in a series of dramatic Corvette-bodied (see 'VETTE) DRAG car crashes, fires, and mechanical failures during the late 1960s and early 1970s.

**Couldn't pull a sick whore off a piss pot.** Negative commentary on the relative power of any automotive engine or vehicle. Most often used by HOT RODDERS during the 1940s and 1950s.

THE **County**
TRADITIONAL OCIR LOGO

the **County** *n.* Orange County International Raceway. Alternately referred to as the COUNTY, SUPERTRACK, and OCIR, the NHRA-sanctioned Orange County International Raceway opened on August 5, 1967. In addition to its state-of-the-art DRAGSTRIP, the upscale million-dollar complex initially featured motorcycle, sports car, and go-kart road-racing facilities. Despite its auspicious, ultraprofessional beginnings, the Southern California track quickly fell on financial hardships and by 1973 had shifted to an AHRA sanction. After experiencing a series of managers (including a brief stint by the legendary C. J. "Pappy" Hart), sporadic financial success, and an eventual return to NHRA sanctioning, the COUNTY finally succumbed to the pressures of nearby suburbia on October 30, 1983.

**coupe** (KOOP) **1.** *n.* Vintage (generally 1930s or earlier) automobile body style configured as a closed, two-door passenger car with a two-person seating capacity (not including optional RUMBLE SEAT). The traditional COUPE roof is much shorter than that of a contemporary SEDAN, covering only the model's single bench seat area. Behind the passenger compartment, a trunk or RUMBLE SEAT lid arches rearward to the back of the vehicle. During much of the 1930s, COUPES were produced in both THREE-WINDOW and FIVE-WINDOW variations with the THREE-WINDOWS being perceived as the more-streamlined, sportier models. The COUPE body style has been a perennial favorite in a broad range of hot rodding and racing applications. **2.** *n.* Nineteen-forties and later model two-door automobile designated as a COUPE while incorporating a second bench seat within its closed passenger compartment. By the 1940s and 1950s, the earlier, obvious distinction between COUPE and SEDAN began to blur with COUPE-designated models becoming physically larger and including an inside seating capacity of four to six passengers. These latter-era COUPES nevertheless maintained a somewhat shorter roof area and generally sportier overall lines than those of contemporary SEDAN models. **3.** *n.* Any sports car featuring a two-passenger seating capacity and fixed, enclosing roof. Chevrolet Corvette (see 'VETTE), Dodge Viper, and Ford-powered Shelby sports cars have all been created in closed-roof COUPE form.

**Coupes are for chickens.** (KOOPS) Early HOT RODDER's expression of preference for open cars (generally ROADSTERS) over closed COUPE models. Prior to 1950, SCTA events would not allow COUPES or other closed cars to race. With their heavier weight and presumed aerodynamic handicap, closed cars were not considered viable in high-performance applications. By the late 1940s and early 1950s, attitudes began to shift as severely CHOPPED and streamlined COUPES proved highly aerodynamic and posted outstanding performance marks on the DRY LAKES and at BONNEVILLE.

RAY ANDEREGG'S AMBR-winning **coupester**

**coupester** (KOOP-ster) *n.* Any vintage (generally 1930s or earlier) COUPE model converted to an open car, or makeshift ROADSTER, through the complete removal of its closed roof area. Though relatively rare, these COUPE-derived "ROADSTERS" date to hot rodding's earliest era. In 1955, RODDER Ray Anderegg's topless 1927 Model T (see T-BONE) COUPE tied for the coveted America's Most Beautiful Roadster title (see AMBR), sharing the award with Blackie Gejeian's 1927 Model T, *Shish Kabob Special*. Anderegg's unique HOT ROD featured a custom-frame, CHANNELED body (with filled doors), FLATHEAD engine, and pale yellow paint.

**cowboy rake** *n.* Any highly exaggerated vehicle body/chassis RAKE featuring a very low FRONTEND and high rear-body position.

**cowl induction** *adj.* Relating to any fresh-air induction system (see RAM AIR) with its air intake near the vehicle's cowl area. Taking

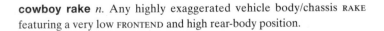

Cowl Induction HOOD ON
1970 CHEVELLE SS 454

advantage of the inherent low-pressure area beneath a vehicle's windshield, COWL INDUCTION systems were utilized sporadically during the 1960s in high-performance and racing applications, but were most closely associated with the 1970 through 1972 Chevrolet Chevelle SS MUSCLE CARS. Available as an option, the bubbled COWL INDUCTION hood on the Chevelle SS featured a vacuum-operated flap that tipped open under full throttle.

**C-pillar** *n.* On any SEDAN model automobile, the rigid structural body member supporting the vehicle's roof, typically at a point where it meets the BACKLIGHT. Some four-door SEDANS and station wagons feature D-PILLARS, placing the C-PILLARS farther forward.

**crab-claw flames** *n.* Custom flame paint treatment (see FLAMES) featuring two-tipped splits resembling the claws of a crab. Initially popularized during the mid-1950s, variations of the theme have maintained continual favor to the present day.

**cracker box** *n.* Any Autolite 4100 model FOUR-BARREL carburetor (see CARB). The CRACKER BOX is a small (465-CFM) moderate-performance CARB featured as original equipment on many 1960s-era SMALL-BLOCK V8 Ford engines. Name derived from its compact size and rectangular shape.

**crank 1.** *n.* Any automotive piston engine's crankshaft, the rotating shaft at the core of most HOT ROD engines. All engine components and systems ultimately serve to spin the crankshaft, whose motion, in turn, is harnessed to propel the vehicle. **2.** see HAUL

**crash box** *n.* Any manual transmission featuring modified synchronizers to facilitate positive, high-speed shifts in PERFORMANCE applications. Derived from the type's tendency to balk or grind when shifted in a normal manner.

**crate motor** (also **crate engine**) *n.* Any complete, or very nearly complete, automotive engine as produced by an original manufacturer or AFTERMARKET engine builder and sold on a retail basis to the general public. High-performance CRATE MOTORS have experienced strong popularity in STREET ROD, STREET MACHINE, and even racing applications from the 1980s through the turn of the twenty-first century. Advantages include convenience, but also oftentimes cost-effectiveness when compared to one-off custom engine machining, modification, and assembly.

**crazy stacks** *n.* Any high-performance fuel-injection VELOCITY STACKS featuring canted tubes of unequal length that aid in precision tuning. The type's seemingly random appearance accounts for its name.

crazy stacks

**crinklewalls,** see WRINKLEWALLS

**crock**, see CRUTCH

**Cross Boss** *n.* Any FoMoCo Autolite inline FOUR-BARREL carburetor (see CARB) and manifold assembly. The unique CROSS BOSS features all four venturis in a single row, unlike the conventional FOUR-BARREL's square pattern. Released by Ford as an OVER-THE-COUNTER complement to their BOSS 302 high-performance package, the CROSS BOSS was produced in two sizes: 850 CFM for SCCA Trans-Am series racing and 1400 CFM for unlimited class racing applications.

**crossed-up** *adj.* Relating to a vehicle traveling somewhat sideways rather than fully forward, generally due to an overpowering of its driven rear wheels and the resulting traction loss. In some forms of racing, it is normal and preferable for a vehicle to be CROSSED-UP and pitched sideways in order to negotiate turns more quickly.

**cross-over springs**, see BUGGY SPRINGS

**cross ram** (also **cross-ram**) *n.* High-performance V8 induction system featuring a FOUR-BARREL carburetor (see CARB) positioned above or outboard of each engine valve cover. The CROSS RAM's unique carb placement provides exceptionally long power-enhancing intake runners, with each FOUR-BARREL feeding air/fuel mixture to the opposite cylinder bank. Unlike the vertical TUNNEL RAM design, the CROSS RAM's generally horizontal runner configuration allows for reasonable hood clearance on many production vehicles. CROSS RAMS achieved their greatest popularity during the 1960s in both OEM FACTORY-installed and AFTERMARKET forms.

**cruise** *v.* To drive a vehicle, usually executing "laps" on one predetermined stretch of urban road, without a specific destination. Most often functions as a type of mobile social event, with adolescent drivers and passengers meeting and communicating between vehicles. HOT RODS, STREET MACHINES, and CUSTOM CARS are sometimes cruised solely for the purpose of being displayed or shown off by their owners. Occasionally, serious HOT RODDERS CRUISE in attempts to CHOOSE OFF an opponent for a STREET RACE. The practice experienced its first widespread popularity during the 1950s, and has continued to the present day. Historically, the term CRUISE has related to the pursuit of a romantic or sexual partner (streetwalking prostitutes were referred to as "cruisers" as early as 1900).

**cruise night** *n.* Typically an organized, prearranged gathering of STREET RODS, STREET MACHINES, or CUSTOM CARS rather than cruising in the traditional sense.

**cruiser gears**, see FREEWAY GEARS

**cruiser skirts** *n.* Unique, elongated style of FENDER SKIRT especially compatible with, and popular on, late-1950s model CUSTOM CARS. The

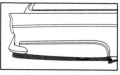

**cruiser skirt** ON
1957 FORD RANCHERO

term and long, graceful proportions are both derived from the SKIRTS provided as original equipment on 1957 and 1958 Mercury Turnpike Cruiser automobiles.

**cruise the gut** *v.* Generally 1950s-era expression for cruising the main street or downtown district of any town.

**crutch** *n.* Early (generally 1940s-era) expression for any vehicle exhibiting poor performance.

**cubes** *n.* The measure of an automotive engine's displacement, either in cubic inches (the traditional American method) or in cubic centimeters (the traditional foreign or import method). Although American manufacturers have recently adopted a policy of rating their engine displacements by the international metric standard (centimeters or liters), it is most common for HOT RODDERS to use the more traditional cubic inches when referring to American-made engines. Example: "I'd have to put my money on the GOAT to win that race. He's still got major CUBES over the 'STANG."

1970 AAR **'Cuda**

**'Cuda** (KOO-duh) *n.* Any Plymouth Barracuda or 'CUDA model. Initially conceived as a sporty FASTBACK version of the compact Plymouth Valiant, the Barracuda was introduced on April 1, 1964, beating the legendary Ford Mustang (see 'STANG) to market by a scant two weeks. (Although not directly inspired by the Mustang, some consider the early-model Barracuda to be the first of Detroit's PONY CARS.) PERFORMANCE variants of the Barracuda include the Formula S models (see BUBBLE-BACK BARRACUDA), the legendary 426 HEMI-powered cars (see HEMICUDA), 'CUDA 440-CID SIX-BARRELS of 1970 and 1971, and 1970's limited-edition AAR 'CUDA (produced to HOMOLOGATE a Trans-Am series racing package and featuring a potent SIX-BARREL 340-CID motor). The Barracuda experienced two major body redesigns during its production run, the first occurring for the 1967 model year and again for 1970. From 1969 until the Barracuda's 1974 demise, Plymouth actually used the abbreviated 'CUDA name as the official designation for various Barracuda-based production models.

**cue ball** *n.* Any white, spherical shift knob. Most commonly associated with the Hurst-brand manual floor-shift linkages introduced and initially popularized during the 1960s, the type's name comes from its similarity in appearance to a white billiards "cue ball."

**curb appeal** *n.* The overall external appearance of any vehicle as perceived on an emotional or visceral level and without close or methodical scrutiny. The initial impression that a car gives when parked by the curb of a street.

**custom car** (also **custom**) **1.** *n.* Any vintage-bodied automobile modified expressly to achieve a CLEAN, streamlined custom appearance.

In its most traditional sense, the term relates to any mid-1930s through early-1960s production automobile employing mild-to-radical body modifications, custom paint, lowered suspension, custom ROLLING STOCK, and/or a custom interior, all to provide a distinctive, graceful, and elegant style or character. The CUSTOM CAR phenomenon largely originated during the late 1930s as an outgrowth of the pre-existing HOP UP culture. While the popular stripped-down HOP UP ROADSTERS of the 1930s and 1940s offered exceptional performance, they were largely impractical for everyday or all-weather driving, so enthusiasts with greater means began to experiment with the modification of newer production cars. Compared with the Spartan 1920s and early-1930s vehicles favored for HOP UP and racing applications, the larger, heavier FAT-FENDER cars of the mid-1930s and 1940s were at a distinct performance disadvantage, thus greater emphasis was placed on a smooth, integrated overall appearance. The CUSTOM style evolved and expanded during the early 1950s, with contemporary production cars being variously lowered, dechromed, FRENCHED, CHOPPED, SECTIONED, and/or treated to elaborate fender extensions. Detroit's radical mid- to late-1950s designs upstaged even these extensively reworked cars, rendering virtually all earlier-bodied CUSTOMS obsolete. During the late 1950s and early 1960s, CUSTOM CARS were seldom subjected to radical body modifications, but instead treated to mild dechroming, lowering, exotic paint jobs, LAKES PIPES, and custom wheels. The popularity of 1960s-era MUSCLE CARS and personal-luxury vehicles effectively ended the original CUSTOM era. During the late 1960s through the mid-1970s, customizing was almost exclusively perpetuated through LOWRIDER CUSTOMS, with only small-scale and localized activity occurring within the Anglo community (see BELLFLOWER CRUISER). Following this long period of diminished activity, a traditional CUSTOM CAR revival began during the late 1970s and has steadily gained in strength into the early twenty-first century. **2.** *n.* Any automobile modified from its OEM, FACTORY configuration to achieve a distinctive, unique outward appearance. Reaching beyond the established parameters of traditional CUSTOMS, the LOWRIDER style in particular tends to express itself in a more varied manner. (LOWRIDERS are commonly based on non-traditional and modern body types and are often finished in more diverse and eclectic styles.)

**customizer** *n.* Any individual involved in the building, driving, and/or showing of CUSTOM CARS.

**custom rod** (also **custom hot rod**) *n.* Any vintage-bodied HOT ROD incorporating CUSTOM CAR-style body elements or modifications. During the 1940s and 1950s, a number of strong distinctions existed between HOT RODS and CUSTOM CARS. Where traditional RODS were most commonly based on 1920s through early-1930s models, the CUSTOM CAR style favored the vehicles of the mid-1930s through the 1950s. Modifications also differed, with RODS being stripped down and hopped up for improved performance and CUSTOMS being treated to extensive body makeovers to enhance their

LATE-1950S **custom rod**

appearance. While HOT RODS were often radically CHOPPED and/or CHANNELED, these changes originated in, or were inspired by, a desire to improve performance. Beginning in the late 1950s, radical SHOW-oriented HOT RODS began to integrate CUSTOM CAR-type bodywork strictly for the sake of aesthetics. Based on early HOT ROD body types, these elaborate showpieces often featured fully custom and exotic nose sections, FRENCHED custom taillights, molded and sculptured fenders, and sometimes even fully custom body structures. The new genre of CUSTOM ROD was born. After experiencing their strongest popularity during the early 1960s, CUSTOM RODS were upstaged by still wilder SHOW-oriented RODS bearing little or no resemblance to any production vehicles whatsoever.

**Customs are for gettin' the girls, hot rods are for forgettin' about the girls.** Traditional expression describing the relative merits of CUSTOM CARS and HOT RODS.

**cut a light on** *v.* To execute a superior REACTION TIME over a DRAG racing competitor. Example: "He ran a better ET. I only won because I CUT A LIGHT ON him."

**cut donuts** *v.* To perform multiple DONUT maneuvers in a vehicle.

**cutouts** *n.* Removable plates or valves incorporated into a vehicle's exhaust system to release engine exhaust before it reaches the muffler(s). CUTOUTS reduce exhaust back-pressure, thereby increasing power levels as well as noise. Even though the use of CUTOUTS is illegal in STREET applications, major domestic automobile manufacturers made systems with CUTOUTS available to the buyers of some high-performance vehicles during the 1960s MUSCLE CAR era.

**cut a good** (or **bad**) **light** *v.* At the outset of a DRAG RACE, to execute a relatively good (or bad) REACTION TIME.

# D

**dagmars** *n.* Large bullet-shaped protuberances featured as front-bumper ornamentation (and supposedly functioning as bumper *guards*) on 1950s-era luxury and CUSTOM CARS. Derived from the popular (and, significantly, buxom) 1940s and 1950s entertainer Virginia Ruth Egnor (a.k.a. "Dagmar") who came to prominence as a singer and dancer on Broadway and later as an early television performer, first on Milton Berle's *Texaco Star Theater* and later on *Broadway Open House*.

**dagmar** ON 1956 CADILLAC

**dago axle** (DAY-go) *n.* Traditional HOT RODDER's expression for any beam-type DROPPED AXLE. Historically, the "dago" expression was used in reference to the city of San Diego, California, thus, in a hot rodding context, DAGO AXLE originally described the popular DROPPED AXLES produced by San Diego RODDER Ed "Axle" Stewart during the 1940s and 1950s.

**dagoed** (DAY-goed) **1.** *adj.* Modified by the inclusion of a DROPPED AXLE, a.k.a. DAGO AXLE. **2.** *adj.* Relating to the general lowering of a vehicle by any means. Example: "The OLDS is lookin' a lot tougher now with a DAGOED FRONTEND."

**daily driver** (also **daily ride**) *n.* Any vehicle street-driven on a daily basis (for transportation to and from work, school, shopping, etc.). Often used as a means of distinction when a HOT RODDER owns more than one vehicle. A HOT ROD or CUSTOM CAR may serve as a DAILY DRIVER or may function as a second vehicle that is driven only on special occasions.

**daisy mags** (also **daisy-spoke mags**, **daisy-petal mags**, or **daisies**) *n.* Any American Racing Equipment 200-S five-spoke MAG WHEELS, which feature a spoke shape reminiscent of a daisy flower's petals. The aluminum 200-S design was introduced by American in 1969 and experienced its greatest popularity from the early to mid-1970s.

**daisy mag**

**dead axle** *n.* Any solid vehicle axle not functioning to propel a vehicle. In hot rodding applications, generally relates to a traditional front BEAM AXLE or TUBE AXLE.

**Dearborn** *adj.* Relating to any Ford Motor Company product. Derived from Ford's major manufacturing facilities in Dearborn, Michigan. Example: "I've always been partial to DEARBORN IRON, myself."

**deck 1.** (also **deck lid**) *n.* Any passenger car's rear trunk lid. **2.** *v.* To remove STOCK rear-DECK emblems, ornamentation, or handles from an auto body, followed by the filling of existing holes and refinishing to achieve a smoother, cleaner appearance. **3.** *v.* To lower the DECK surface of a cylinder block (see BLOCK) through machining. **4.** *n.* In any passenger

SEDAN, the "package tray" area between the back seat and the rear-window glass. [Rare]

**deep gears** (also **deep gearing**) *n.* Any relatively low (numerically high) automotive final-drive ratio (see REAREND). Example: "Those 4.88s are some pretty DEEP GEARS to be using on the street."

**deep staging** *n.* In organized DRAG racing, to STAGE a vehicle slightly farther forward than the normal starting position by activating both the CHRISTMAS TREE's pre-STAGE and STAGE lights, then inching forward to a point where the pre-STAGE light is no longer lit. Serves to reduce REACTION TIME but also makes a competitor more vulnerable to REDLIGHT starts.

**delivers the mail**, see HAULS THE MAIL

**delivery**, see SEDAN DELIVERY or PANEL DELIVERY

**detail 1.** *v.* To thoroughly and meticulously clean and/or mildly refurbish a vehicle that is already in appreciably good condition. The overall process may include rubbing or buffing paint to restore its original luster; repairing minor paint scratches or dings; painstakingly cleaning the interior, underhood, and/or chassis areas; and repairing minor upholstery imperfections. **2.** *v.* To modify any vehicle or vehicle component with a level of detail beyond its original FACTORY-STOCK condition. To customize any vehicle with small, distinct, personal changes that enhance its appearance or functionality.

**Detroit iron** (DEE-troit) *n.* Very generally, any American-made vehicle but most often referring to the traditional larger, heavier automobiles produced in the U.S. during or prior to the 1960s. Derived from Detroit, Michigan, the established center of American automobile manufacturing.

**Detroit locker** *n.* Heavy-duty differential type employing an overriding mechanical ratcheting clutch to effect a positive differential lockup in straight-line applications. DETROIT LOCKER-type differentials have been made factory-available in a variety of PERFORMANCE and MUSCLE CAR applications.

**deuce 1.** *n.* Any automobile produced by the Ford Motor Company during the 1932 model year. A perennial favorite of HOT RODDERS from its introduction to the present day, the DEUCE's strong appeal stems from its simple, classic styling and practical status as the first model year offering Ford's popular FLATHEAD V8. The type's name is derived from the numeral "2," the last in the vehicle's model year. (In common usage, the term may describe the two of any suit within a deck of playing cards, the two-spotted face on a gaming die, a two-year prison sentence, etc.) **2.** *n.*

Any Chevrolet Chevy II, Chevy II Nova, or Nova model produced from 1962 through 1979. The compact Chevy IIs were made available with a number of significant PERFORMANCE engines and options during the 1960s and early-1970s MUSCLE CAR era. Standouts include: **a.** 1966's 350-BHP 327-powered cars; **b.** the 375-BHP 396 and 402 BIG-BLOCK-powered models of 1968 through 1970; and **c.** 425-BHP 427 cars of 1969 and the 360-BHP LT1 350 "Yenko DEUCE" models of 1970, both specially prepared by the renowned Yenko Chevrolet dealership in Canonsburg, Pennsylvania. **3.** *n.* Any TWO-BARREL carburetor (see CARB). Most often used in a plural form to describe a high-performance, multiple-carburetor induction system (three DEUCEs, four DEUCEs, etc.). **4.** *n.* Any non-Ford vehicle produced for the 1932 model year. [Rare]

**dial-in** *n.* In BRACKET RACING, the unique elapsed time (see ET) estimate established by each racer prior to a ROUND of competition. Numerical DIAL-INS are typically painted on a competing vehicle's windows with white shoe polish.

**diff**, see REAREND

**dig**, see WEIGHT TRANSFER

**digger** *n.* Any purpose-built DRAGSTER, but most often relating to a 1950s- or 1960s-era SLINGSHOT. Derived from a DRAGSTER's tendency to DIG IN (experience WEIGHT TRANSFER) at the start of a race.

**the digger** *n. National Dragster,* the official weekly newsletter of the NHRA, first published in 1960.

**dig in** *v.* To achieve traction-enhancing WEIGHT TRANSFER at the outset of a DRAG RACE.

**dig out** (also **dig off**) *v.* At the beginning of a DRAG RACE, to accelerate quickly and aggressively from a standing start. The terms DIG OUT and DIG OFF were most popular during the 1950s.

**the digs** *n.* Generally 1950s through 1960s expression for any organized DRAG racing meet or event.

**dinosaur 1.** *n.* Any complete vehicle or vehicle component (most often an engine) perceived to be primitive, archaic, and/or of an exceptionally large size. Term also tends to evoke a sense of brutish, unrefined power. Example: "Tearin' up the road in a HEMI-STOKED, late-50s DINOSAUR is about as close to heaven as I'll ever get." **2.** *n.* Any Buick Dynaflow automatic transmission. Produced from 1948 through 1963, the Dynaflow was often disparaged by 1950s-era HOT RODDERS for its heavy weight and sluggish, inefficient performance. Dynaflows were also installed in 1953 Oldsmobiles and Cadillacs following a disastrous fire at GM's Hydra-Matic plant.

**dipped**, see ACID-DIPPED

the **dirty two club** *n.* The EL MIRAGE dry lake's 200 MPH Club, a derivative of the venerable BONNEVILLE 200 MPH CLUB. Name attributed to EL MIRAGE's hard dirt surface.

**dish mags** (also **dished mags**) *n.* Any AFTERMARKET slot-type MAG WHEELS, but most often referring to the less-expensive, STREET-oriented SLOT MAGS as generally produced during the 1960s and 1970s.

**D.O.** (pronounced as separate letters) *adj.* Early HOT RODDER'S expression relating to any high-performance double-overhead camshaft (see CAM) engine configuration. Most commonly used during and prior to the 1950s, and later replaced by the term DOHC.

**dog** *n.* Highly general and long-lived expression for any vehicle exhibiting inferior performance.

**dog dishes** (also **dog dish caps** or **dog dish hubcaps**) *n.* Any automotive hubcaps with the simple unadorned appearance of a metallic dog dish (see POVERTY CAPS).

**DOHC** (pronounced as separate letters) *adj.* Relating to any double-overhead camshaft (see CAM) engine configuration.

**domehead** *n.* Generally 1950s and 1960s expression for any HEMI-type engine.

**dometopper** *n.* Custom HOT ROD type featuring a large, clear "bubble" in place of a conventional glass GREENHOUSE or ROADSTER soft top (see BUBBLE TOP, Definition 2).

**donor car**, see PARTS CAR

**donut** (also **doughnut**) *n.* The deliberate act of breaking traction or BURNING RUBBER in a vehicle while traveling in a very tight circle. While performing a DONUT, the driver generally pitches the vehicle somewhat sideways (CROSSED UP) with only its front wheels pointed in the actual direction of travel. Most often executed for the purpose of entertainment or spectacle.

**donuts** (also **doughnuts**) **1.** *n.* General term for any automotive tires but most often referring to the large rear tires commonly used in DRAG racing and hot rodding applications. **2.** *n.* Multiple DONUT maneuvers.

**doorslammer** (also **door car**) *n.* Any DRAG racing vehicle constructed from or based on an actual production vehicle with functioning doors (as distinguished from a purpose-built DRAGSTER). Initially coined during

1968 CAMARO **doorslammer**

the 1960s and used by DRAGSTER racers to berate slower, production-based vehicles. Over time the term's negative connotations have substantially diminished.

**double stick,** see D.O.

**drag 1.** *adj.* Relating to DRAG racing. **2.** *v.* To engage in a DRAG RACE.

**drag chute** *n.* Any parachute deployed from the rear of a DRAG racing vehicle to assist in slowing it from exceptionally high terminal speeds. (DRAG CHUTES are also recognized for their ability to "pull" an out-of-control car back to a straight and true attitude in high-speed emergency situations.) The use of parachutes to slow vehicles dates to the mid-1930s when chutes were tested as an emergency means of slowing runaway diesel trucks. By 1945, the U.S. military was using tail chutes to slow fighter aircraft on short runways. The first use of a parachute in a hot rodding application came in 1958 when racer Abe Carson contracted chute engineer Jim Deist to adapt a chute to the FLATHEAD-powered *Hartman and Carson* DRAGSTER. By 1960, big-name drivers like Tommy Ivo and Art Chrisman were strong chute proponents, furthering the system's popularity. During the mid-1960s, dual parachute systems were introduced, providing still greater slowing potential. Today, DRAG CHUTES are typically mandated on vehicles capable of speeds exceeding 150 miles per hour in the quarter-mile.

MID-1960S CROSSFORM
**drag chute**

**Drag City 1.** *n.* Abbreviated reference to Fontana DRAG CITY, a popular Southern California DRAGSTRIP in operation from 1960 through 1972. **2.** *n.* Mythical DRAG racing utopia as described by recording artists Jan & Dean in their similarly titled 1963 single and 1964 album (see HOT ROD MUSIC).

**draggin' wagon** *n.* Any purpose-built or extensively modified vehicle constructed exclusively for maximum DRAG racing performance. Term dates to the formative early-1950s period of organized DRAG racing. (The May 1952 issue of *Hop Up* magazine included a feature entitled "Drag'in Wagon" about an early purpose-built DRAGSTER. Capable of 11.14-second ETs, RODDER Otto Ryssman's stripped-down THINGIE featured FLATHEAD MERC power, 1925 Chevrolet frame RAILS, and, according to *Hop Up,* a "neat installation of battery and fuel tank . . . accomplished with aid of plumber's tape.")

**drag hag** *n.* Any male DRAG RACER's wife or girlfriend. May serve as a part of a competitor's pit crew or simply support his efforts by attending races.

**drag it out** *v.* Generally late-1940s through early-1950s expression for DRAG racing. May have been derived from one driver's challenging another to bring his car out (i.e., "DRAG IT OUT") to race.

**drag-out job** (also **drag-out special**) *n.* Early-1950s term for any vehicle expressly built for DRAG racing.

**drag race 1.** *n.* Any straight-line acceleration contest between two vehicles, most often beginning from a standing start. May occur on a public road (illegal street racing) or on a legal, sanctioned DRAGSTRIP. While contest distances may vary, most DRAGSTRIPS are currently one-quarter mile in length, with eighth-mile tracks also being reasonably common. Originating in the late 1940s, the term DRAG RACE may have been derived from the expression "main drag" (the main street through any town where early illegal STREET RACES often took place), or from the phrases DRAG IT OUT or DRAG THE GEARS. Although the practice of spontaneous and illegal acceleration racing undoubtedly dates to the earliest years of the motor vehicle, the first legal off-highway DRAG racing began in the late 1940s with the Goleta DRAGS (held on Santa Barbara airport property at Goleta, California). Widely regarded as the first truly organized DRAG events, the Goleta DRAGS were organized by a group of local RODDERS who formed the Santa Barbara Acceleration Association to present semi-regular, insured, and legal meets from 1949 through 1951 (illegal meets were held at the airport in 1948). Additional regularly scheduled DRAG racing events debuted in 1950, including the Pomona and Santa Ana (see SANTA BANANA) DRAGS. **2.** *v.* To engage in a DRAG RACE.

**the drags** *n.* Any organized DRAG racing meet or event.

**drag slicks,** see SLICKS

**dragster 1.** *n.* Any elongated, skeletal vehicle constructed expressly for optimum DRAG racing performance. Term was in popular use by the early 1950s. **2.** *n.* Any purpose-built DRAG racing vehicle regardless of configuration or body and chassis type.

**dragstrip** (also **drag strip**) *n.* Any formal, organized DRAG racing course as generally authorized or sanctioned by a major racing organization. Many early DRAG racing events were presented on the vast expanses of abandoned World War II-era airfields. Term is thus considered by many to have its origins in the aviation terms "airstrip" and "landing strip."

**drag the gears** *v.* To hold a transmission in a given gear longer than normal before upshifting to the next higher gear (the opposite of a SHORT-SHIFT). Expression was most commonly used during the 1940s and 1950s and is sometimes credited with inspiring the term DRAG RACE. Delayed shifting correlates directly to higher engine RPM, generally an advantage in acceleration contests.

**Dragway** (also **Drag-O-Way**) *n.* Alternative and generally archaic term that has most commonly been used in conjunction with an established DRAGSTRIP facility name, e.g., Caddo Mills DRAGWAY (Caddo Mills, Texas),

Detroit DRAGWAY (Detroit, Michigan), and DRAGWAY 42 (West Salem, Ohio). The term DRAG-O-WAY has also been employed in some instances: Carlisle DRAG-O-WAY (Little Rock, Arkansas) and York US 30 DRAG-O-WAY (York, Pennsylvania).

**dressed**, see FULLY DRESSED

**drilled** *adj.* Relating to any automotive component with holes bored or cut into it for the purpose of performance-enhancing lightening. (Early DRAG and LAND-SPEED RACING vehicles sometimes featured DRILLED exterior body panels to release trapped air at speed.) In DRAG racing applications, the practice of drilling parts was most popular during the 1950s. As DRAG technology rapidly evolved throughout the 1960s, DRILLED OEM parts were more often replaced entirely by stronger, more efficient custom- and purpose-built racing components. Traditionally styled STREET RODS sometimes feature DRILLED parts solely to achieve a vintage, racy appearance.

drilled VISOR ON
1931 MODEL A FORD

**drilled and filled** *adj.* Relating to any beam-type DROPPED AXLE modified by the boring of holes across its central lower expanse for the purpose of lightening, and by the "filling" of its turned-up end segments. Traditionally, the process of dropping STOCK axles stretched and often significantly distorted the axle's end portions. The original-manufacture depressions normally found in BEAM AXLE ends were sometimes filled with weld material then ground flush after the dropping process. The filling procedure was believed to improve both the axle's strength and appearance.

**driveability** *n.* In any vehicle, the relative qualities of comfort, responsiveness, and pleasure provided to the driver. A STREET ROD or STREET MACHINE is said to possess good DRIVEABLITY when it can be driven comfortably and reasonably on an everyday basis or on a long road trip. Good DRIVEABILITY may be achieved by the inclusion of updated but practical running gear, modern independent suspension, disc brakes, radial tires, ergonomic seating and interior layout, etc. Conversely, a vehicle is said to have poor DRIVEABILITY when featuring a temperamental race-style engine and/or drivetrain, exceptionally stiff or outdated suspension, awkward and uncomfortable seating, excessive fuel consumption, loud exhaust, etc.

**drive around** *v.* In DRAG racing, to overtake and pass a competitor to win a race. Example: "With my horsepower advantage, I was able to DRIVE AROUND him on the BIG END."

**driver** *n.* Any HOT ROD or CUSTOM CAR that is driven on an everyday basis and/or on regular road trips. Differentiated from a ROD or CUSTOM (most often a temperamental race-type ROD or SHOW-oriented TRAILER QUEEN) that is seldom or never driven on the street. Example: "The

'32's been a real DRIVER for me. I've put over 50,000 miles ON THE CLOCK in just four years."

**drive the wheels off** (also **drive the tires off**) *v.* To cover long distances and log many hours of actual road time in a vehicle. Example: "As soon as the ROADSTER's finished, I fully intend to DRIVE THE WHEELS OFF of it."

droop-snoot
FORD TORINO TALLADEGA

**droop-snoot** *adj.* Relating to any Ford Torino Talladega (named for the famous Talladega [Alabama] Superspeedway) or Mercury Cyclone SPOILER II PERFORMANCE car produced by Ford Motor Company during the 1969 model year. A limited number of Talladega and SPOILER II AERO WARRIORS were marketed to the general public to HOMOLOGATE a highly successful NASCAR racing package. Both models were based on a SLIPPERY FASTBACK design but were treated to additional aerodynamic improvements, including rolled rocker panels, a flush grill, and extended, narrowed and lowered front body components (the inspiration for the DROOP-SNOOT name). Ford tests indicated that their body revisions added nearly 5 miles per hour to the Talladega's TOP END. STREET Talladegas and SPOILER IIs were powered by 428 Cobra Jet engines (see CJ).

**drop kick** *v.* To abruptly and aggressively launch a vehicle into forward motion at the outset of a DRAG RACE. Derived from the popular American football expression.

**dropped axle** *n.* Any automotive front axle of either tubular (see TUBE AXLE) or I-beam (see BEAM AXLE) construction and featuring a more pronounced dip or "drop" to its overall shape than one of STOCK configuration that results in the lowering of a vehicle's FRONTEND. During the 1940s and 1950s STOCK BEAM AXLES were modified by heating and reshaping, but by the 1960s, AFTERMARKET TUBE AXLES became available with appropriate drops integrated during manufacture.

dropped headlight bar ON
1930 FORD

**dropped headlight bar** *n.* Any automotive HEADLIGHT BAR reshaped from STOCK so as to lower the relative position of the vehicle's headlights. From the mid-1920s through the early 1930s, production vehicles commonly mounted headlights by means of a straight or arch-shaped, steel bar. Typically, this headlight bar was mounted between front fenders immediately forward of a vehicle's radiator, with headlights affixed to the bar just outboard of the vehicle's GRILL SHELL. Achieving the sleeker, custom appearance of lowered headlights has traditionally been accomplished by recontouring STOCK bars with lowered portions or "drops" in the areas where the headlights are mounted. In more recent years, AFTERMARKET bars have been manufactured with custom drops integrated during original manufacture.

**drop tank**, see BELLY TANK

**drop the clutch**, see POP THE CLUTCH

**drop the hammer** *v.* To abruptly engage the engine power to a vehicle's driven wheels (most often refers to popping the clutch in a manual-transmission HOT ROD or PERFORMANCE car). Typically occurs from a standing start to perform a BURNOUT or to effect a positive vehicle LAUNCH.

**drop top** *n.* Any HOT ROD, CUSTOM CAR, or STREET MACHINE featuring a convertible soft top that may be easily lowered or "dropped" at any time.

the **dry lakes**, see the LAKES

**dualie** (DOOL-ee) *n.* Any heavy-duty pickup truck equipped with dual rear wheels for additional load capacity and traction. Commonly used as tow and support vehicles for DRAG RACE or SHOW vehicles, and sometimes highly customized in a STREET MACHINE or SPORT TRUCK style.

**dual manifold** (also **dual intake** or **dual**) *n.* Any high-performance intake manifold mounting two carburetors (see CARB). Most often used in reference to a dual TWO-BARREL carburetor system during hot rodding's 1940s through 1950s FLATHEAD era.

**dual quads** *n.* Any high-performance induction system featuring two FOUR-BARREL carburetors (see CARB). Beginning in the mid-1950s, DUAL QUADS were a common feature on STOCK American PERFORMANCE V8 engines. By the early 1970s, multiple FACTORY carburetion of any kind had generally been displaced by more efficient single FOUR-BARREL induction systems. DUAL QUADS have remained popular to the present day in full-competition applications.

**duals** *n.* Any automotive exhaust system featuring two separate sets of head pipes, mufflers, and sometimes tailpipes. DUALS improve a vehicle's performance by reducing the back-pressure common with a single-exhaust system.

**dual setup** *n.* Any high-performance induction system featuring two carburetors (see CARB). Term was most commonly used during or prior to the 1950s to describe AFTERMARKET dual TWO-BARREL manifolds and CARBS.

**dual spots**, see TWIN SPOTS

**dual-throat carb**, see TWO-BARREL

**ducktail spoiler** (also **ducktail**) *n.* Any automotive SPOILER consisting of a relatively short vertical extension or "kick-up" projecting from the

ducktail spoiler ON
LATE-1970S CAMARO Z/28

rearmost portion of a vehicle's DECK LID and quarter panels. Unlike other SPOILER types employing a horizontal WING mounted on vertical pedestals, DUCKTAILS fit flush with existing body panels. DUCKTAIL SPOILERS were optionally available on most manufacturers' late-1960s through early-1970s PONY CAR offerings.

**dummy block** *n.* Any hollow, one-piece artificial engine produced in lightweight plastics and used for chassis fabrication and setup or for display purposes.

**dummy spot** *n.* Any non-functional spotlight (see SPOTS) affixed to the A-PILLAR of a traditional CUSTOM CAR exclusively for aesthetic purposes.

**dump** *v.* To lower a vehicle or a portion of a vehicle, generally through suspension modifications. Example: "I'd need to DUMP the FRONTEND a couple more inches to get the right STANCE."

**dumps** (also **dump tubes**), see CUTOUTS

**dump the clutch**, see POP THE CLUTCH

**dust** someone (also **dust** someone **off**) *v.* To soundly beat an opponent in a DRAG RACE. Dates to at least the 1950s. Example: "The Camaro dude thought he was all hot shit, but I DUSTed his ass big time."

**Dutch**, see VON DUTCH

Duvall windshield[1] ON
1932 FORD ROADSTER

**Duvall windshield** (also **DuVall windshield** or **DuVal windshield**) (doo-VAHL) **1.** *n.* Custom ROADSTER windshield featuring a two-pane "V'd" design and back-swept styling, as introduced by George DuVall during the late 1930s to fit a 1936 Ford cowl. The first recognized instance of a DUVALL WINDSHIELD in a true hot rodding application came in the early 1940s when Jack Dorn contracted CUSTOMIZER Jimmy Summers to adapt the streamlined windscreen to his FULL-FENDERED DEUCE ROADSTER (later the renowned Doane Spencer HIGHBOY). The style subsequently proved a highly desirable addition to 1940s through early-1950s HOT RODS. **2.** *n.* Any modern windshield produced in the classic Duvall style, which gained renewed popularity in the 1970s and has continued into the early twenty-first century.

# E

**E&J headlights,** see TORPEDOES

**early Hemi** (HEM-ee) *n.* Any hemispherical combustion chamber-type V8 engine produced by the greater Chrysler Corporation from the 1951 through 1958 model years. While Chrysler Division 331-, 354-, and 392- (see '92) CID EARLY HEMIS achieved unparalleled DRAG racing successes from the 1950s through the 1960s, smaller Dodge and DeSoto EARLY HEMIS (see BABY HEMI) experienced moderate popularity in PERFORMANCE applications.

**early iron** *n.* Any complete early-vintage automobile or grouping of early autos. Most often used to describe vehicles modified in a STREET ROD style.

**East Coast stance** *n.* Unique STANCE as traditionally applied to vintage-bodied HOT RODS on the East Coast (especially the New England region). Commonly practiced during the 1950s, the EAST COAST STANCE is characterized by an extreme overall vehicle lowness, largely achieved through a severely CHANNELED body.

East Coast stance
ON MODEL A ROADSTER

**E-body 1.** *n.* Chrysler Corporation's designation for the common body/chassis type shared by the Dodge Challenger and Plymouth Barracuda (see 'CUDA) PONY CARS from 1970 through 1974. The highly distinctive E-BODY MOPARs were derived from Chrysler's more conventional B-BODY intermediate series, with the B-BODY's ample engine compartment dimensions employed to accommodate virtually all of Chrysler's engine options. **2.** *n.* Official General Motors corporate designation for its series of personal-luxury cars produced during the 1960s and 1970s MUSCLE CAR era. At various times, Buick Riviera (see RIV), Cadillac Eldorado, and Oldsmobile Toronado models were all based on GM's E-BODY platform.

**echo cans** *n.* Custom, large-diameter exhaust tips as popularized in 1950s-era CUSTOM CAR and STREET MACHINE applications. ECHO CANS' large size serves to amplify a vehicle's exhaust tone.

**effie** (EF-ee) *n.* Any Ford F-100 model light-duty pickup truck produced during the 1953 through 1956 model years. The unique, bulbous styling of the mid-1950s F-100s drew immediate favor among RODDERS and CUSTOMIZERS and has remained a constant favorite to the present day. The most coveted of all F-100s is the rare 1956-only BIG-WINDOW. While most first-generation EFFIES featured a small, flat BACKLIGHT, the optional BIG-WINDOW employed a large wraparound rear window in addition to the standard 1956 wraparound windshield. In the early twenty-first century, fiberglass (see 'GLASS) replica bodies of the 1956 F-100 have

1956 BIG-WINDOW **effie**

become available in both small- and BIG-WINDOW variations, affirming the model's strong popularity.

1955 CHEVROLET
eggcrate grill

**eggcrate grill** *n.* Any automotive grill assembly featuring evenly spaced rows of horizontal and vertical flat bars. The small rectangular divisions created by the grill's intersecting bars are reminiscent of the openings in a traditional egg-shipping crate.

**eight** (also **eight holer** or **eight lunger** [LUNG-er]) *n.* Any eight-cylinder automotive engine.

**eight-barrel**, see DUAL QUADS

**Eight for Show, Four for Go.** Generally 1940s-era expression of preference for FLATHEAD four-cylinder engines over FLATHEAD V8s in PERFORMANCE applications. Although the Ford FLATHEAD V8 possessed greater inherent PERFORMANCE potential than the earlier FLATHEAD fours, little PERFORMANCE development had been accomplished (or speed equipment produced) for the engine by the mid-1940s. By contrast, RODDERS had been successfully hopping up 'BANGERS since the Model T (see T-BONE) era of the 1910s and 1920s, assisted by the abundance of four-cylinder speed equipment available at the time.

Eighty-Eight
1949 ROCKET 88 CONVERTIBLE

**Eighty-Eight** *n.* Any Oldsmobile Rocket 88 model. Introduced for the 1949 model year, the EIGHTY-EIGHT was the first American PERFORMANCE-based automobile of the POSTWAR period. Teaming the lightweight 76-series body with a revolutionary new overhead-valve V8 engine (see KETTERING V8), Oldsmobile's FACTORY HOT ROD embodied the essence of what would one day be known as the MUSCLE CAR. In 1951, R & B artist Jackie Brenston recorded the Ike Turner-penned "Rocket 88," extolling the virtues of Oldsmobile's HOT PERFORMANCE model. As a hit single (and some claim the first rock 'n' roll recording), "Rocket 88" served to further the EIGHTY-EIGHT'S PERFORMANCE image.

**elephant** (also **elephant motor**) *n.* Any Chrysler Corporation-manufactured 426-CID, LATE HEMI engine. Term derives from the engine's substantial size and weight.

**elephant ears** *n.* Unique engine-mounting system as traditionally adapted to Chrysler Corporation-based DRAG racing vehicles. ELEPHANT EARS consist of a single plate sandwiched between an engine's water pump and BLOCK while extending outward to mounting positions at each side of the vehicle's chassis. In competition applications, ELEPHANT EARS offer greater strength and overall rigidity when compared with FACTORY OEM mounting systems. ELEPHANT EARS were initially popularized in LATE HEMI-engined DRAG cars (hence the type's ELEPHANT name) but were later applied to other SMALL-BLOCK and BIG-BLOCK MOPAR V8 engine types.

**elkie** (also **elky**) *n.* Any Chevrolet El Camino model (see CAMINO).

**El Mirage** *n.* EL MIRAGE dry lake in Southern California, a popular venue for LAKES racing, especially in the post-World War II period (see the LAKES).

**engine setback** *n.* Modification performed to a DRAG racing vehicle to enhance its WEIGHT TRANSFER properties and accomplished by relocating a vehicle's engine farther rearward in its chassis than would be normal in a STOCK application. The resulting additional rear-weight bias places more weight on the vehicle's rear tires during acceleration, thus improving traction and performance.

**engine swap** *n.* The exchanging of a vehicle's engine for a type that was never available to the model in an OEM FACTORY installation. Typically involves the installation of a more modern, efficient engine or one that was originally intended for use in a larger, heavier vehicle to create a more favorable power-to-weight ratio and thereby improve a given vehicle's performance. Some ENGINE SWAPS are relatively simple BOLT IN affairs while others require extensive fabrication and reengineering.

**ET** (also **E.T.**) (pronounced as separate letters) **1.** *n.* Elapsed time. The time that it takes for a competing vehicle to traverse any DRAG RACE course (typically clocked to one-thousandths of a second). ET is measured from the instant that a vehicle begins to move until it reaches the track's finish line. Barring disqualification, ET together with REACTION TIME determine a DRAG RACE's winner and loser. **2.** *v.* To record a relatively low elapsed time while DRAG racing. Example: "We've been pullin' a good MILE-AN-HOUR with the new combination, but just can't seem to get the thing to ET."

**ET car** (ET pronounced as separate letters) *n.* Any DRAG racing vehicle purpose-built to compete in elapsed-time BRACKET RACING.

**ET racing** (also **ET bracket racing** or **ET handicap racing**) (ET pronounced as separate letters), see BRACKET RACING

**exhaust cutouts**, see CUTOUTS

**exhaust note**, see NOTE

**exhibition stocker**, see MATCH BASH STOCKER

**exhibition wheelstander**, see WHEELSTANDER

**experimental stocker**, see MATCH BASH STOCKER

# F

**fab** *v.* To fabricate.

**factory** *adj.* Relating to any complete vehicle or automotive component as produced by the original manufacturer "at the factory" (see STOCK). Example: "You're best off sticking with your FACTORY manifolds. They work pretty well in STREET applications."

**factory altered** (also **factory experimental**), see MATCH BASH STOCKER

**factory hot rod** *n.* General term for any vehicle FACTORY-equipped with an exceptionally powerful engine and/or other performance-enhancing equipment so as to emulate the performance of a custom-built HOT ROD. Term dates to at least November 1960, when *Hot Rod* magazine used it to describe the relatively new Chevrolet Impala line (see IMPY).

**factory mags** *n.* Any wheels produced by an automobile manufacturer to loosely imitate the style of AFTERMARKET or racing MAG WHEELS. Commonly featured as original equipment on American MUSCLE CARS and high-performance vehicles from the mid-1960s to the present day.

**fadeaway**
ON 1947 CHEVROLET CUSTOM

**fadeaways** (also **fadeaway fenders**) *n.* Any smooth-flowing front-fender extension as generally applied to 1940s production era CUSTOM CARS. Prior to the 1949 introduction of fully SLAB-SIDED body styles, most 1940s cars featured front-fender shapes terminating abruptly either immediately forward of, or partially into, the vehicle's front door area. CUSTOMIZERS in the late 1940s and early 1950s often reconfigured these front fenders to gradually "fade" rearward, in a streamlined integration with the overall body shape (see FULL FADEAWAYS). During the late 1940s, the Jimmy Summers Company of Los Angeles offered comprehensive 1942 through 1948 Chevrolet fender extension kits for $69.50 each.

**fades** *n.* Custom automotive paint effect wherein one color gradually and subtly fades into another. Often featured as part of traditional graphic treatments such as FLAMES or SCALLOPS.

**fad-T** (also **fad car**) *n.* Any T-BUCKET ROADSTER constructed entirely from new, prefabricated components, including a reproduction fiberglass (see 'GLASS) body. The first AFTERMARKET fiberglass ROADSTER bodies featured in hot rodding and street rodding applications were introduced (notably by Cal Automotive) in the late 1950s. From the early to mid-1960s, T-BUCKET ROADSTER kits gained in sophistication and completeness; the resulting FAD-T trend peaked in popularity in the late 1960s and has maintained moderate favor to the present. FAD-Ts offer the advantages of simpler construction and lower initial cost when compared with other STREET ROD types, but are sometimes discounted by RODDERS who prefer genuine VINTAGE TIN bodies and components.

**fairgrounds queen** *n.* Derogatory term for any HOT ROD, STREET ROD, or CUSTOM CAR that is seldom driven on roadways. A FAIRGROUNDS QUEEN may frequently be trailered and is driven only marginally during major rodding events (often presented at vast outdoor fairgrounds complexes). A FAIRGROUNDS QUEEN shares much in common with a TRAILER QUEEN in that it is generally street-legal and fully functional but is so pristine in nature that its owner avoids situations that expose it to the hazards of everyday driving.

**fan the clutch**, see SLIP THE CLUTCH

**fast 1.** *adj.* Most often relating to any vehicle capable of exceptional maximum terminal speed (see TOP END). **2.** *adj.* Though most often relating to TOP END speed, the term FAST is sometimes used to describe strong vehicle acceleration.

**fastback** *n.* Any automobile with its roofline flowing in a graceful, uninterrupted curve from the windshield to the rear of the DECK LID. In the mid-1960s through mid-1970s MUSCLE CAR era, most major U.S. manufacturers produced high-performance vehicles in FASTBACK or semi-FASTBACK body styles.

fastback
1969 FORD TORINO GT "SPORTSROOF"

**fat-block**, see BIG-BLOCK

**fat-fender** (also **fat-fendered** or **fatty**) **1.** *adj.* Relating to any vehicle produced with decidedly round, bulbous fenders. The type was initiated in the mid-1930s when vehicle design began to more fully integrate fenders with the primary body structure. FAT-FENDER styling evolved (with a break for World War II) until it was eclipsed by the revolutionary SLAB-SIDED cars of the late 1940s. Since their introduction, FAT-FENDER models have maintained moderate-to-strong popularity as foundations for both HOT ROD and CUSTOM CAR modification. FAT-FENDER RODS peaked in favor in the 1980s (when the term experienced its first widespread popularity) and were often treated to the MONOCHROMATIC and PRO STREET themes of the time. The traditional practice of fender removal (see FENDERLESS) is seldom performed on FAT-FENDER HOT RODS. **2.** (also **fat car**) *n.* Any FAT-FENDER style vehicle.

fat-fender[1]
1946 FORD CLUB COUPE

**fat Ford** *n.* Any FAT-FENDER vehicle as originally produced by the Ford Motor Company from 1935 through 1948.

**fatties**, see MEATS

**F-body** *n.* Official General Motors designation for the common body/chassis type shared by all Chevrolet Camaro and Pontiac Firebird (see 'Bird) PONY CARS produced from 1967 through 2002. The GM F-BODY experienced four distinctly different body types during its long production run (1967–1969, 1970–1981, 1982–1992, and 1993–2002), with relatively minor facelifts occurring between major restyles.

**FC** (usually written, not spoken), see FUNNY CAR

**feather the clutch**, see SLIP THE CLUTCH

**feather the throttle** (also **feather-foot it**) *v.* During the course of a DRAG RACE, to apply throttle with subtlety and finesse so as to not overpower the vehicle's tires and lose traction.

**fender flare** ON
1969 CORVETTE

**fender flare** *n.* Custom auto body modification consisting of an extended lip beveled or "flared" away from a vehicle's front or rear quarter panel to surround a tire in a semicircular fashion. Along with their perceived aesthetic value, FENDER FLARES provide practical coverage to the portion of any large tire and wheel combination that would otherwise protrude beyond a STOCK wheel opening. FENDER FLARES experienced strong popularity in the mid- to late 1970s in a variety of STREET MACHINE applications, but had appreciably lost their favor by the 1980s, when the growing trend toward narrowed REAREND/WHEEL TUB combinations more often tucked large wheels and tires well within the confines of OEM body panels.

**fenderless** *adj.* Relating to a HOT ROD style wherein all fenders and related hardware (brackets, splash aprons, etc.) are entirely removed for weight savings, improved aerodynamics, and/or aesthetic purposes. Because fenders typically became a more integral part of overall auto bodies by the mid-1930s, fender removal is most often performed on pre-1935 model year vehicles.

**fender lizards** *n.* Any group of observers slouching low over, or clinging to, an automobile's front fenders while admiring or discussing the vehicle's open engine compartment.

**fender skirts** *n.* Accessory body panels covering the wheelwell openings of an automobile body's (generally rear) quarter panels solely for aesthetic purposes. Available in a broad variety of styles, FENDER SKIRTS are usually removable to allow for wheel access and have long experienced popularity in OEM and, especially, CUSTOM CAR applications.

**fenderwell headers** *n.* Unique steel-tubing exhaust header type commonly featured on 1960s-era full-bodied STREET MACHINE and DRAG vehicles. While most header designs tuck tightly between the cylinder block (see BLOCK) and the frame, FENDERWELL HEADERS arch upward and outward, crossing *above* the frame before turning downward and joining in a collector immediately behind the vehicle's front wheels. FENDERWELL HEADERS offer the advantages of long, equal-length primary tubes, reduced clearance problems with spark plugs and chassis components, and easy access to head-pipe flanges. In order to accommodate FENDERWELL HEADERS, a vehicle's STOCK inner fenders, or "fenderwells," must be either modified or removed altogether (the removal of fenderwells was a common GASSER-era weight-saving measure).

fenderwell headers ON
1955 CHEVROLET SEDAN

**FH** (usually written, not spoken), see FLATHEAD

**Fiestas** (also **Fiesta caps** or **Fiesta flippers**) **1.** *n.* Unique tri-bar style hubcaps as originally featured on the exclusive 1953 Oldsmobile Fiesta convertible model. Original FIESTA CAPS are distinguished by their three decorative bars radiating outward from an elegant central crest. Beneath the bars lies an evenly spaced series of concentric ribs or rings. True Fiesta-type caps were also available on various 1954 and 1955 Oldsmobile products and were commonly adapted to CUSTOM CARS and sometimes to HOT RODS during the 1950s. **2.** *n.* Any vintage hubcaps featuring the FIESTAS' signature element of three evenly spaced ornamental bars. The popularity of Oldsmobile's original three-bar design led to many similar AFTERMARKET caps during the late 1950s and early 1960s. In 1958 advertising, Honest Charlie's Speed Shop offered two different AFTERMARKET tri-bar variations, both referred to as "fiesta type chrome wheel covers." While more appropriately named STARFIRE CAPS, the tri-bar caps included on Oldsmobile's 1956 Starfire models are commonly referred to FIESTAS or FIESTA CAPS as well.

**filled 1.** *adj.* General term relating to the filling of STOCK holes or openings in any auto body panel during the course of custom modifications. **2.** *adj.* Relating to the filling of a BEAM AXLE's end portions (see DRILLED AND FILLED).

**filled grill shell** (also **filled shell**) *n.* Any STOCK automotive GRILL SHELL that has been modified by having its original radiator cap and/or ornamentation removed, followed by the filling of existing holes and refinishing. In hot rodding applications the term FILLED GRILL SHELL most often applies to the extremely popular unit from the 1932 Ford (see DEUCE) passenger car.

**finesse** *v.* To subtly and artfully alter any STOCK body component to achieve a cleaner, more aesthetically pleasing appearance. Example: "That car's lines would look so much better if he were to FINESSE the wheel openings to complement the tire size."

**fingerprint slicks**, see PIE-CRUST SLICKS

**fire burnout** *n.* Any BURNOUT performed by a high-powered DRAG racing vehicle through a burning pool of gasoline. To initiate a FIRE BURNOUT, a standing pool of gas is ignited by the heat and friction of free-spinning DRAG SLICKS. With the gasoline burning, the rear portion of the vehicle is briefly engulfed in a wall of brilliant yellow and orange flames before accelerating clear of the fire and avoiding damage. First popularized in the early 1970s, FIRE BURNOUTS were featured at DRAG events solely for the purpose of dramatic spectacle. Photos were commonly published in magazines and sometimes marketed as posters or on T-shirts. Due to obvious safety concerns, the FIRE BURNOUT phenomenon was relatively short-lived.

**fired**, see STOKED

**fire 'em off** (also **fire 'em up**), see BURN RUBBER

**fire-shooters**, see FLAMETHROWERS

**First On Race Day** *adj.* A mnemonic-like endorsement of Ford Motor Company products.

**fish**, see 'CUDA

**five-pane**, see FIVE-WINDOW

**five-spokes** (also **five-spokers**) *n.* Any AFTERMARKET MAG WHEELS featuring five distinct spokes to connect the wheel's central hub with its outer rim. American Racing Equipment's popular Torq-Thrusts, Astro Supreme chrome custom wheels, and the venerable Cragar S/S MAGS are all considered five-spoke wheels or, more simply, FIVE-SPOKES.

**five-window[1]**
1934 FORD COUPE
DRAG CAR

**five-window 1.** (also **five-window coupe**) *n.* Any vintage COUPE model automobile featuring five windows (not including the windshield). Term is most often used to describe COUPES from the 1930s, when manufacturers commonly produced both three- and FIVE-WINDOW models. FIVE-WINDOWS have experienced strong and consistent opularity in hot rodding applications from their introduction to the present day. **2.** *n.* Any non-COUPE vehicle featuring a FIVE-WINDOW configuration. One common usage of the term FIVE-WINDOW relates to the "Advance Design" Chevrolet and GMC light trucks produced from 1947 through early 1955 (1954 for GMC). Deluxe-cab models featured small curved "quarter windows" between their side door glass and BACKLIGHT. These trucks are relatively popular in STREET ROD and sometimes CUSTOM CAR and LOWRIDER applications. **3.** *adj.* Relating to any vehicle with five windows, not including the windshield.

**Fixed Or Repaired Daily** *adj.* A mnemonic-like negative commentary on Ford Motor Company products.

**flagman** (also **flag starter**) *n.* The established method for starting organized, sanctioned DRAG RACES from the sport's late-1940s origins to the advent of the automated CHRISTMAS TREE system in 1963. During this era, races were signaled by a track crew member standing in front of the competing vehicles and usually on the track's centerline. Typically, this FLAGMAN would wave a green flag to start races and a red flag to indicate foul starts. In the interest of showmanship, FLAG STARTERS often leaped high in the air as they waved the green flag skyward.

1950S-ERA **flagman**

**'flake,** see METALFLAKE

**flame job** *n.* Any custom paint scheme that includes stylized FLAMES.

**flames** *n.* Custom automotive paint treatment depicting a stylized representation of actual flames, usually licking rearward from a vehicle's leading edges. Although there were earlier examples (notably on 1930s-era midget race cars), FLAMES found their first widespread popularity on the HOT RODS and CUSTOM CARS of the 1950s.

**flame the tires,** see BURN RUBBER

**flamethrower** *n.* Any vehicle equipped with flame-throwing exhaust devices (see FLAMETHROWERS).

**flamethowers** *n.* Custom devices producing flames shooting rearward from a vehicle's exhaust system exclusively for the purpose of dramatic spectacle. Typically, ignition devices (traditionally automotive spark plugs) are fitted to the rearmost portion of a vehicle's exhaust tips. To activate the system, the driver REVS the engine, then suddenly disables the ignition spark. With the engine still turning, unburnt fuel is pumped through the engine and exhaust system and finally burned in the form of exhaust-tip flames. Although FLAMETHROWERS date as far back as the 1930s, their first large-scale popularity came in association with the TAILDRAGGER CUSTOMS of the 1950s. FLAMETHROWERS have once again gained favor with the revival of traditional ROD and CUSTOM practices in the 1990s and early twenty-first century.

**flares,** see FENDER FLARES

**flat-ass floored** (also **flat-assed floored**) *adj.* Relating to an absolute full-throttle condition. Inspired by depressing an accelerator pedal "flat" against a vehicle's floorboards or firewall.

**flathead 1.** (also **flat-knocker**) *n.* Traditional term for any VALVE-IN-BLOCK Ford or Mercury V8 engine produced in the U.S. from the 1932 (Ford) and 1939 (Mercury) through 1953 model years (see FLATMOTOR and FLAT-TOP). FLATHEAD Ford and MERC V8s were extremely popular in hot rodding and various racing applications until they were eclipsed by more modern, efficient OHV V8s in the mid- to late 1950s. **2.** *n.* Any engine configured to house both its intake and exhaust valves within its cylinder block (see BLOCK). Name derived from the relatively flat slab of metal functioning as the cylinder head or HEADS.

**Flatheads forever!** *interj.* Common expression of favor for the venerable FLATHEAD Ford/MERC V8 engine. In the late 1960s, *Rod & Custom* magazine published a regular column entitled "Flatheads Forever." Most often written by veteran HOT RODDER Don Francisco, the feature was dedicated to the nuances of the by-then obsolete FLATHEAD engine.

**flatmotor** (also **flatty** or **flattie**) *n.* Alternative and more modern expressions for any Ford or Mercury FLATHEAD V8 engine.

**the flats** *n.* General term for any of several LAND-SPEED RACING venues. May describe either one of Southern California's dry lake beds (see the LAKES) or the BONNEVILLE Salt Flats in western Utah.

**flat-top** *n.* Traditional East Coast expression for any FLATHEAD V8 engine.

**flat tow** (also **flat-tow**) *v.* To tow any vehicle while it rolls "flat" on its own four wheels through the use of a specialized tow bar or similar device. Distinguished from towing a vehicle while fully on a trailer or with two wheels raised off the road surface. Though potentially more dangerous than other methods, FLAT TOWING was commonly employed to transport even high-end race vehicles during hot rodding's formative years (generally the 1950s and earlier). Oftentimes, street-legal roadworthy tires and wheels would be used strictly for transportation purposes, traded for specialized competition-only ROLLING STOCK while racing, then switched back again for the trip home.

**flexi-flyer** (FLEX-ee) *n.* Any DRAG racing vehicle frame or chassis displaying excessive deformation or "flex" when in motion. Often used to describe the mid- to late-1960s SLINGSHOT DRAGSTERS featuring long-wheelbased, custom tube-chassis with extreme flexing properties engineered into them. Such chassis flex was believed to improve traction-enhancing WEIGHT TRANSFER while keeping front wheels on or near the track's surface. The FLEXI-FLYER name is derived from the venerable Flexible Flyer children's snow sled featuring flexible runners for steering.

**flip-flop paint** *n.* Any exterior automotive paint treatment that appears to change color with varying light conditions. Though traditionally applied to the classic Murano-brand PEARLS, the term FLIP-FLOP PAINT is sometimes used to describe modern "color-changing" paints as well (see CHAMELEON PAINT).

**flip-front** *adj.* Relating to any vehicle with a TILT FRONTEND.

**flippers** (also **flipper caps** or **flipper hubcaps**) *n.* Any OEM or AFTERMARKET hubcaps featuring one or more raised styling "bars" across their outer surfaces. The earliest FLIPPERS consisted of a mildly convex full wheel cover with only a single raised bar spanning its width. Introduced in the late 1930s, these AFTERMARKET SINGLE-BAR FLIPPERS were a near-requisite feature on 1940s-era CUSTOMS. During the 1950s and early 1960s, three- and four-bar FLIPPERS upstaged the earlier single-bar types. The highly general term FLIPPER has been applied to a wide variety of 1950s-era caps including tri-bar Oldsmobile FIESTAS and STARFIRES, four-bar Dodge LANCER CAPS, and any AFTERMARKET caps featuring similar three- or four-bar designs. Typically chrome-plated or of brightmetal construction, all FLIPPER HUBCAPS are noted for their effect of reflecting and scattering light when in motion.

SINGLE-BAR **flipper**

**flip-top** *adj.* Relating to any racing vehicle featuring a one-piece body hinged at the rear of its chassis so as to open and close as a single unit. Most often used to describe FUNNY CARS.

**floor it** (also **floorboard it**) *v.* To aggressively and fully depress a vehicle's accelerator pedal.

1969 **flip-top** FIREBIRD

**flopper** (also **flop**) *n.* Any FLIP-TOP FUNNY CAR. Derived from the FUNNY CAR's one-piece fiberglass (see 'GLASS) or carbon-fiber replica auto body, hinged to "flop" open or closed from the back of its chassis.

**flush skirts** *n.* Any automotive FENDER SKIRTS fitting "flush" with a vehicle's existing quarter panels so as to form a consistent, integrated plane. Traditionally popular in both OEM and custom applications.

**fly**, see HAUL

**flying eyeball** *n.* Stylized, winged human eyeball, the signature icon of famed automotive pinstripe artist Ken "VON DUTCH" Howard. VON DUTCH claimed that his design was based on an ancient Macedonian or Egyptian symbol meaning "the eye in the sky knows and sees all."

VON DUTCH **flying eyeball**

**fogbank** *n.* Any exceptionally large and dense cloud of tire smoke as produced by an intense BURNOUT.

**fogged in** *adj.* Inundated by dense, thick tire smoke. Most often used to describe early- to mid-1960s SLINGSHOT DRAGSTERS. While on actual PASSES, vintage RAILS produced vast and intense clouds of burning-rubber smoke; drivers were said to be FOGGED IN when completely obscured during the course of a run.

**fogs** *n.* Custom automotive paint treatment wherein an opaque base coat is partially covered and obscured by a differing accent color. FOGS initially appear as an extremely light mist or veil and very gradually grow denser until they themselves appear opaque or semi-opaque. FOGS are often used to delineate the outlines of individual body panels or to otherwise accent bodylines within an overall custom paint scheme.

**fog the tires,** see BURN RUBBER

**FoMoCo** (FOE-MOE-COE) *n.* Ford Motor Company, the producer of Ford, Lincoln, and Mercury products. FoMoCo is a formal abbreviation that was originally created by Ford Motor Company but is sometimes used in spoken language by HOT RODDERS as well.

**Fordillac** (FORD-il-lack) *n.* Any Ford vehicle modified by the inclusion of a Cadillac engine. Term was most commonly used during the 1950s when HOT RODDERS and CUSTOMIZERS would frequently swap contemporary, large-displacement OHV Cadillac V8s into early Ford HOT RODS and CUSTOM CARS for improved performance.

**Fords for gow** (GOW)**, Chevys for plow.** Early HOT RODDER's expression suggesting the performance superiority of Ford products over those produced by Chevrolet (see GOW).

**forked eight,** see BENT EIGHT

**Found On Road Dead** *adj.* A mnemonic-like negative commentary on Ford Motor Company products.

**four banger** (also **four, four holer**, or **four lunger** [LUNG-er]) *n.* Any four-cylinder automotive engine.

four bar

**four bar** *n.* Any custom or AFTERMARKET parallel-link radius-rod suspension system. A suspension that employs two parallel steel tubes with one pair of ends located at points affixed to a suspended axle and the opposite ends located at equidistant points on an automotive frame. Widely regarded as the most efficient of solid-axle STREET ROD suspensions, FOUR BAR allows each axle end to move independently of the other without experiencing suspension bind or axle twist. Although the use of FOUR BAR dates to at least the 1950s, the type's popularity increased dramatically during the 1970s and 1980s. While still commonly featured for its practicality, the FOUR BAR's favor has diminished somewhat during the 1990s and early twenty-first century as traditionally styled RODS have once again opted for the look of WISHBONE or HAIRPIN suspension systems.

**four-barrel 1.** (also **four-barrel carb**) *n.* Any carburetor (see CARB) featuring a four-venturi configuration. Since the mid-1950s, a common and fundamental feature in most hot rodding and DRAG racing applications, the production FOUR-BARREL carburetor was first introduced with the Buick Roadmaster and Oldsmobile Super 88 models of 1952. **2.**

*n.* Early expression for any four-cylinder engine. The use of the term FOUR-BARREL to describe four-cylinder motors was most common during and prior to the 1940s, when FOUR-BANGERS were favored in high-performance applications and production FOUR-BARREL carburetors had yet to be introduced.

**four on the floor** *n.* Any four-speed manual transmission with a floor shifter configuration.

**four-throat** (also **four-throat carb**) *n.* Alternative expression for any FOUR-BARREL carburetor. Term most popular during the 1950s and 1960s.

**four twos** *n.* Any high-performance induction system featuring four TWO-BARREL carburetors (see CARB).

**foxhunt** *n.* Any of a series of DRAG racing events allowing free-of-charge admission to all female spectators. The term was originally coined as a promotional gimmick by famed DRAG announcer and track manager Steve Evans. The first FOXHUNT events were presented at the Evans-managed Irwindale (California) Raceway during the early 1970s.

**frag** *v.* To explode in a major, destructive mechanical failure (said of any automotive engine or metallic component or mechanical system). Expression originated in Vietnam War-era American military usage, where it meant to kill or wound with the use of a fragmentation grenade. Example: "Miss a shift at that RPM and you're likely to FRAG the whole BOTTOM END."

**frame horns** *n.* The front- or rearmost portions of a classic (generally late-1920s through early-1930s vintage) automobile frame consisting of approximately the last foot of each frame RAIL extending beyond the main body to support fenders, bumper brackets, gas tank, etc. In a STOCK, FULL-FENDERED application, HORNS are hidden by fenders and sheetmetal splash aprons, but on a FENDERLESS HOT ROD they are exposed as gently curving, horn-shaped appendages. FRAME HORNS are sometimes BOXED to improve their appearance, while HIGH-TECH, ultra-CLEAN RODS often omit HORNS entirely.

**frame-off**, see BODY-OFF

**free horsepower** *n.* Any horsepower with no perceived disadvantages. While some horsepower-producing components or modifications come at a cost (PEAKY unstreetable power band, excessive fuel consumption, etc.), those delivering FREE HORSEPOWER are considered to have no "down sides." FREE HORSEPOWER may be derived from free-flowing exhaust systems, precision engine balancing and/or blueprinting, ROLLER CAMS, cold-air induction systems, etc.

**freeway gears** *n.* Any relatively high (numerically low) automotive final-drive ratio (see REAREND). High gearing, while generally detrimental to acceleration, is advantageous to high-speed cruising or "freeway" applications.

frenched TAILLIGHT

**frenched** (also **frenched in**) *adj.* Relating to the replacement of STOCK headlight or taillight housings with smooth, continuous extensions of body panels. When FRENCHED, body edges or lips are smoothed and rounded inward with the lighting components generally being recessed and installed from behind. Term is sometimes applied to other external body components (radio antennas, grill elements, door hinges, etc.) that are dechromed and blended or recessed into a vehicle's body panels. Popular CUSTOM CAR expression derived from the resulting similarity in appearance to French cuffs.

**front clip 1.** *n.* Any complete automotive front chassis assembly, including frame, suspension, and braking components, generally forward of a vehicle's firewall. In many street rodding applications, replacing the original FRONT CLIP of an older vehicle with one from a more modern chassis may provide the improvement of many components, systems, and features, including independent suspension, a lowered RIDE HEIGHT, disc brakes, power steering, sway bar, mounts for a modern engine, etc. **2.** *n.* Any automotive front body component assembly, including fenders, hood, and related hardware. In PERFORMANCE applications, the term FRONT CLIP often refers to a lightweight, fiberglass (see 'GLASS) replacement for standard OEM sheetmetal body components.

**frontend 1.** *n.* The overall front portion of any vehicle, including body and chassis. **2.** *n.* Any vehicle's front body components (fenders, hood, grill and headlight assemblies, etc.). **3.** *n.* Any vehicle's front suspension assembly and related components.

**fry 'em** (also **fry 'em off** or **fry the tires**), see BURN RUBBER

**fry the baloneys,** see BURN RUBBER

**fuel 1.** *n.* Nitromethane racing fuel (see NITRO). **2.** *n.* Any racing fuel (including nitromethane, methanol [see ALKY], or mixtures thereof), but excluding gasoline. (HOT RODDERS and DRAG racers tend not to refer to gasoline as FUEL, instead using the term to distinguish more exotic FUEL types *from* gasoline.)

Fuel Altered[1] WITH
1932 AUSTIN ROADSTER BODY

**Fuel Altered 1.** *n.* The legendary vintage-bodied DRAG racing cars of the 1960s through early 1970s that burned nitromethane racing FUEL (see NITRO) and typically featured: **a.** Custom tube chassis; **b.** Supercharged (see BLOWER) FUEL racing engines (with a maximum of 25 percent ENGINE SETBACK); **c.** Small, lightweight automotive bodies or fiberglass (see 'GLASS) body replicas (most often based on a 1932 American Austin ROADSTER, Fiat

Topolino [see Topo] coupe, or Model T Ford [see T-bone] roadster); **d.** Tube axle frontends; and **e.** High-gear-only drives. The dangerous and unwieldy Fuel Altereds were disallowed for much of their existence by the NHRA. After being sanctioned by various other organizations (principally the United Drag Racers Association [UDRA] and American Hot Rod Association [AHRA]), Fuel Altereds were accepted into the NHRA ranks for the 1967 season. With relatively primitive suspensions, wheelbases averaging between 95 and 100 inches, and maximum-horsepower engines, the popular Fuel Altereds consistently delivered unpredictable "guardrail-to-guardrail" action. **2.** *n.* Any altered class drag racing vehicle burning nitromethane racing fuel (see nitro).

**Fuel Altereds forever!** *interj.* Expression of favor for Fuel Altered drag racing and/or its vehicles.

the **fuel ban** *n.* Period of 1957 through 1963, during which the NHRA prohibited competitors from burning any fuel other than gasoline at its sanctioned events. The NHRA cited safety and cost controls as reasons for the ban, but the popularity of fuel-burners at non-NHRA events led to the reinstatement of fuel classes beginning in 1964.

**Fueler 1.** *n.* Any purpose-built, ultimate-performance dragster burning nitromethane fuel (see nitro). **2.** *n.* Any drag racing vehicle burning nitromethane fuel, regardless of body or chassis configuration.

**fuelie 1.** (also **fuelie motor**) *n.* Any high-performance small-block Chevrolet V8 engine (see Mouse) factory-equipped with Rochester mechanical fuel injection. Introduced for 1957, Chevrolet's "Ramjet" fuel injection helped its new 283-cid motor produce a milestone 283 bhp (one horsepower per cubic-inch of displacement). With steadily increasing power figures throughout their production run, Chevy fuelies peaked with the 1964 and 1965 327-cid engines developing 375 bhp. **2.** *n.* Any Chevrolet vehicle produced during the 1957 through 1965 period and powered by a Rochester fuel-injected engine. While Chevrolet initially offered its fuel-injected small-blocks in both Corvette (see 'Vette) and passenger-car models, the fuelies were dropped from the passenger-car line after 1959. Corvettes exclusively carried fuel-injected power until the type's 1965 discontinuance. During their period of manufacture, fuelie-motored Chevy vehicles were highly revered for their outstanding performance. **3.** *n.* Any non-Rochester/Chevrolet engine or vehicle equipped with fuel injection. [Rare]

**fuel leak** *n.* Any automotive carburetor (see carb). Term most popular during the 1950s when used to describe the two-barrel carbs used in high-performance, multiple-carburetion induction systems.

**full-blown** *adj.* Extensively modified for improved performance (generally said of an engine).

**full fadeaways** *n.* Custom fender treatment with front fenders extending fully to rear fenders (see FADEAWAYS).

**full-fendered** (also **full-fender**) *adj.* Relating to a style of HOT ROD featuring all original fenders and related hardware. Example: "I love the HIGHBOY style, but I just see a FULL-FENDERED ROD as being more practical."

**full-house** *adj.* Relating to any engine that has been extensively modified for maximum performance. Most commonly used in association with the FLATHEAD Ford V8 engine (FULL-HOUSE FLATHEAD).

**full moons** *n.* Custom hubcap type featuring a smooth, chrome-plated convex surface and often a slight outward flare to their rims. Differing from BABY MOONS, the larger FULL MOONS cover the entire outer surface of a steel wheel. Experienced their strongest popularity in the 1950s.

**full-race** *adj.* Relating to any vehicle or vehicle component designed for full competition, maximum-performance usage.

**full row of ducks** *n.* Any induction system featuring four TWO-BARREL carburetors (see CARB) in an inline configuration. Term was most often used from the late 1940s through the 1950s in association with the FLATHEAD Ford/MERC V8 engine. With their excessive capacity, FLATHEAD four-CARB SETUPS were only compatible with true racing applications.

**fully dressed** (also **full dress**) *adj.* Relating to any engine that has been thoroughly accessorized with appearance- and/or performance-enhancing BOLT-ON external components. A FULLY DRESSED engine may include polished-aluminum AFTERMARKET HEADS, chrome acorn nuts, a polished-aluminum multi-CARB INTAKE, chrome AFTERMARKET air cleaner(s), etc. Term most often relates to early-vintage engines (especially the FLATHEAD Ford V8) when used in hot rodding or street rodding applications.

EARLY-2000S ERA **Funny Car**[2]

**Funny Car** (also **Funny**) **1.** *n.* Mid-1960s DRAG racing vehicle based on an actual production HARDTOP or SEDAN but featuring extreme modification to provide ultimate DRAGSTRIP performance. Although directly evolved from the popular STOCK-class racers of the early 1960s, the first FUNNY CARS often boasted such radical modifications as severely altered WHEELBASES (see AWB), dramatically raised centers-of-gravity, and maximum-performance FUEL racing engines. The awkward appearance of these early STOCK-class derivatives was the original impetus for their FUNNY CAR name. Jack Chrisman is generally credited with producing the first true FUNNY CAR by running a BLOWN, INJECTED, FUEL-burning 427-CID Ford motor in a compact Mercury Comet HARDTOP during the 1964 racing season. Chrisman's Comet was forced to race in the B/FUEL DRAGSTER class but created a sensation with its smokey, mid-

nine-second passes. **2.** *n.* DRAG racing vehicle employing the lightweight facsimile of a late-model passenger-car body over a purpose-built front-engined DRAGSTER chassis. The first FLIP-TOP, tube-chassis FUNNY CAR iterations appeared during the 1966 DRAG season with the most successful being campaigned by "Dyno" Don Nicholson. Nicholson's 'GLASS-bodied, CAMMER-motored Mercury Comet replica was the archetype for all FUNNY CARS to follow. Constantly evolving, modern FUNNY CARS feature highly aerodynamic bodies that bear little resemblance to any production vehicles. Though abstract, the FUNNY CAR's SLIPPERY shape yields tremendous performance benefits. FUEL FUNNY CARS consistently post numbers (both speeds and ETs) only slightly behind DRAG racing's ultimate performers, TOP FUEL DRAGSTERS. **3.** *n.* Any professional DRAG racing class campaigned by FUNNY CARS.

**fun pedal** *n.* Any automotive accelerator pedal.

# G

**gangster whitewalls** *n.* Any tires featuring exceptionally wide white sidewall bands. Term derived from the perception that 1920s-era "gangsters" featured such tires on their vehicles.

1941 WILLYS **gasser**[1]

**gasser 1.** *n.* Late-1950s through 1960s DRAG racing vehicle based on an extensively modified early (generally 1930s through 1950s vintage) production COUPE or SEDAN and burning gasoline for fuel. **2.** *n.* Any DRAG racing vehicle burning gasoline for fuel.

**gasser stance** *n.* Any high overall and generally level (sometimes slightly FRONTEND-up) body STANCE as originally popularized as a means of WEIGHT TRANSFER on 1960s-era gas-class DRAG racing vehicles. Sometimes applied to STREET RODS or STREET MACHINES solely to achieve a traditional or nostalgic DRAG RACE look.

**gasser style** *adj.* Featuring the look and overall character of a 1960s-era GASSER. Elements may include a GASSER STANCE, STRAIGHT AXLE front suspension, big 'n' little Halibrand wheels (see HALS), removed front bumper, front-mounted MOON TANK, etc.

**the Gasser Wars** *n.* Extremely popular period of gas-class DRAG racing history (generally the late 1950s through mid-1960s) in which highly publicized personal and speed-equipment rivalries, fast and intense racing action, and wildly aggressive-looking equipment (most notably Willys COUPES and Anglia and Austin SEDANS) combined to create one of DRAG racing's classic eras. The term GASSER WARS was not used in the 1960s but was coined later to describe the period in retrospect.

**Gas, Tires, and Oil** *n.* A mnemonic-like negative commentary on the Pontiac GTO's (see GOAT) allegedly excessive nature.

**gate** *v.* In a DRAG RACE, to attain a lead over an opponent by virtue of a GATE JOB. Example: "He's easily two-tenths quicker. My only chance is to GATE him OFF THE LINE."

**gate job** (also **gate shot**) *n.* In a DRAG RACE, the act of gaining an advantage during the first moments of the race (OUT OF THE GATE). Generally the result of a driver's superior REACTION TIME. Example: "He pulled a solid GATE JOB and held on for the win."

**gearbox** *n.* Any automotive manual transmission.

**gear-grabber 1.** *n.* Any automotive shifter (transmission gear selection mechanism). **2.** *n.* Any driver of a manual-transmissioned DRAG RACE vehicle. [Rare]

**gearhead** *n.* Any especially avid or passionate automotive enthusiast, but particularly one who is active with hands-on mechanics.

**gennie** (JEN-nee) *adj.* Genuine. Term is most often used to describe an OEM automotive part and serves to draw a distinction between new and reproduction components. Example: "That GRILL SHELL's GENNIE '32 Ford."

**get loose** (also **get out of shape** or **get squirrelly**) *v.* During the course of a DRAG RACE, to partially lose control of a vehicle, generally by breaking traction and getting somewhat sideways or CROSSED UP.

**get off of it** (also **get out of it**) *v.* To fully release or ROLL OFF of a vehicle's accelerator pedal.

**get on it** someone (also **get into it**) *v.* To aggressively depress a vehicle's accelerator pedal.

**get out on** someone *v.* To gain an early advantage in a DRAG RACE by virtue of a superior REACTION TIME and/or greater initial acceleration.

**get rubber** *v.* To BURN RUBBER. Term most often describes the generally short period of rubber-burning experienced when upshifting during hard acceleration. Example: "The thing's an absolute TORQUE MONSTER. It'll GET RUBBER easy in all four gears."

**get the drop on** someone, see GET OUT ON

**get the power to the ground**, see PUT THE POWER TO THE GROUND

**gets on** (also **gets with it** or **gets with the program**) *v.* Exhibits outstanding performance (said of any engine or complete vehicle).

**Gets Tickets Often** *adj.* A descriptive commentary on any Pontiac GTO model (see GOAT).

**ghost flames** *n.* Any custom-paint flame treatment (see FLAMES) that is only subtly visible because its color very nearly matches the vehicle's overall paint scheme.

**giggle gas** (also **giggle juice**) *n.* Nitrous oxide (see NITROUS). Term refers to nitrous oxide's effect of intoxication or giddiness when intentionally inhaled by humans.

**Gimmy** (JIM-mee), see JIMMY

**'glass** (also **glass**) *n.* Fiberglass. Product based on fine strands of actual glass fiber permeated with a liquid resin and chemically solidified into sheet form. Fiberglass is commonly used to produce complete automobile bodies or various auto body components. Advantages of 'GLASS over steel include lighter weight (especially when applied to thin-gauge or low-resin-content, race-type body panels); rust- and dent-free replica bodies (in street rodding applications); and relative ease of construction in hobbyist or one-off custom work. In cutting-edge racing applications, traditional fiberglass has largely been eclipsed by advanced composite materials such as Kevlar and carbon fiber, which offer significantly greater strength and weight savings when compared with traditional 'GLASS. Body-shop owner and ROD-builder Dee Wescott pioneered the use of fiberglass body components in hot rodding applications. An August 1958 *Hot Rod* magazine article titled "GLASS Rods For Tomorrow?" described Wescott's operation and the many advantages of his early Ford replica components (fenders, dashboards, splash aprons, running boards, etc.). HRM assured readers that, "The fender shortage is over."

**'Glass is class.** In street rodding applications, an expression of preference for fiberglass (see 'GLASS) auto bodies over their original, VINTAGE TIN counterparts. A lyrically convenient (though often regarded as empty) rebuttal to the condescending STEEL IS REAL.

**glass-packs** (also **glass-pacs**) *n.* Any high-performance exhaust mufflers in which exhaust gasses pass directly through a ventilated tube surrounded by a tight packing of fiberglass material. Notable for their unique "mellow" sound, GLASS-PACKS were especially popular in 1950s and 1960s HOT ROD, CUSTOM CAR, and STREET MACHINE applications.

**'glide,** see SLIP 'N' SLIDE

**G-machine** *n.* Any customized STREET MACHINE capable of outstanding overall performance (including TOP END speed, acceleration, and braking) but with a particular emphasis on handling. Term derived from the lateral G-force rating system that stands as a common measure of a vehicle's handling capabilities. The term G-MACHINE and vehicle style were introduced and popularized in the early twenty-first century.

**GNRS,** see OAKLAND ROADSTER SHOW

**go 1.** *n.* Generally 1950s- and 1960s-era expression for any significant DRAG meet. **2.** *n.* A specific race or ROUND within a greater DRAG event, also generally of 1950s and 1960s usage.

**Goat**
1965 GTO CONVERTIBLE

**Goat** *n.* Any Pontiac GTO model. The GTO debuted for 1964 as a high-performance option package on the Tempest intermediate line. By installing a 389-CID BIG-BLOCK motor (with available 348 BHP) into a lightweight, mid-size SEDAN, HARDTOP, or convertible, Pontiac established a blueprint for the quintessential MUSCLE CAR. Enhancing its PERFORMANCE image, the GTO's sporty name was borrowed from the popular Ferrari 250 GTO (in Italian *Gran Turismo Omologato*, meaning "homologated for grand touring or racing"). For 1966, the strong-selling GTO was designated a separate Pontiac series, with its 389-CID TRI-POWER motor then developing 360 BHP. GTO performance peaked during the 1969 and 1970 model years with the 400-CID RAM AIR IV engine producing an advertised 370 BHP. The GTO "Judge" subseries was offered from 1969 through 1971, with standard features including RAM AIR power, vinyl appearance stripes, and rear DECK SPOILER. By the 1972 model year, the GOAT had, once again, reverted to option status as both performance and production began to wane. Carrying on through 1974, the GTO eventually succumbed to tightening governmental regulations and a changing marketplace. Although GTOs performed well in STOCK-class DRAG competition, their real impact was felt on the streets. While never the fastest cars produced, the plentiful GTOs were nonetheless very strong performers in STOCK trim, and quicker still when modified by enterprising HOT RODDERS. The GTO's GOAT nickname was in popular usage by the mid-1960s.

**goat** *n.* Early HOT RODDER's term (most often used during the 1940s and 1950s, significantly predating the Pontiac GTO) for an older, uncompetitive race car or any vehicle with poor performance.

**go-box** *n.* Any automotive manual transmission, but especially one that is heavy-duty or high-performance in nature.

**go-buggy** *n.* Any exceptionally FAST or QUICK vehicle. Term most popular during the 1950s and 1960s.

**goer** (GO-er) *n.* Any vehicle capable of strong performance. An exceptionally FAST or QUICK car. Term most commonly used by HOT RODDERS during the 1950s and 1960s.

**go-fast goodies** *n.* Any automotive speed equipment, but generally AFTERMARKET replacement parts and components engineered to improve a vehicle's performance.

**go juice** (also **gogo juice**) *n.* Any liquid fuel as burned in an internal-combustion engine, but most often referring to gasoline.

**the gold** *n.* Any trophy or trophies as awarded to DRAG racing class or elimination winners. Derived from the typically bright-plated gold color of such trophies, the term experienced its greatest popularity in the 1950s and 1960s.

**gold dust** *n.* Slang term for traction-enhancing powdered ROSIN.

**goodies** *n.* Highly general term for any, usually AFTERMARKET, components or accessories as applied to a HOT ROD, STREET ROD, or STREET MACHINE. Most popular during the 1960s, the term may describe virtually any PERFORMANCE- or appearance-enhancing parts installed on or affixed to a vehicle. Example: "The engine compartment's TRICKED OUT with the usual chrome GOODIES."

**go off** *v.* To DRAG RACE. Term most often relates to the initial moments of an illegal STREET RACE.

**gook wagon** *n.* Derogatory term for any principally STOCK vehicle adorned with an extreme excess of OEM or, especially, inexpensive AFTERMARKET accessories (trumpet horns, fox tails, bug deflectors, mud flaps, etc.). The GOOK WAGON expression and customizing style were most common from the late 1940s through the mid-1950s and usually applied to 1930s model year vehicles. The proliferation of modern 1950s-era automobiles upstaged the GOOK WAGON, bringing about its general demise. In conflict with prevailing tastes, the GOOK WAGON's appearance was by then often considered tacky, gaudy, or pretentious by contemporary HOT RODDERS and CUSTOMIZERS, for whom common aesthetics suggested that a vehicle's appearance was improved by the removal, rather than addition, of accessories and trim.

**gow** (GOW) *n.* Early HOT RODDER's expression (generally pre-1960s) for any outstanding vehicle performance. Example: "Don't let its looks fool you. That little FIVE-WINDOW packs plenty of GOW."

**gow job** (GOW) *n.* Early (generally pre-World War II era) expression for what would later become known as a HOT ROD, namely a vehicle extensively modified in a "home-built" manner to provide improved performance. Term possibly derived from the expression to GOW OUT, or may be a permutation of "go-job."

**gow out** (GOW) *v.* Early (generally pre-World War II) expression meaning to accelerate quickly.

**gow wagon** (GOW) *n.* Generally 1940s-era term for any vehicle modified for strong performance.

**GP** (usually written, not spoken) *n.* Any Pontiac Grand Prix personal-luxury car as produced from the 1962 model year to the present day. As introduced in 1962, the Grand Prix shared the same General Motors B-BODY platform as the Pontiac Catalina (see CAT) but was unique in its commitment to upscale elegance teamed with ample performance. Early Grand Prix could be outfitted with a host of high-performance options including TRI-POWER versions of the potent 389-CID and 421-CID motors (maximum-performance 421 Super Duty engines were installed in a small number of 1962 and 1963 GPs), four-speed manual transmission with floor shift, and Kelsey-Hayes eight-lug wheels (see KELSEYS). The Grand Prix was significantly redesigned for 1969 with a dramatic long-hood, short-DECK look. Initially dubbed an "A-special" body, the new intermediate type would later be reclassified as the General Motors G-body. In homage to the classic Duesenbergs, G-body Grand Prix were classified as either J models or SJ models, with the Grand Prix SJ offering more luxury and generally greater performance. For 1970 through 1972, Hurst Performance Products modified STOCK Grand Prix J models with a custom luxury/appearance package, resulting in the vehicle that became known as the

Grand Prix SSJ. From 1988 to the present day, the Grand Prix has been based on the smaller, front-drive General Motors W-body platform. A number of PERFORMANCE-oriented W-body GPs have been produced, culminating in the 240-BHP supercharged (see BLOWER) V6-powered GTP versions of the late 1990s and early twenty-first century. Like their Chevy Monte Carlo (see MONTE) cousins, highly modified versions of late-model Grand Prix have experienced considerable success in NASCAR racing applications.

**grab a handful** *v.* To aggressively upshift into a higher transmission gear. Term most often applies to a fast, competition-type POWERSHIFT or speedshift performed with a manual transmission floor shifter. Example: "All I have to do is GRAB A HANDFUL of second, and it'll LIGHT THE TIRES halfway up the block."

**grab some sky** *v.* In any vehicle, to perform or experience a WHEELSTAND.

**grand** *n.* One thousand RPM. Term is always preceded by a number, together indicating a specific RPM level. Example: "The thing's tachin' over eight GRAND IN THE TRAPS."

the **Granddaddy of Them All** *n.* Traditional phrase for the esteemed GRAND NATIONAL ROADSTER SHOW (see OAKLAND ROADSTER SHOW).

**Grand National Roadster Show**, see OAKLAND ROADSTER SHOW

**grand prix gray** *n.* Traditional HOT RODDER term for any gray primer automotive exterior finish.

**granny shift** *v.* To shift a manual transmission's gears in an exceptionally slow, gentle, or conservative manner.

**graphics 1.** *n.* Custom automotive paint scheme featuring colorful, abstract designs that aspire to complement and embellish a vehicle's exterior body panels or individual components. Painted GRAPHICS achieved exceptional popularity during the late 1980s and early 1990s in a broad range of STREET ROD and STREET MACHINE applications. Variations on the GRAPHICS theme include drybrush, neon, splatter, heartbeats, confetti, shock waves, and liquid-like splashes. Some GRAPHICS employ an effective *trompe l'oeil* ("trick the eye") artistic style, creating faux bare-metal finishes (with painted-on screws and rivets), or including lines, objects, and geometric shapes visually suspended over a surface by the use of drop shadows. The GRAPHICS of the 1980s and 1990s were often featured in conjunction with a MONOCHROMATIC overall style (including opaque pastel base colors) and frequently extended to vehicle interiors and engine compartments. Although somewhat diminished in popularity, GRAPHICS have nonetheless been featured in many early-twenty-first-century paint schemes (oftentimes on SPORT TRUCKS and imports). **2.** *n.* Automotive exterior accent treatment as featured on STOCK, FACTORY-produced PERFORMANCE vehicles. STOCK GRAPHICS are almost exclusively

1980S NEON-TYPE **graphics**[1]

presented in a tape or "stick-on" form and may take the form of stripes, engine designation numbers, or make and model names. OEM tape-style GRAPHICS were introduced during the late 1960s and experienced their greatest popularity through the 1970s. Somewhat more subdued graphic themes have endured in a variety of STOCK PERFORMANCE applications to the present day.

**greenhouse** *n*. On any vehicle, the portion of the body extending upward from the BELTLINE and serving to cover the passenger compartment. Depending on the specific model type, the GREENHOUSE may include the windshield, side-window glass, window pillars, BACKLIGHT, and/or roof.

**grenade 1.** *n*. Any automotive engine or component built and/or used in such a way as to be in imminent danger of explosive mechanical failure. **2.** *v*. To explode in a major, destructive mechanical failure.

1932 FORD **grill shell**[1]

**grill shell** (also **grille shell**) **1.** *n*. Metal auto body component (generally of mid-1930s or earlier vintage) serving to house a vehicle's grill assembly and surround its radiator. The smooth, streamlined GRILL SHELLS featured on 1932 Ford (see DEUCE) passenger-car models have long experienced outstanding popularity in hot rodding and street rodding applications. Since the 1930s, RODDERS have commonly fitted the DEUCE GRILL SHELL to earlier Ford Model T (see T-BONE) and Model A (see A-BONE) -bodied vehicles, replacing more angular STOCK SHELLS. **2.** *n*. The indistinct area of sheetmetal surrounding the grill opening of a 1940s or later era automobile. Term is sometimes used when an entire grill assembly (along with surrounding integrated auto body sheetmetal) is removed from one vehicle and grafted as a single unit into another. [Rare]

**grind** *n*. Any specific camshaft (see CAM) type as measured in lift, duration, overlap, etc. Camshafts are generally produced from cast-iron blanks or BILLETS and custom "ground" to their final dimensions with a stone grinding wheel. Example: "What GRIND are you runnin' in the CHEVY?"

**grinder 1.** see GEAR GRINDER **2.** see CAMGRINDER **3.** *n*. Any race-style automotive engine. Generally a 1960s-era term. [Rare]

**grocery getter** *n*. Any smooth-running, reliable vehicle capable of being driven around town on an everyday basis and serving as a practical means of conveyance. Contrasting markedly with its literal meaning, the term is often used sarcastically to describe a street-driven, race-oriented HOT ROD. Example: "Eight hundred horsepower in a street-driven ROD, that ought to make for quite the little GROCERY GETTER."

**gross horsepower** *n*. The traditional method of measuring horsepower (as practiced by American manufacturers prior to the 1972 model year). The gross method of horsepower rating does not account for all power-robbing accessories required in a practical vehicle application (alternator, air cleaner, full exhaust system, etc.).

**ground effects** *n.* General term for any aerodynamics-enhancing accessories applied to a vehicle to improve its high-speed stability. In MUSCLE CAR or STREET MACHINE applications GROUND EFFECTS may come in the form of various SPOILERS, WINGS, and front AIR DAMS.

**ground grazer** *n.* Any HOT ROD, CUSTOM CAR, or STREET MACHINE featuring an extremely low RIDE HEIGHT.

**ground pounder** *n.* Any intensely loud and powerful HOT ROD or DRAG racing vehicle.

**grudge night** *n.* Any legal DRAG racing event open to the general public for participation and presented regularly on a given night of the week.

**grudge races** (also the **grudges**) *n.* Any regularly scheduled legal DRAG racing program open to the general public. GRUDGE RACES provide a venue for any adult with a valid driver's license to race virtually any vehicle capable of passing a TECH safety inspection. Term originally derived from the concept that one driver may harbor a "grudge" against another that could only be resolved through racing. Legal, sanctioned DRAGSTRIPS sought to provide a safe, controlled environment for these races to take place.

**grump lump** *n.* Unique type of hood scoop as introduced by renowned Chevrolet DRAG racer Bill "Grumpy" Jenkins. Jenkins' original GRUMP LUMP consisted of a large, angular sheet-aluminum box positioned to cover his RAT-motored Camaro's Weiand high-ram/dual-QUAD induction system. A small slot at the bottom of the scoop's face allowed fresh air to enter from the front, while a larger rear opening introduced air from the low-pressure area at the base of the car's windshield. GRUMP LUMPS were featured on a series of Jenkins' highly successful Camaro PRO STOCKS during the early 1970s and were sometimes replicated in custom and AFTERMARKET form during the same period.

**grump lump**
HOOD SCOOP

**grunt** *n.* Torque as produced by any engine.

**gun** *v.* To aggressively increase an engine's speed as measured in RPM.

**gut** *v.* To strip a vehicle's interior areas (passenger compartment, trunk, engine compartment, etc.) of all excess weight to improve the vehicle's performance.

**guts 1.** *n.* Power. Horsepower or torque as produced by any engine. **2.** *n.* Any vehicle's interior (carpet, door panels, upholstered seats, etc.).

**gutter sweepers** *n.* Custom exhaust system wherein tailpipes exit a vehicle's underside immediately forward of, and perpendicular to, its rear wheels. Name derived from the implausible concept of engine exhaust blowing or "sweeping" a street's gutters clean. Term and exhaust style were most popular during the 1960s.

# H

**hair blower** *n.* Any open or convertible PERFORMANCE vehicle, but most often referring to a traditional HOT ROD ROADSTER, CABRIOLET, or PHAETON model.

**hairdryer** *n.* Any automotive turbocharger (see TURBO). Refers to the action of a turbocharger's ultra-high-speed rotating vanes. Working in conjunction with a heated flow of exhaust gasses, the TURBO's function is somewhat reminiscent of an operating hairdryer.

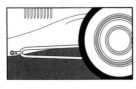

hairpin

**hairpins** *n.* Any custom or AFTERMARKET suspension radius rods constructed from steel tubing and bearing a strong resemblance to actual women's hairpins. HAIRPINS are located at two points affixed to a suspended axle and at one point on an automotive frame. Initially popularized on 1940s- through 1960s-era HOT RODS, HAIRPINS have gained renewed favor with the nostalgia and RETRO ROD trends of the 1990s and early twenty-first century.

**Hals** *n.* Any AFTERMARKET high-performance wheels as produced by the Halibrand Engineering Company (more recently Halibrand Performance Corporation). The business' founder, Ted Halibrand, created his first experimental set of magnesium racing wheels in 1946. The type's successes in circle-track midget racing inspired the formation of Halibrand Engineering the following year. Although varying somewhat in style, race-type magnesium Halibrands most often featured a series of kidney-bean-shaped slots or windows in their surface to provide lightening and brake cooling. Halibrand WINDOW MAGS are easily distinguished by the raised "eyebrows" surrounding each wheel slot or opening. Throughout the 1950s and 1960s, the use of Halibrand wheels was widespread in many forms of circle-track and road racing (specialty Halibrand designs were featured on such significant 1960s-era race cars as Ford GT40s, AC Cobras, and Corvette [see 'VETTE] Grand Sports). Halibrands were also extremely popular in various 1960s-era DRAG racing applications, including SLINGSHOT DRAGSTERS, FUEL ALTEREDS, GASSERS, and early FUNNY CARS. In more recent years, Halibrand has produced a variety of aluminum STREET wheels based on, or inspired by, their classic and traditional racing designs.

**hammered,** see CHOPPED

**hammered-down** *adj.* Generally 1950s-era expression for any vehicle that has been severely lowered through chopping, channeling, and/or sectioning.

**hammer the throttle** (also **hammer it** or **hammer on it**) *v.* To aggressively and fully depress a vehicle's accelerator pedal.

**hammer-weld** (also **hammerweld**) *v.* To cleanly join two sections of sheetmetal through welding and hammering processes. Traditionally practiced with an oxyacetylene torch, HAMMER-WELDing is frequently employed when undertaking radical body modifications (chopping, sectioning, hood-pancaking, etc.) or when adding "patch panels" to rusty or damaged VINTAGE TIN bodies. The HAMMER-WELDing process begins by tack-welding a sheetmetal joint together at short, regular intervals. Next, the entire joint is finish-welded in a series of very short segments so as to reduce heat distortion in the metal. Immediately following each welding procedure, the weld material and adjacent area are beaten flat between a hammer and a steel dolly. Because the metal is worked while still in a red-hot state, the actual weld is hammered even with the overall surface. The nearby sheetmetal is also stretched, counteracting the shrinkage and subsequent warpage that would otherwise occur to the panel. When executed properly, all sheetmetal distortion is eliminated and the welded seam need only be finished with light sanding or filing.

**hand grenade**, see GRENADE

**handicap racing**, see BRACKET RACING

**handler** *n.* Any race-car driver. Example: "He's considered one of the best PRO STOCK HANDLERS in the business."

**hang a left** (also **hang a right** or **hang a U-ie** [YOU-ee]) *v.* While driving a vehicle, to make a left, right, or complete 180-degree U-turn. Terms commonly used by drivers and passengers while cruising.

**hang out the laundry** *v.* To deploy a DRAG CHUTE to assist in the slowing of a vehicle following a DRAG RACE.

**hardtop 1.** *n.* Any closed "pillarless" passenger model automobile manufactured in the POSTWAR period and similar in overall configuration to the traditional closed SEDAN, but significantly different due to its roof construction. A HARDTOP foregoes the SEDAN's requisite window pillars (the rigid structural members and frames surrounding window glass), leaving the sleek, graceful appearance of a convertible model with a steel top grafted onto its body. The earliest POSTWAR American HARDTOP model was offered in 1946 as a special, limited-edition Chrysler Town & Country two-door "hardtop convertible." The first true production HARDTOPS arrived in 1949 in the form of the Cadillac Series 62 COUPE de Ville, Buick Roadmaster Riviera, and Oldsmobile 98 Holiday. By the mid-1950s, HARDTOPS had become standard fare in the lower-priced field and had captured a significant portion of the domestic market. With their sportier, cleaner lines, HARDTOP models of the 1950s and 1960s were frequently designated COUPES by their manufacturers. HARDTOPS (especially those produced in the 1950s and 1960s) have enjoyed perpetual favor as FACTORY HOT RODS, MUSCLE CARS, and as a foundation for high-performance STREET MACHINE modification. **2.** *n.* Any removable hard or rigid roof assembly on a two-seat production ROADSTER model. The first-generation Thunderbirds (see T-BIRD) of 1955 through 1957 and all Corvette (see 'VETTE) ROADSTERS produced from 1956 through 1975 offered detachable HARDTOPS as an option. **3.** *n.* Circle-track racing vehicle type based on generally mid- to late-1930s closed (fixed-roof) passenger cars. The often primitive ROUNDY-ROUND HARDTOPS experienced their greatest popularity during the 1940s and 1950s.

**Harper** *n.* HARPER dry lake, a LAND-SPEED RACING venue in Southern California used intermittently from 1938 through 1946 (see the LAKES).

**hat** *n.* High-performance fuel-injection unit featuring a series of large throttle-actuating butterfly valves in the leading face of a low-profile scoop. Fuel-injection HATS are generally used in race-only applications and most often in conjunction with Roots-type superchargers (see BLOWER). HAT-type units are sometimes applied to NATURALLY ASPIRATED engines as well, usually topping race-style TUNNEL RAMS.

**haul** (also **haul ass, haul booty,** or **haul butt**) **1.** *v.* To demonstrate outstanding performance (said of an engine or vehicle). Example: "Those early A/FX cars could really HAUL ASS for their day." **2.** *v.* To drive at an exceptionally high speed.

**hauler** *n.* Any exceptionally FAST or QUICK vehicle.

**hauls the mail** *v.* Exhibits outstanding performance (said of an engine or vehicle). Expression was most popular during the 1960s.

**haze the tires,** see BURN RUBBER

**header mufflers** (also **header muffs**) *n.* AFTERMARKET exhaust system produced to work in conjunction with steel-tubing exhaust HEADERS. Consisting of only a short length of exhaust pipe, muffler, and turndown, HEADER MUFFLERS function as an abbreviated, self-contained "one-size-fits-all" exhaust system.

**headers** *n.* Any high-performance, free-flowing exhaust manifolds. Term most often refers to AFTERMARKET manifolds constructed of steel tubing (as differentiated from the iron castings used in most STOCK applications). High-performance OEM, cast-iron manifolds are sometimes considered HEADERS, provided they feature a non-restrictive, individual-tube design. Note: When applied to any single-bank (inline) engine configuration, the singular term "header" is appropriate. Due to the dominance of high-performance V-type engines from the 1950s to present, the plural expression HEADERS is more commonly used.

**headlight bar** *n.* A straight or arch-shaped steel bar mounted between front fenders immediately forward of a vehicle's radiator, with affixed headlights just outboard of the vehicle's GRILL SHELL. Common on production vehicles of the mid-1920s through early 1930s.

**headlight bucket** *n.* Formed sheetmetal housing serving to contain and seal the rear portion of a headlight assembly. HEADLIGHT BUCKETS were employed prior to the time when lighting assemblies were fully integrated into a vehicle's bodywork, generally the late 1930s and earlier. The term bucket is derived from the housing's roundish shape and frontal opening to accommodate a headlight unit. Bucket-type headlights are featured on most early-bodied HOT RODS and STREET RODS.

**heads** *n.* Any automotive cylinder heads. The cast (or sometimes machined) metal components capping each bank of cylinders on an internal-combustion engine. Depending on the specific engine configuration, HEADS may also include engine valves, intake and exhaust ports, or complete valve/camshaft (see CAM) systems. V-configured engines feature two cylinder heads, one for each bank of cylinders.

**heads-up** *adj.* Relating to the traditional form of DRAG racing wherein both participants are signaled to begin simultaneously and race through the finish line. Barring disqualification (REDLIGHT start or the crossing of the track's centerline), the first car to reach the finish line wins the race. The term HEADS-UP serves to draw a distinction from any form of handicap or BRACKET RACING that features a staggered start or limitation on elapsed times (see ET). The quickest and most professional of DRAG racing classes are all run on a HEADS-UP basis. Example: "I still believe that *real* DRAG racing is run HEADS-UP, but it's just too expensive to field a competitive car these days."

**heap 1.** *n.* Any old, substantially dilapidated vehicle. Term derived from the expressions "scrap heap" and "junk heap." **2.** *n.* Highly general term for virtually any vehicle but most often suggesting one modified for improved performance. A HOT ROD, STREET ROD, or STREET MACHINE. The term HEAP was most popular in the 1950s and 1960s.

**heat 1.** (also **heat race**) *n.* In circle-track competition, any preliminary race to determine participants or starting positions in subsequent events. **2.** see ROUND

**helmet air cleaner** *n.* Any custom or AFTERMARKET air cleaner of a small (generally $4^1/2$-inch diameter) size and featuring an enclosed bulbous, helmet-like top and sides tapering gently inward until finishing in a slightly outward-flared base. Air enters the unit beneath its chrome-plated external shell. The most notable of the helmet-type air cleaners were produced by Hellings Company in the 1950s, but modern interpretations have been made available in the 1990s and early twenty-first century as well. HELMET AIR CLEANERS experienced their greatest popularity when used on the high-performance, multi TWO-BARREL induction systems of the 1950s.

helmet air cleaners

1965 PLYMOUTH
**Hemi** VALVE COVER

**Hemi** (also **Hemi-head**) (HEM-ee) *n.* Any V8 engine featuring hemispherical (dome-shaped) combustion chambers as produced by Chrysler Corporation in two distinct series: EARLY HEMI (1951 through 1958 model years) and LATE HEMI (1964 through 1971 model years), both of which achieved considerable popularity in PERFORMANCE applications for their efficient, power-producing designs. Chrysler's traditional HEMI V8s are easily recognized by their exceptionally broad valve covers with distinctive mid-cover spark plug placement. With the turn of the twenty-first century, DaimlerChrysler has revived the HEMI name while using it in reference to a modern 345-CID HEMI-HEAD V8 engine.

**hemi** (also **hemi-head**) (HEM-ee) *n.* Any non-Chrysler engine featuring hemispherical-shaped combustion chambers. The highly efficient HEMI design has been applied to a variety of automotive production engines as well as fully AFTERMARKET competition engines since the time of the original Chrysler HEMI V8s.

**Hemicuda** (also **Hemi-Cuda**) (HEM-ee KOO-duh) *n.* Any Plymouth Barracuda or 'CUDA PERFORMANCE model equipped with a 426-CID HEMI engine. Although a number of first-generation Barracudas had received HEMI transplants at the hands of private owners (see BUBBLE-BACK BARRACUDA), it wasn't until 1968 that Plymouth engaged Hurst Performance to modify a limited number of Barracudas expressly for DRAG racing. With their light weight and highly tuned 426-CID HEMI engines, these FACTORY race cars proved extremely successful in Super Stock DRAG competition. For the 1970 and 1971 model years, the general public could purchase a STREET HEMI-equipped 'CUDA directly from the showroom floor. During this same period, HEMI-powered 'CUDAS were successfully campaigned in the new PRO STOCK DRAG class. The June 1965 issue of *Car Craft* magazine featured an article entitled "HEMI-CUDA" showcasing an early mid-engined HEMI/Barracuda conversion and thus dating the term to at least that period.

**Hemified** (HEM-ee-fyed) *adj.* Relating to any vehicle originally produced with, or modified to include, a HEMI engine.

**Henry 1.** *n.* Any vehicle produced by the Ford Motor Company, but most often referring to early-model Fords manufactured during the lifetime of company founder Henry Ford (1863–1947). Term experienced moderate popularity with HOT RODDERS and STREET RODDERS during the 1960s and 1970s era. **2.** *n.* Any engine produced by the Ford Motor Company. [Rare]

**herd** *v.* To drive any vehicle in a high-performance or racing context, generally with the implication that the vehicle performs poorly. Most common during the 1940s, the term HERD was frequently used in conjunction with the term GOAT (a contemporary reference to a badly performing vehicle).

**hides** *n.* HOT RODDER's expression for any automotive tires.

**highboy** (also **hiboy**) **1.** *n.* HOT ROD type, most often consisting of a mid-1920s through mid-1930s ROADSTER body mounted in the STOCK location (un-CHANNELED or "high") on a production passenger-car frame. The quintessential HIGHBOY has traditionally been created by combining either a 1928/1929 or 1932 Ford ROADSTER body with the elegantly sculpted 1932 Ford frame. HIGHBOYS do not have fenders and are generally minimalist and PERFORMANCE-oriented in style. The HIGHBOY type found its first widespread popularity during the 1940s in Southern California, where favorable year-round weather was conducive to ROADSTER (and significantly FENDERLESS ROADSTER) driving. **2.** *n.* Any mid-1920s through mid-1930s vintage, non-ROADSTER HOT ROD constructed in the FENDERLESS and un-CHANNELED HIGHBOY style. **3.** *n.* Generally 1960s-era term for any HOT ROD or STREET MACHINE featuring an exceptionally high, NOSE-BLEED RIDE HEIGHT. [Rare]

1932 FORD **highboy**[1] ROADSTER

**high-gear** someone *v.* During the course of a DRAG RACE, to overtake and defeat an opponent while in high gear. The passing of a vehicle in high gear most often occurs as a direct consequence of superior horsepower.

**highrider** (also **hi-rider**) *n.* Any STREET MACHINE featuring an exceptionally high RIDE HEIGHT.

**High Riser** (also **427 High Riser**) *n.* Maximum-performance 427-CID V8 engine produced by FoMoCo in 1963 and 1964. Ford's HIGH RISERS shared much in common with the concurrently produced 427 LOW RISERS, but differed in several significant respects. The 427 HIGH RISERS featured exceptionally tall, rectangular intake ports with an accompanying high-rise intake manifold, the inspirations for their name. All HIGH RISERS also incorporated larger valves and cross-bolted main-bearing caps for additional BOTTOM END strength. Like LOW RISERS, 427 HIGH RISERS were made available in both single FOUR-BARREL and dual-QUAD configurations. During the 1964 DRAG season, HIGH RISER-equipped LIGHTWEIGHT GALAXIE, THUNDERBOLT, and A/FX Mercury Comet DRAG cars all used Ford's unique TEARDROP HOOD to provide the necessary clearance for the unusually tall HIGH RISER engine. The dual-QUAD HIGH RISERS were FACTORY-rated at the same 425 BHP as the 427 LOW RISER, but true HIGH RISER output was generally considered well beyond 500 BHP.

**high-tech** (also **hi-tech**) *adj.* HOT ROD or CUSTOM CAR style characterized by an ultra-CLEAN, highly modern overall construction and appearance. Elements of the style include cutting-edge sophisticated chassis and drivetrain; a proliferation of machined BILLET-aluminum components; CLEAN, smooth external body surfaces entirely devoid of ornamentation; and simple sculptured, often "Euro"-styled, interiors. Celebrated DRAG car and STREET ROD builder "Li'l" John Buttera largely originated and

**high-tech**
THE *ALUMA COUPE*

strongly influenced the HIGH-TECH style with his revolutionary 1928 Ford HIGHBOY ROADSTER in 1976. With its extraordinary craftsmanship and stark "form-follows-function" appearance, Buttera's white Model A (see A-BONE) was a radical departure from the OVER-DETAILed RODS of the time. The HIGH-TECH HOT ROD style reached its pinnacle with an exotic, custom-bodied FENDERLESS COUPE conceived by designer Larry Erickson and realized by renowned builder Boyd Coddington. Introduced in 1992, the *Aluma Coupe* (so named for its aluminum-panel body construction) featured a transversely mounted mid-engine Mitsubishi four-cylinder, sophisticated one-off independent suspension, and Coddington's signature BILLET aluminum wheels.

**highway gears** (also **hiway gears**), see FREEWAY GEARS

**hi-po** (also **hi-pro, hi-perf,** or **hi-per**) *adj.* High-performance (see HY-PO).

**hired gun** *n.* Any individual contracted expressly to drive a DRAG racing vehicle in competition. Term is more generally used in reference to any person hired to commit a crime with a gun, or to protect individuals and/or property with the use of firearms. Expression evokes an association with the mythological gunfighters of the nineteenth-century American West, perceived to be highly skilled, cool, and calculating specialists.

**his-and-hers shifter** (also **his 'n' hers shifter**) *n.* Automatic transmission shifter type featuring two possible modes for gear changing. In the "hers" mode, the shifter works in the manner of a conventional automatic shifter, while the "his" mode provides an isolated, forward-gears-only "gate," allowing the TRANS to be manually upshifted without the possibility of a misshift. Beginning in the early 1960s, Hurst Performance Products marketed their "Dual Gate" automatic shifter, describing the unit as a HIS-AND-HERS SHIFTER in print advertising. Hurst's system came complete with a personal lockout key, preventing the "his" mode from being used by anyone other than the key holder. Hurst noted: "HIS ONLY—This key on his personal key ring prevents use of the competition gate by the curious parking lot attendant, or the automatic minded little lady." During the 1960s and early-1970s MUSCLE CAR era, Dual Gate shifters were available in AFTERMARKET form and as original equipment in many FACTORY high-performance models.

**hit it** *v.* To aggressively and fully depress a vehicle's accelerator pedal.

**hockey stick stripe** (also **hockey stick**) **1.** *n.* OEM accent stripe optionally available on 1969 Chevrolet Camaro models and featuring the overall shape of an actual hockey stick. The Camaro's HOCKEY STICK STRIPE consists of a broad vertical band at the leading edge of each front fender curving sharply rearward to form a long horizontal stripe along the vehicle's BELTLINE. **2.** *n.* Hockey stick-shaped accent stripe as featured on 1970 Plymouth 'CUDA models. Although similar to the Camaro's HOCKEY STICK, Plymouth's stripe appears as a reverse or "mirror" image to CHEVY's. The stripe's vertical band is, instead, at the trailing edge of each rear quarter panel, and its horizontal stripe follows the BELTLINE forward until terminating on the vehicle's door. The 'CUDA's HOCKEY STICK also includes the vehicle's numerical engine displacement within its vertical band (on 426 HEMI-powered cars, the word HEMI substitutes for the displacement figure).

'CUDA **hockey stick stripe**[2]

**hog's head**, see PUMPKIN

**hold off** someone *v.* To win a DRAG RACE by reaching the finish line before a competitor who is steadily or rapidly gaining in position.

**hole** *n.* Any single cylinder within an engine. Example: "The best we can hope for is to get through this ROUND with a dead HOLE."

**holeshot 1.** (also **hole job**) *n.* In a DRAG RACE, the act of gaining an advantage during the initial moments of the race (OUT OF THE HOLE). The term HOLESHOT strongly relates to a superior REACTION TIME. Example: "You're gonna need a solid HOLESHOT to beat the times he's been running." **2.** *v.* To execute a HOLESHOT at the outset of a DRAG RACE.

**Hollywood hauler** *n.* Any Chevrolet El Camino (see CAMINO) or Ford Ranchero (see 'CHERO) light truck/passenger car hybrid model.

**homologate** (huh-MAUL-uh-gate) *v.* To qualify a PERFORMANCE model or PERFORMANCE option as truly STOCK by selling a specified number to the general public. Major automotive manufacturers have traditionally campaigned representative vehicles in STOCK-class auto racing (circle-track, DRAGS, etc.) to enhance brand prestige and to bolster sales. In the pursuit of victories, however, highly exotic, limited-edition vehicles are commonly created, often straying far from true production-line STOCKERS. These handcrafted FACTORY race cars are never cost-effective to produce, leading manufacturers to build only the few necessary for racing. In order to legitimize these "ringers," governing racing organizations (NASCAR, NHRA, etc.) dictate that a reasonable number be produced and sold through established dealer networks. Example: "MOPAR had to build 1,000 each of its 1970 Challenger T/As and AAR 'CUDAS in order to HOMOLOGATE the models for Trans-Am series racing."

**honeycomb wheels** (also **honeycomb mags** or **honeycombs**) *n.* Unique Pontiac "poly cast" wheels featuring an interlocking pattern of hexagonal shapes. Although HONEYCOMBS have the outward appearance of cast-aluminum mag-type wheels, they actually consist of conventional 15x7-inch steel RIMS with rubberized metallic-silver "honeycomb" centers. HONEYCOMB WHEELS were available on various Pontiac PERFORMANCE models for the 1971 through 1976 model years.

honeycomb wheel

**honk,** see HAUL

**honker** *n.* Any exceptionally FAST or QUICK vehicle. Term most popular during the 1950s and 1960s.

**honkin' on** *n.* The act of driving in a very fast or aggressive manner.

1956 CHEVROLET **hood bird**[1]

**hood bird 1.** *n.* Any of several chrome-plated, diecast hood ornaments optionally available on Chevrolet passenger cars during the early- to mid-1950s. CHEVY's popular HOOD BIRDS integrated the stylized head of an eagle with the swept wings of a jet plane in an elegant, futuristic design. **2.** see SCREAMING CHICKEN.

**hood pin** ON
1970 DODGE CHALLENGER

**hood pins** *n.* Chrome-plated steel pins affixed to a vehicle's underhood substructure and positioned in such a way as to protrude through small holes in the vehicle's hood (one near each front hood corner) when the hood is closed. The hood is secured by placing clips through holes in each of the pins immediately above the hood level. The clips themselves are generally attached to the vehicle by light-gauge cable to prevent being misplaced. Working to supplement a conventional underhood latching system, HOOD PINS positively and securely prevent an automobile's hood from opening while driving at high speeds. While obviously serving a practical function, HOOD PINS are sometimes valued for their racy appearance as well. Most American manufacturers offered HOOD PINS as a PERFORMANCE model option during the late-1960s through early-1970s MUSCLE CAR era.

**hood tach** FROM
1970 PONTIAC GTO

**hood tach** *n.* Any automotive tachometer mounted directly to a vehicle's hood in a special integrated pod. HOOD TACHS were provided as original equipment on various General Motors, FoMoCo, and Chrysler Corporation MUSCLE CARS during the late 1960s and early 1970s.

**hook up** (also **hook**) *v.* To achieve full and complete traction with virtually no tire spinning or slippage. Term most often relates to a DRAG racing vehicle under hard acceleration. Example: "We're having a tough time getting the thing to HOOK UP on the new track surface."

**hoops** *n.* Any automotive wheels, but most often referring to the large-diameter AFTERMARKET BILLET-aluminum wheels popularized from the late 1990s to the early twenty-first century.

**hop 1.** *n.* Any organized contest wherein LOWRIDER-type CUSTOM CARS use adjustable hydraulic suspension systems to "hop" their wheels completely clear of a road's surface (see HOPPING). **2.** *v.* To participate in a LOWRIDER HOPPING activity.

**hop a Tall Boy** *v.* To HOP a LOWRIDER car the height of a "Tall Boy" beer can. During the 1970s, STREET LOWRIDERS found the $7^1/2$-inch height of a

24-ounce Schlitz Tall Boy beer can to be a significant challenge to their RIDE's vertical HOPPING capability. At that time, it was a matter of considerable pride for a LOWRIDER to HOP A TALL BOY.

**hopper** *n.* Any LOWRIDER-based CUSTOM CAR specifically designed to compete in HOPPING events.

**hopping** *n.* Unique sport wherein LOWRIDER-type CUSTOM CARS use adjustable hydraulic suspension systems to "hop" their wheels completely clear of a road's surface. Derived from impromptu street contests, HOPPING evolved during the 1970s through organized competitive events. The traditional contest consists of vehicles striving to achieve the greatest measured clearance between ground surface and airborne front wheels. From the 1980s to the present, HOPPING has grown in popularity and sophistication to include multiple classes and purpose-built exhibition vehicles.

**hop up 1.** (also **hop-up job** or **hopped-up job**) *n.* Early (generally pre-1960s) expression for a vehicle extensively modified for improved performance. During the late 1940s and 1950s, the term HOP UP was largely displaced by the more modern term HOT ROD. **2.** *v.* To modify any vehicle for improved performance. Traditional. **3.** *n.* Generally 1940s through early-1950s term for any individual involved in modifying vehicles in a HOP UP or HOT ROD style. A HOT RODDER.

**Hop Up** *n.* Early small-format magazine (see the LITTLE PAGES) showcasing "HOT RODS, CUSTOM CARS (American), motorcycles, speed boats, and various forms of American speedway racing." Introduced in August 1951, *Hop Up* originally sold for just 15 cents per issue, and by 1953 the popular magazine had become the first sponsor of the famed BONNEVILLE 200 MPH CLUB. In the year 2000, the *Hop Up* name was resurrected and adopted by a modern magazine dedicated to ultratraditional HOT RODS and CUSTOM CARS.

**Horning 1.** (also **Horning head**) *n.* High-performance cylinder HEAD designed and produced by Wayne F. Horning as an AFTERMARKET complement to the inline GMC six-cylinder engine. After selling his rights to the original WAYNE HEAD, Horning created a new design to work with the superior GMC SIX's SHORTBLOCK. As with the earlier WAYNE HEADS, HORNINGS featured a "cross-flow" TWELVE-PORT design but differed somewhat by their altered valve sequence (necessitating a special BILLET camshaft [see CAM]). HORNING HEADS were considered exceptional performers for their era, achieving strong popularity during the early 1950s. **2.** *n.* Any complete high-performance GMC engine equipped with a HORNING TWELVE-PORT HEAD.

**horns,** see FRAME HORNS

**horse** *adj.* Horsepower. Abbreviated term is always used in conjunction with a numerical horsepower rating. Example: "The little 350-HORSE 327 in a lightweight Chevy II [see DEUCE, Definition 2] proved highly competitive in the A/STOCK class."

**horsepressure** *n.* Alternative expression for horsepower most often used in reference to the power produced by a supercharged (see BLOWER) engine.

**hot 1.** *adj.* Powerful. Possessing outstanding performance capabilities (said of an engine or vehicle). **2.** *adj.* Stolen, especially recently. Term may relate to any contraband automotive parts or to a complete vehicle.

**hot iron** *n.* Early (generally late-1940s and earlier) expression describing a vehicle modified for improved performance. The term HOT IRON would be effectively replaced by the term HOT ROD in the POSTWAR era.

**hot licks**, SEE FLAMES

**hot rod 1.** *n.* Any vintage automobile (most often a 1920s- or 1930s-era passenger car) extensively modified to improve its appearance and, especially, performance. In its strictest and most traditional sense, the term relates to a style of vehicle originally popularized during the 1920s through 1940s but maintaining a constant favor to the present day. The quintessential HOT ROD features upgraded suspension and drivetrain as well as body modifications immediately derived from PERFORMANCE or racing applications (e.g., CHOPPED top, fender removal, LOUVERS, NERF BARS, etc.). The actual mid-1940s origins of the term HOT ROD are unclear, but many perceive it to be a lyrical contraction of "hot ROADSTER," the most popular PERFORMANCE model of the era. By the late 1940s, the term HOT ROD was in common but negative use in the Southern California press. As portrayed in print, HOT RODDERS were considered reckless, irresponsible, and dangerous to the greater public's welfare. Through the diligent efforts of the National HOT ROD Association (see NHRA), together with publications like *HOT ROD* magazine, HOT RODS and HOT RODDERS gradually achieved societal acceptance during the 1950s. **2.** *n.* Any vehicle constructed or extensively modified in a non-production, "home-built" manner to provide exceptional overall performance, with a particular emphasis on acceleration and/or TOP END speed. The use of brute horsepower and/or torque (often provided by a large-displacement V8 engine) to dramatically enhance performance is one prevailing characteristic of the American HOT ROD. **3.** *v.* To modify any vehicle in a HOT ROD style or fashion; to improve a vehicle's performance through custom modification.

***Hot Rod*** *n.* Traditionally and consistently hot rodding's leading periodical. Introduced in January 1948, HRM was the first magazine dedicated specifically to the street, DRY LAKES, and circle-track racing interests of true HOT RODDERS. (Interestingly, *HOT ROD* magazine's beginnings actually predate organized DRAG racing.)

**hot rodder** *n.* Any individual involved in the building, driving, racing, and/or showing of HOT RODS.

**hot rod louvers** *n.* Custom vents as applied to a HOT ROD's exterior body panels. Term is used to distinguish the type from the STOCK, original-manufacturer louvers found on most vintage production vehicles (usually as a single row of very long vents) to dissipate underhood heat. As a distinctive adaptation to this practical feature, HOT ROD LOUVERS consist of multiple rows of much shorter vents.

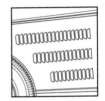

hot rod louvers

**hot rod music** *n.* Type or genre of rock 'n' roll music featuring lyrics and/or themes directly relating to HOT RODS, MUSCLE CARS, and DRAG racing. While cars and, to a lesser degree, HOT RODS have been a relatively common and enduring theme in American popular music, the term HOT ROD MUSIC is most often associated with the unique "California sound" music of the early to mid-1960s, which gained strong national popularity beginning in 1962 and was defined by its rich vocal harmonies, amplified (generally Fender brand) electric guitars, and youth-oriented lyrics (most often celebrating HOT RODS and, more broadly, surfing and "girls"). Released in June 1962, the Beach Boys' single "409" (see '09) is often credited with initiating the HOT ROD MUSIC craze, which lasted in varying intensity through 1965. During its relatively brief period of favor, HOT ROD MUSIC was recorded by hundreds of bands, many consisting only of studio musicians brought together for a given project and dubbed with a HOT ROD-oriented name (Super Stocks, Four Speeds, QUADS, etc.). In attempts to further capitalize on the HOT ROD MUSIC trend, a number of spin-off genres were also attempted. With varying success, albums and/or single records were produced relating to motorcycles, WEIRDO cartoon characters, skateboarding, go-karts, and even miniature slot-car racing. Significant contributors to the HOT ROD MUSIC phenomenon include: Gary Usher (highly prolific writer, producer, and performer); the Beach Boys' Brian Wilson (writer or co-writer, producer, and performer on virtually all of the group's HOT ROD material); Los Angeles radio station KFWB disc jockey Roger "HOT ROD ROG" Christian (a.k.a. "The Poet of the STRIP," who wrote or co-wrote many HOT ROD hits); and Jan Berry of the popular Jan & Dean surf/HOT ROD band (a co-writer, producer, and performer of numerous successful HOT ROD records). With the 1960s being an extraordinarily tumultuous period in popular music history, by mid-decade the HOT ROD music fad was effectively replaced by new and evolving forms of pop music. The actual expression HOT ROD MUSIC was in record industry usage by 1963.

**hot rod primer** *n.* Any flat-black primer as applied to an automotive exterior finish (see SUEDE).

**hot rods from hell** *n.* Popular and descriptive name for 1960s-era Fuel Altered drag racing vehicles.

**hot-shoe** *n.* Any exceptionally fast and/or aggressive driver.

**HP** (pronounced as separate letters) **1.** *adj.* High-performance. **2.** *n.* Horsepower.

**HRM** (usually written, not spoken) *n.* Hot Rod magazine.

**huffer**, see BLOWER

**hummer**, see GOER

**hurt** *v.* To damage an automotive part or component through use in a demanding competition application. Example: "Looks like we HURT the motor bad enough where we won't be making the next ROUND."

**'Hyde** *n.* Naugahyde. Traditionally a popular, vinyl-based automotive upholstery material with a presumed resemblance to real leather. Naugahyde is currently marketed as a product of Uniroyal Technology Corporation.

**hy-po** (also **hy-pro, hy-perf**, or **hy-per**) *adj.* High-performance (see HI-PO).

# I

**I6** (also **I-6**) *n.* Any "inline" six-cylinder automotive engine (see STRAIGHT SIX).

**If it don't go, chrome it.** Traditional HOT RODDER's expression implying a strong distinction between PERFORMANCE-oriented RODS and those that are more influenced by aesthetics.

**Impy** (also **Imp** or **Impaler**) *n.* Any Chevrolet Impala model as produced on and off from 1958 to the present day. The Impala was conceived as Chevrolet's ultimate full-size offering, incorporating top-of-the-line luxury, power, and appearance features. Ed Cole, CHEVY's chief engineer during the late 1950s, described the Impala as a "prestige car within the reach of the average American Citizen." America's bestselling car during virtually every year of the 1960s, the Impala's market position weakened in subsequent decades, eventually resulting in the model's retirement after its 1985 production run. The Impala name was resurrected for 1994 through 1996 and assigned exclusively to the PERFORMANCE-oriented Impala SS (see B-BODY), retired once more for several years, and finally revived with the modern GM W-bodied Impalas of the early twenty-first century. PERFORMANCE standouts within the greater Impala line include: the W Series (see LUMPY HEAD) -engined cars of 1958 through 1965; the 427-CID BIG-BLOCK (with up to 425 BHP) models of 1966 through 1969; and the Impala SS, as produced from 1994 through 1996. The Impala has also proven a highly popular base for CUSTOM CAR modification. The radical styling of the 1958 through 1960 models drew immediate favor with contemporary CUSTOMIZERS, and early- to mid-1960s Impalas have long been considered the ultimate LOWRIDER CUSTOM foundation.

**Impy**
1958 IMPALA MILD CUSTOM

**Indy** *n.* The NHRA Championship DRAG races (see the BIG GO). While in a mainstream context, INDY generally describes the legendary Indianapolis 500 open-wheel race, DRAG racers more often relate the term to the NHRA's foremost DRAG meet.

**injected** *adj.* Relating to any automotive engine or complete vehicle equipped with a fuel-injection system.

**intake** *n.* Any generally cast metallic manifold serving to distribute air/fuel mixture from a carburetor (see CARB) or fuel-injection unit to the individual cylinders of an engine. Custom AFTERMARKET INTAKE manifolds have long been popular additions to high-performance STREET and race-type engines.

**in the traps** (also **in the lights** or **in the eyes**) *adj.* Relating to any DRAG racing vehicle entering or traversing the timing-device area near the finish line of a DRAGSTRIP (see the TRAPS).

**in the weeds** *adj.* Relating to a vehicle (or portion of a vehicle) that has been severely lowered, generally through suspension modifications.

**iron 1.** *n.* Highly general term for any type, grouping, or gathering of vehicles. Most often describes vintage, American-manufactured HOT RODS, high-performance, or CUSTOM CARS. Example: "There was some really tits IRON on display at PASO this year." **2.** *n.* Any individual automobile or vehicle, but most often referring to one modified for improved performance or appearance. [Rare]

# J

**jacked-up** *adj.* Relating to any vehicle with its body/chassis assembly raised through suspension modifications. In the late 1950s, a group of Chrysler employees (initially calling themselves the "Ram Chargers," and later the "Ramchargers") created a highly innovative DRAG racing vehicle based on a 1949 Plymouth Business COUPE. Team members surmised that raising the vehicle's center of gravity would tend to increase (traction-enhancing) WEIGHT TRANSFER. With its CHOPPED top, tunnel-rammed 354-CID HEMI, and bizarre megaphone-tipped exhaust HEADERS, the aptly named *High & Mighty* performed exceptionally well in the C/Altered DRAG class. The car's 1959 and 1960 successes established a trend of high-riding DRAG machines that would last through the mid-1960s. (Excessive RIDE HEIGHTS were quickly abandoned when safer, alternative methods of traction enhancement [improved tire and chassis technology] came into being.) Street machiners adopted a version of the JACKED-UP style purely for aesthetic purposes during the late 1960s and early 1970s, sometimes pushing the trend to extreme heights (see NOSE-BLEED RIDE HEIGHT). Though relatively rare, some retro or nostalgia-inspired STREET MACHINES have included a high-and-level, JACKED-UP STANCE in the 1990s and early twenty-first century.

**jacked-up**
THE RAM CHARGERS'
*HIGH & MIGHTY*

**jack job** *n.* Any vehicle featuring a raised body/chassis assembly through suspension modifications (see JACKED-UP).

**jag rearend** *n.* Any independent REAREND assembly (see WIGGLY REAREND) originally manufactured by Jaguar Cars Ltd. of Great Britain, traditionally the most popular type of independent REAREND adapted to hot rodding and street rodding applications. Independent JAG REARENDS were introduced with the popular XKE models imported to the United States beginning in 1961. An important attribute of the JAG REAREND is its "inboard" disc brakes. Fitted near the unit's center-section, inboard discs reduce unsprung weight while enhancing the unit's overall exotic appearance.

**jalopy** (also **jallopy** or **jalop**) (ja-LOP-ee) **1.** *n.* Any old, substantially dilapidated automobile. Although its origins are uncertain, the term JALOPY may relate to Jalapa, a city in Mexico where many American used cars were sent. Term experienced its greatest popularity during the 1940s and 1950s. **2.** *n.* Any rough, oftentimes crudely constructed, early-vintage automobile used in circle-track racing applications during the 1940s and 1950s.

**Jav**
1971 JAVELIN AMX

**Jav** *n.* Any American Motors Corporation Javelin model PONY CAR. Throughout the Javelin's 1968 to 1974 production run, the sporty AMX represented the ultimate PERFORMANCE model within the greater

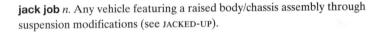

Javelin line. Initially conceived as a challenger to the Chevrolet Corvette's (see 'VETTE) market, the 1968 through 1970 AMX models were actually a shortened version (by approximately 1 full foot) of the standard Javelin, with seating for just two passengers. Though clearly Javelin-based, the first-generation AMXs were not considered Javelins but rather an altogether separate AMC model. For 1971, the two-seat AMX was discontinued, with the AMX model becoming an option package in the redesigned Javelin series. In the PONY CAR tradition, AMX models exhibited well-balanced road manners (good handling as well as strong acceleration when equipped with AMC's potent 390-CID [1968 through 1970] and 401-CID [1971 through 1974] V8 engines). AMXs experienced moderate success in late-1960s STOCK class DRAG racing, but the Javelin's greatest PERFORMANCE achievement came by winning both the 1971 and 1972 titles in the prestigious SCCA Trans-Am road-racing series.

**jelly bean mags** (also **jelly beans**) *n.* Alternative and colloquial expression for any small-window Halibrand DRAG racing wheels (see KIDNEY BEAN MAGS). Name derived from the unique shape of its surface windows.

**jet**
CRAIG BREEDLOVE'S 1963
*SPIRIT OF AMERICA*

**jet** (also **jet car**) *n.* Any DRAG or LAND-SPEED RACING vehicle propelled solely by the thrust of one or more jet engines. On August 5, 1963, 26-year-old HOT RODDER Craig Breedlove drove his three-wheeled *Spirit of America* JET CAR to a new ultimate world speed record of 407 miles per hour on Utah's BONNEVILLE Salt Flats. Breedlove's effort bested the 394-mile-per-hour LSR record established by Englishman John Cobb in 1947 (though Cobb's record, based on four wheels and driven-wheel technology, was recognized by the international FIA governing body while Breedlove's was not). For several years, Breedlove traded world speed records with both Walt and Art Arfons, with the rivalry culminating in a 600-mile-per-hour average by Breedlove in his new *Spirit of America—Sonic One* machine on November 15, 1965. During the 1990s, Breedlove went on to create a new jet-powered *Spirit of America* in an attempt to be the first to break the sound barrier on land. While experiencing sporadic success, Breedlove's bid for the title of first supersonic land vehicle was eventually thwarted by Richard Noble's *Thrust SSC* car. (With Andy Green at the controls, the British LSR vehicle successfully eclipsed the speed of sound by averaging 763 miles per hour across Nevada's Black Rock Desert on October 15, 1997. *Thrust SSC* employed two Rolls-Royce jet engines with a combined 55,000 pounds of thrust.) During the late-1963 height of the HOT ROD MUSIC craze, the Beach Boys surf-rock band recorded a ballad titled "Spirit of America" in recognition of Breedlove's initial LSR accomplishment.

**Jetbird** *n.* Any Ford Thunderbird as produced from the 1964 through 1966 model years. Fully redesigned from the futuristic BULLETBIRDS of

1960 through 1963, JETBIRDS featured a more elegant and subdued overall styling. These fourth-generation Thunderbirds were also treated to a completely new interior, including a cockpit-like "Flight Deck" instrument panel. While no "Sports ROADSTER"(see BULLETBIRD) JETBIRDS were officially produced, approximately 50 convertible T-BIRDS were equipped with the model's signature tonneau and Kelsey-Hayes (see KELSEYS) wire wheels for the 1964 model year. During 1964 and 1965, JETBIRDS were powered by a 300-BHP version of the 390 V8, but for 1966 the 390 was upgraded to 315 BHP and Ford's new 428-CID FE Series iteration (with 345 BHP) was made available as an option.

**Jetbird**
1965 THUNDERBIRD HARDTOP

**jet job 1.** *n.* Any vehicle equipped with FLAMETHROWER exhaust devices. **2.** see JET or JETSTER

**jetster** *n.* Any jet-propelled DRAG racing vehicle (a combining of the words "jet" and "DRAGSTER"). A variety of jet-powered DRAG vehicles have maintained strong popularity from the early 1960s to the present. While thrust-motivated versions of DRAGSTERS and FUNNY CARS are most favored, jet-propelled DRAG exhibition vehicles have also included semitrucks, pickup trucks, go-karts, motorcycles, quad ATVs, and at least one stretch limousine. The first jet-powered DRAG car was campaigned by Walt Arfons and featured a military-surplus Westinghouse J46 turbo-jet engine. Arfons debuted his *Green Monster* at Union Grove, Wisconsin, on August 1, 1960 (the Arfons brothers, Walt and Art, had successfully campaigned a series of piston aircraft-engined *Green Monster* DRAG cars during the 1950s). The jet DRAGSTERS of the 1960s were often pitted against conventional SLINGSHOTS in exhibition MATCH RACES, creating a sensation with their sheer spectacle and fantastic performance. With the NHRA reluctant to recognize the type, early JETS frequently ran at non-NHRA sanctioned tracks like Southern California's San Gabriel and Lions (see the BEACH). Popular standouts from the 1960s include: **a.** Bill Frederick's J47-powered and Gary Gabelich-piloted *Valkyrie 1,* which was also prominently featured in the 1964 Universal film *The Lively Set,* starring James Darren and Doug McClure; **b.** The *Green Mamba* campaigned by "Mr. Jet Car" Doug Rose, who, prior to his involvement with the *Mamba,* lost both of his legs in an accident while driving Walt Arfons' *Green Monster*; and **c.** A series of JETSTERS created by Romeo Palamides, each named *The Untouchable* and most often handled by "Jet Car Bob" Smith, who set a then-astounding 287-mile-per-hour quarter-mile speed record at Lodi, California's Kingdon DRAGSTRIP on January 13, 1963.

**jiggler** *n.* Any automotive engine rocker arm. In a traditional OHV engine, a pivoting device that transfers camshaft-actuated (see CAM) pushrod motion to engine valve movement. The term JIGGLER was most often used during and prior to the 1950s.

**Jimmy 1.** *n.* Any GMC (the truck division of General Motors Corporation) inline six-cylinder engine as significantly popularized in early-1950s PERFORMANCE applications. During the POSTWAR period, JIMMY six-cylinders were often favored for their relatively large displacement and FACTORY overhead-valve configuration. GMC power levels could also be substantially increased with the addition of superior AFTERMARKET HEADS. **2.** *n.* Any complete truck or truck component (most notably a GMC positive-displacement supercharger, a.k.a. a JIMMY BLOWER) produced by the GMC division of General Motors.

**job** *n.* Highly general term for any vehicle, but especially one that has been modified for improved performance. Term is often preceded by a modifier to indicate a more specific vehicle type, e.g., RAIL JOB, BOB JOB, TRACK JOB, SOUP JOB, etc.

**jug** *n.* Any automotive carburetor (see CARB), but most often the TWO-BARREL types commonly featured in high-performance, multiple-CARB applications. Term experienced its strongest popularity during and prior to the 1960s.

**juice brakes** (also **juice binders** or **juicers**) *n.* Hydraulic brakes. Most of the early vehicle types popular in hot rodding and street rodding applications were originally equipped with inferior mechanical braking systems (Ford did not introduce hydraulic brakes until the 1939 model year). The term JUICE BRAKES was most often used during the 1940s and 1950s, when RODDERS commonly converted vehicles to more reliable and efficient hydraulic brakes. Over time, the existence of OEM mechanical brakes has diminished to the point where the term JUICE BREAKS holds little distinction. Virtually all modern RODS are equipped with hydraulic braking systems.

**juicer**, see HAT

**jumping jacks** *n.* Unique system employed by early DRAG racers (including the renowned "Sneaky Pete" Robinson) to facilitate quicker starting line LAUNCHes. With such a system, a vehicle's rear wheels were actually lifted clear of a track's surface after staging had occurred. At the precise instant of the race's signaled start, the already spinning wheels were dropped to the track, abruptly thrusting the vehicle into motion. Although JUMPING JACKS were entirely vehicle-contained and showed good performance potential, their bizarre nature soon led to their prohibition by all major sanctioning organizations.

**jump juice**, see NITROUS

**jump on it** *v.* To aggressively and fully depress a vehicle's accelerator pedal.

**junior muscle car** (also **Jr. muscle car**) *n.* Any of a series of downscaled MUSCLE CARS produced by major American manufacturers from the mid-1960s through the mid-1970s. JUNIOR MUSCLE CARS were offered as lower-priced, more practical alternatives to the manufacturers' various big-cube, maximum-performance offerings. While expressing much of the same visual appeal and overall character of their large-displacement counterparts, JUNIOR MUSCLE CARS were generally powered by smaller, more-economical V8 engines. Examples of JUNIOR MUSCLE CARS include Buick's GS340 (1967) and GS350 (1968–1970); the Plymouth Duster 340 (1970–1973) and Dodge Demon 340 (1971–1973); Oldsmobile's W-31 package Cutlass (1968–1970); and Pontiac's Firebird 350 HO (1968–1969).

junior muscle car
1971 PLYMOUTH DUSTER 340

# K

**kandy apple** (also **kandy**) **1.** *n.* Alternative spelling of CANDY APPLE. The variation was inspired by customizer George Barris' often-used "K" spellings (see KUSTOM) and by his own line of KANDY Kolor paint products. In mainstream culture, the KANDY term is perhaps most widely known for its use in the title of author Tom Wolfe's 1965 bestseller, *The Kandy-Kolored Tangerine-Flake Streamline Baby,* a collection of articles exploring various aspects of early-1960s American pop culture. **2.** see CANDY APPLE, Definition 2

**KB** (pronounced as separate letters) *n.* Any high-performance engine or significant engine component produced by Keith Black Racing Engines, but especially referring to the company's legendary TOP FUEL DRAG racing engines. Company founder Robert "Keith" Black established a strong reputation as a successful FUEL DRAG engine builder during the 1960s. In 1974, Black introduced the first of his fully AFTERMARKET aluminum racing engines. Based on the Chrysler's 426-CID LATE HEMI, Black's design virtually dominated FUEL DRAGSTER racing over the next decade. KB HEMI FUEL BLOCKS are currently in their 15th stage of development and are popularly raced in modern land and boat DRAG applications.

**Kelseys** *n.* Any automotive wheels produced by the Kelsey-Hayes Company. Formed in 1927 by the merger of the Kelsey and Hayes wheel companies, Kelsey-Hayes produced a wide variety of quality automotive wheels during the early HOT ROD era. The unique bent-spoke wire wheels made by the company during the 1930s were a popular addition to the HOP UPS and GOW JOBS of the PREWAR years. During the 1950s and early 1960s, Kelsey-Hayes created exotic chrome-plated wire wheels for high-end domestic sports and luxury cars (including the exclusive early- to mid-1950s Buick Skylark, Oldsmobile Fiesta, and Cadillac Eldorado, and the early-1960s Ford Thunderbird [see BULLETBIRD]) that have become desirable ROLLING STOCK for STREET and SHOW-type CUSTOM CARS as well. Kelsey-Hayes also manufactured wheels for PERFORMANCE cars during the 1960s, notably their Mag Star five-spoke MAG WHEELS (sold in AFTERMARKET form and optionally available on 1967 Shelby Mustangs [see 'STANG]) and the eight-lug, aluminum-wheel/brake-drum sets featured on early- to mid-1960s full-size Pontiac PERFORMANCE models.

**kemp** *n.* Late-1950s and early-1960s beatnik or hipster jargon for virtually any car or truck. The term KEMP was significantly popularized through its usage in small-format (see the LITTLE PAGES) CUSTOM CAR magazines. Since the 1980 organization of the Kustom Kemps of America (see KKOA), the term KEMP has sometimes been taken as a synonym for CUSTOM or CUSTOM CAR.

**Kettering V8** (KETT-er-ing) *n.* Highly revolutionary, overhead-valve V8 engine introduced by General Motors for the 1949 model year. Named for the eminent "GM vice-president in charge of research" Charles F. Kettering, this first completely new post-World War II engine set design standards for all engines to follow. Lighter in weight and more powerful than comparable engines of its time, the KETTERING V8's innovative features included overhead valves, hydraulic valve lifters, an OVERSQUARE design, crankshaft (see CRANK) with six counterweights (as opposed to the eight counterweights used on previous V8 engines), and a full-flow oil filter. The initial release of the KETTERING V8 came in the form of the Oldsmobile "Rocket V8" with 303 CID and 135 horsepower. All of the popular V8 PERFORMANCE engines featured in subsequent hot rodding applications trace their lineage back to the KETTERING V8 design.

**kickdown crease** *n.* Highly distinctive styling element featured on all 1949 through 1951 Mercury (see MERC) passenger-car models. Created as the vehicle's front fender line blends smoothly into its front door area, turning abruptly downward near the rear of the door, then straightening to flow level to the rear of the vehicle. Interestingly, the STOCK Mercury KICKDOWN CREASE was often removed from classic MERC CUSTOM CARS of the early 1950s era, with CUSTOMIZERS blending the front fender line into a continuous, uninterrupted FADEAWAY FENDER treatment.

kickdown crease ON
1949 MERCURY

**kicked** (also **kicked up**) *adj.* Relating to an automotive frame that has been modified with an elevated "kick-up" serving to raise a portion of the frame above either the front or rear suspension components and thereby severely lowering the vehicle's body/chassis assembly.

**kick out the rods** (also **kick the rods out**) *v.* To experience major and destructive engine failure in the form of connecting rods (see RODS) that break free and depart through the cylinder block (see BLOCK) and/or the engine pan's external surfaces.

**kickstands** *n.* Alternative term for any CUSTOM CAR-style LAKES PIPES. Term derived from a similarity in appearance to a bicycle kickstand in the raised position.

**kidney bean mags** (also **kidney bean wheels** or **kidney beans**) **1.** *n.* Any of several mag wheel types produced by Halibrand Engineering (later Halibrand Performance Corporation) and featuring a uniform series of small, kidney bean-shaped holes or "windows" for lightening and brake-cooling purposes. While a number of different Halibrand designs are popularly called KIDNEY BEANS, the Halibrand Corporation recognizes only those wheels based on their classic road racing "knockoff" design as true KIDNEY BEAN WHEELS and formally designates them as such. Original knockoff KIDNEY BEANS were featured in a multitude of racing applications during the 1950s and early 1960s, significantly including Kurtis Kraft and Watson Indy ROADSTERS,

kidney bean mag[1]
EARLY-1960S
HALIBRAND DRAG WHEEL

Cunningham road racers, and the SR-2 and Sebring SS racing Corvettes (see 'VETTE). The small-window, BOLT-ON Halibrands popularized in early-1960s gas class (see GASSER) DRAG racing are also commonly referred to as KIDNEY BEANS by the rodding and DRAG communities. Halibrand has trademarked both its specific kidney bean shape and the kidney bean name. **2.** *n.* Any AFTERMARKET MAG WHEELS produced in the essential style of original Halibrand KIDNEY BEAN WHEELS.

**kill the light** *v.* In DRAG racing, to execute an exceptionally short or "tight" REACTION TIME. While good REACTION TIMES are vital to success in DRAG racing, the term KILL THE LIGHT often carries with it a negative connotation; under some circumstances, taking the risk of cutting an extremely close REACTION TIME may be ill-advised. Example: "There's no need for you to try to KILL THE LIGHT with the numbers we've been running today."

**King Bees** *n.* Headlight type as popularized in 1950s-era hot rodding applications. AFTERMARKET King Bee-brand lights were favored over early STOCK headlights for their desirable bucket shape (see HEADLIGHT BUCKETS) and, especially, for their smaller size.

**king kong** (also **king kong motor**), see ELEPHANT

**KKOA** (pronounced as separate letters) *n.* The Kustom Kemps of America. Founded in 1980, the KKOA claims the title of "America's oldest running CUSTOM CAR and truck association." By organizing traditional CUSTOM CAR enthusiasts and producing regular CUSTOM-oriented shows, the KKOA in large part initiated a 1980s-era CUSTOM CAR revival. Based in the Midwestern United States and continually governed by President Jerry Titus, the KKOA has developed a strong membership base and overall popularity that continues to the present day.

**Kookie Car**
NORM GRABOWSKI'S
MODEL T HOT ROD

**Kookie Car** (also **Kookie Kar** or **Kookie T**) (KOO-key) *n.* Alternative term for any T-BUCKET ROADSTER derived from a highly influential Model T (see T-BONE) Ford HOT ROD originally constructed by RODDER Norm Grabowski in the early and mid-1950s. Grabowski's trend-setting ROADSTER was actually based on a cut-down 1922 Model T Touring Car body and featured a severely shortened pickup bed (a revolutionary design element), 1952 Cadillac (see CADDY, Definition 2) engine, 1939 Ford transmission, SUICIDE FRONTEND, and a pronounced body RAKE. The car achieved a high level of exposure on the popular ABC television series *77 Sunset Strip* (1958–1964) as the steady RIDE of character Gerald Lloyd Kookson III (a.k.a. "Kookie"), played by actor Edd Byrnes. To a large degree, Grabowski's ROADSTER established a HOT ROD style that would be reproduced en masse during the 1960s and beyond as the FAD-T. Note: By the inclusion of a pickup bed, Grabowski's T (and the many T-BUCKETS with highly abbreviated truck beds that were to follow) may, in some ways, be considered a ROADSTER PICKUP. The term ROADSTER

PICKUP, however, is seldom used to describe any T-BUCKET HOT ROD. Instead, the expression is reserved for RODS that more closely conform to the true-production ROADSTER PICKUP type (most often 1928 through 1934 model year Fords).

**kustom** (also **kustom kar**) *n.* Alternative spellings of CUSTOM and CUSTOM CAR as originated and popularized by renowned builder, entrepreneur, and showman George Barris during the late 1940s and 1950s. The first incidence of Barris using the KUSTOM spelling came in the May 1948 issue of *HOT ROD* magazine in a Barris Shop print advertisement that included the phrases "Barris's Custom Shop KUSTOM Automobiles" and "KUSTOM Auto Painting."

# L

**lace painting** *n.* Custom automotive paint treatment and technique in which paint is sprayed through actual lace fabric to reproduce its pattern on a vehicle's body panels. LACE PAINTING achieved its greatest popularity during the 1960s and 1970s.

**LADS** (also **L.A.D.S.**) (LADS) *n.* Lions Associated DRAGSTRIP (see the BEACH).

**lady luck** *n.* Stylized caricature of a scantily clad young woman holding an adjustable wrench in one hand and a four-leaf clover in the other. Experienced strong popularity from the 1950s through the early 1960s as an icon and mascot closely tied to the hot rodding and circle-track racing cultures. Successfully marketed in T-shirt, felt emblem, and water decal form, LADY LUCK can still be found on HOT RODDERS' jackets, toolboxes, window glass, etc.

lady luck

**the lakes** *n.* Group of dry lakebeds (see ROSAMOND, HARPER, EL MIRAGE, and MUROC) located in the Antelope Valley region of Southern California's Mojave Desert. From as early as the 1920s, PERFORMANCE enthusiasts ran their vehicles for TOP END speed across the LAKES' level, hard dirt surfaces. Formal timed speed trials began by the late 1920s and increased in popularity (with a break during World War II) until the early 1950s. With the 1950s advent of organized DRAG racing, HOT RODDERS largely abandoned the LAKES for the comfort and convenience of localized DRAGSTRIPS. Though not experiencing the widespread popularity of earlier times, meets continue even today at EL MIRAGE and MUROC (now renamed Rogers Dry Lake). Many consider the LAKES to be the birthplace of what we now call hot rodding.

**lakes modified,** see MODIFIED

**lakes pipes** (also **lake pipes** or **lakers**) **1.** *n.* Any traditionally styled custom exhaust HEADERS, including CUTOUTS or LAKES PLUGS, that release exhaust in racing applications. Term derived from the type's usage in early dry lakes competition. **2.** *n.* Any long, narrow chrome-plated SIDE PIPES as most often fitted to CUSTOM CARS. Employed solely for aesthetic reasons, the low and sleek CUSTOM CAR LAKES PIPES are often of a non-functional variety. CUSTOM CAR LAKERS were originally popularized on SHOW-type vehicles during the late 1950s.

**lakes plugs** (also **lake plugs** or **lakes caps**) *n.* Any exhaust CUTOUTS employed to improve vehicle performance. Inspired by the CUTOUTS featured on early dry lakes (see the LAKES) racing vehicles.

**lakester 1.** *n.* Any LAND-SPEED RACING vehicle featuring custom, streamlined bodywork while maintaining an open-wheel configuration. Term first popularized during the early 1950s as a means of distinguishing the type from full-bodied, covered-wheel STREAMLINERS. **2.** *n.* Any vehicle purpose-built for LAND-SPEED RACING on Southern California's dry lake beds (see the LAKES).

**Lancers** (also **Lancer caps** or **Lancer flippers**) **1.** *n.* Unique crossbar hubcap type as originally featured on 1957 Dodge Lancer models. Dodge's popular LANCER CAPS were commonly fitted to CUSTOM CARS and sometimes HOT RODS during the late 1950s. **2.** *n.* Any of a large number of AFTERMARKET hubcap types produced in the general intersecting crossbar design of the original 1957 Dodge LANCER CAPS.

1957 DODGE **Lancer**[1] HUBCAP

**land-speed racing** (also **land-speed record racing**) *n.* Any automotive racing with straight-line TOP END speed as its ultimate objective. In its hot rodding context, the term LAND-SPEED RACING most often applies to BONNEVILLE and DRY LAKES competition (see LSR).

**lap 1.** *n.* In ROUNDY-ROUND or road-racing competition, the completion of one full circuit of any closed race course (a series of LAPS constitutes a complete race). **2.** *n.* Any singular DRAG RACE or PASS as performed by an individual vehicle (differentiated from the many races typically occurring at a DRAG racing meet or event). In DRAG applications, the term LAP is often used in relation to a TEST AND TUNE session. Example: "I'm hoping we can get in enough LAPS this afternoon to have things dialed in for Saturday." **3.** *v.* In ROUNDY-ROUND or road-racing competition, to overtake an opponent and in the process increase one's own lead to a full circuit.

the **last drag race** *n.* Popular expression describing the last event ever presented at the venerable LIONS DRAGSTRIP (see the BEACH) on December 1–2, 1972.

**late great Chevrolet** (also **late great Chevy**) *n.* Any Chevrolet vehicle produced during the 1958 through 1964 model years, but especially relating to the full-sized passenger cars of the period. Designated Impala (see IMPY), Bel Air, Biscayne (see BISCUIT), and Delray in their various series, these full-sized SEDANS and HARDTOPS maintained a strong PERFORMANCE reputation when powered by top-of-the-line SMALL-BLOCKS and, particularly, CHEVY's revered W Series BIG-BLOCK motors (see LUMPY HEAD).

**late great Chevrolet**
409-POWERED 1962 BEL AIR

**late Hemi** (HEM-ee) *n.* Any hemispherical (dome-shaped) combustion-chamber V8 engine produced by Chrysler Corporation from 1964 through 1971 model years. All production LATE HEMIS featured a 426 CID and were significantly based on Chrysler's conventional RB Series cylinder block (see BLOCK). LATE HEMIS were produced in both RACE HEMI and STREET HEMI configurations.

**launch** *n.* The act or occurrence of a vehicle being abruptly propelled forward into motion at the outset of a DRAG RACE. Term is generally used in reference to a purpose-built or extensively modified DRAG vehicle equipped with a high-horsepower engine, traction-enhancing suspension, racing SLICKS, etc.

**lay a patch** (also **lay a strip**), see LAY RUBBER

**lay down** *v.* To produce flat, below-potential performance due to mechanical failure or poor tuning (said of an engine or vehicle). Example: "It kicked ass OUT OF THE HOLE then gradually began to LAY DOWN after half-track."

**lay rubber** *v.* To BURN RUBBER on a paved road surface, leaving behind a dark mark or stripe of solidified rubber as semipermanent evidence of the act.

**lead-foot** *n.* Any exceptionally fast or aggressive driver. From the obvious premise that a foot made of lead would be heavier and thus tend to keep an accelerator pedal fully depressed.

**lead-foot it** *v.* To drive fast or aggressively.

**lead head** *n.* Any ardent devotee or builder of traditional LEAD SLED CUSTOM CARS.

**lead sled** *n.* Traditional term for the extensively modified CUSTOM CARS of (generally) the 1950s era. Term was originally used by HOT RODDERS to disparage heavy, slow, and sometimes crudely constructed CUSTOM CARS finished with liberal amounts of lead filler. (Though polyester-based body fillers were introduced during the late 1950s, their initial quality was poor, leading most CUSTOMIZERS to use long-proven lead for finishing.) In more recent years, the popular term LEAD SLED has lost its former derogatory tone, referring in a positive manner to any thoroughly restyled vintage-bodied CUSTOM.

**leaker** *n.* Any amateurish and/or underfunded DRAG racing vehicle. Name derived from the type's tendency to leak oil or other fluids onto a race track's surface.

**leave** *v.* To foul or REDLIGHT at the outset of a DRAG RACE, i.e., to "leave" early, resulting in immediate disqualification.

**leave on** someone *v.* To gain an advantage at the outset of a DRAG RACE, i.e., to "leave" the starting line first by virtue of a superior REACTION TIME.

**letter car** (also **letter series car**) *n.* Any Chrysler 300 "letter series" luxury/PERFORMANCE car. Introduced for the 1955 model year, the exclusive Chrysler C-300 was named for its COUPE status (HARDTOP COUPE models only were produced in 1955) and its then-remarkable 300 BHP. With a dual-QUAD, solid-lifter 331-CID HEMI engine, the C-300 claimed the title of "America's most powerful STOCK CAR," and the 300's early dominance in NASCAR racing only served to corroborate Chrysler's advertising hype and bolster its strong PERFORMANCE image. For 1956, Chrysler released the 300B, beginning the practice of sequential letter identity for each subsequent model year. 300Bs were available with the new 354-CID HEMI and optional 355 BHP. For 1957 and 1958, the respective 300C and 300D models were equipped with the last V8 in the EARLY HEMI series, the legendary 392 (see '92). Notably in 1958, the 300D introduced Bendix electronic fuel injection on a scant 35 cars, but the systems proved highly troublesome and most were replaced with conventional QUADS. For 1959, the 300E featured Chrysler's new 413-CID WEDGE MOTOR in place of the discontinued HEMI, while 1960's 300F added LONG RAM and SHORT RAM (Definition 1) induction systems (the potent 413 WEDGE would go on to power all remaining LETTER CARS). During the 1962 model year, Chrysler first shared the revered 300 name with a new lower-priced series dubbed the Sport 300. By 1965, the distinction between the 300 LETTER CAR and Sport 300 had blurred to the point where the production of separate series was considered impractical. The last true LETTER CAR was produced in the form of the 1965 Chrysler 300L (the letter "I" was skipped, with 1962 models being designated 300Hs and 1963 editions being named 300Js). Interestingly, Chrysler resurrected the 300 letter series concept for the 1999 model year with its 300M four-door SEDAN.

letter car
1958 CHRYSLER 300D

**licks,** see FLAMES

**lid** *n.* Early HOT RODDER's expression for any cylinder head (see HEADS). Term was most often used during or prior to the 1950s and in relation to a FLATHEAD-type component.

**lift** *v.* To fully release a vehicle's accelerator pedal during the course of a DRAG RACE. Generally executed when a vehicle gets out of control, experiences a mechanical failure, or is in danger of BREAKING OUT. The term differs from the expression BACK-PEDAL, which refers to a partial releasing of throttle. Example: "I got so CROSSED UP when I hit second that I had to LIFT."

**lifted** *adj.* Equipped with a hydraulic-type suspension system to provide instantaneous and comprehensive RIDE HEIGHT adjustments. Term most often relates to LOWRIDER CUSTOM CARS.

**light** *n.* Any recorded DRAG racing REACTION TIME. Example: "You've got yourself a race this time around. He's been really good with his LIGHTS all afternoon."

**light 'em up** (also **light 'em off**), see BURN RUBBER

**light the tires** (also **light up the tires**, **light the skins**, or **light the hides**), see BURN RUBBER

**lightweight Catalina** *n.* Any Pontiac Catalina model produced with lightweight components expressly for improved DRAG racing performance (see CAT).

**lightweight Galaxie** *n.* Any of the limited-edition 1962 through 1964 Ford Galaxie models produced exclusively for STOCK-class DRAG racing. The 1962 and 1963 LIGHTWEIGHT GALAXIES slashed body weight through the extensive use of fiberglass (see 'GLASS) body panels. Special aluminum components were also featured, variously including bumpers, bumper brackets, inner fender panels, four-speed transmission cases, and bellhousings. The LIGHTWEIGHT GALAXIE's weight-reduction method was changed significantly for 1964, with original steel bodies ACID-DIPPED to achieve the desired lightening. The only holdover from the earlier fiberglass treatment came in the form of the 1964's TEARDROP HOOD. At various times, LIGHTWEIGHT GALAXIES were powered by 406-CID and 427-CID (both Low Riser and High Riser) versions of Ford's FE Series BIG-BLOCK. During the 1962 and 1963 seasons, LIGHTWEIGHT GALAXIES competed in the FX and S/S classes with only marginal success, while 1964 models raced in the then-new AA/Stock class where they were consistent winners.

limefire headers

**limefire headers** (also **limefires**) *n.* Distinctive, outside-chassis HEADERS of the type featured on the influential *Limefire* DEUCE HIGHBOY ROADSTER. Celebrated HOT ROD builders Pete and Jake (Pete Chapouris and Jim Jacobs) created *Limefire* during the early months of 1987. The trend-setting HIGHBOY featured an overall 1960s-era DRAG RACE theme as well as the outrageous tangerine FLAME JOB over metallic lime-green paint that inspired its name. Jim Jacobs crafted *Limefire*'s distinctive, megaphone-style HEADERS, resurrecting an exhaust type previously favored during the 1950s. On each cylinder bank, the individual primary tube exiting from the front-most cylinder curves gracefully rearward, straightens once clear of the chassis, and gradually expands in diameter until terminating adjacent to the vehicle's cowl. Exhaust primary tubes branch forth from subsequent cylinders and join the conical shape created by the first primary tube. The HEADER's open end is capped during normal STREET usage. With the cap in place, exhaust is routed through a separate flanged tube exiting the bottom of the cone and then passing through a conventional exhaust system beneath the car. When full-performance, open exhaust is desired, the end caps are simply removed or replaced with short open "turn-outs" directing exhaust away from the vehicle's body.

**limited slip** (also **limited slip rearend**), see POSI

**line job** *n.* In a DRAG RACE, the act of gaining an advantage during the first moments of the race (OFF THE LINE). Generally the result of a driver's superior REACTION TIME.

**line lock** *n.* AFTERMARKET device used in DRAG racing to facilitate BURNOUTS and to hold a manual-transmissioned car absolutely stationary (on the "line") immediately prior to the start of a race. With a LINE LOCK system, a driver-actuated electronic switch serves to hydraulically lock a vehicle's front brakes, freeing both feet for use on the clutch and accelerator pedals. The lock is released at the precise instant of the race's signaled start. Some modern LINE LOCK systems provide for a four-wheel lock during actual race staging. Hurst Performance Products introduced and heavily promoted their "Line/Loc" system in 1965.

**'liner,** see STREAMLINER

**Lions** *n.* Lions Associated DRAGSTRIP (see the BEACH).

the **little pages** (also **little book**) *n.* Any of a large number of HOT ROD and CUSTOM CAR magazines produced in a small pocket-size format during the 1950s and early 1960s, but most often referring to Petersen Publishing's *Rod & Custom* magazine. (*Rod & Custom* switched to a standard magazine format beginning with its August 1961 issue.) Additional small-format titles included: *Hop Up, Honk!, how to Hop-Up your engine* [*sic*], *Car Speed and Style, Speed and Custom, Rod Builder & Customizer, Custom Rodder, Custom Craft, Custom Cars,* and *Customs Illustrated.*

**live** (LIV) *v.* To last or endure without experiencing mechanical failure, debilitating damage, or significant wear (said of an automobile part or component, especially when taxed in a punishing high-performance application). Example: "There's no way the STOCK REAREND's gonna LIVE behind that RAT MOTOR."

**lizard nose** *n.* Unique and highly distinctive nose treatment as commonly applied to the stylish aluminum-bodied SLINGSHOT DRAGSTERS of the 1960s. The typical LIZARD NOSE featured a sleek, rounded or mildly pointed leading edge with sweeping bulges arching rearward and downward to each body side immediately behind the front axle position. While offering some structural rigidity, the LIZARD NOSE served more to enhance a DRAGSTER's overall appearance. The shape of an actual lizard's head was the obvious inspiration for the type's name.

EARLY-1960S **lizard nose**

**loaded** *adj.* Highly modified for improved performance (most often said of an automotive engine). Term experienced its greatest popularity during the 1950s and 1960s. Example: "He's runnin' a DEUCE FIVE-WINDOW with a LOADED CHEVY V8."

**locked rearend** *n.* Any driven rear-axle assembly (see REAREND) allowing for no differential action whatsoever. With a LOCKED REAREND, both axle shafts (and consequently wheels) are effectively "locked" together as a single rigid unit, transferring the driveshaft's rotational motion directly, equally, and simultaneously to both rear wheels. A LOCKED REAREND may be achieved by the crude and ineffective method of welding STOCK differential pinion and side gears together, or by installing a solid "spool" in their place. While LOCKED REARENDS serve to provide improved traction in many DRAG applications, they are impractical and potentially dangerous in STREET use.

**locker**, see DETROIT LOCKER

**Loewy coupe** (LOW-ee), see SLIPPERY STUDE

**log manifold 1.** (also **log**) *n.* Any high-performance INTAKE manifold incorporating round, tubular castings (in V8 applications, two parallel tubes are used, one feeding each cylinder bank). LOG MANIFOLDS achieved strong popularity during the 1950s and early 1960s for their ability to accommodate large numbers of TWO-BARREL carburetors (see CARB). The type's round, log-like shape inspires its name. **2.** *n.* Any exhaust manifold featuring a round, tubular construction.

**long arm**, see BIG ARM

**longblock** *n.* Partial engine assembly including cylinder block (see BLOCK), all components housed within the cylinder block, and complete cylinder head (see HEADS) assemblies, but excluding other external components. A SHORTBLOCK plus HEADS. Term is generally used in reference to a new or remanufactured unit.

**long-legged 1.** *adj.* Relating to any vehicle capable of exceptionally high TOP END speeds (sometimes at the expense of strong acceleration). **2.** *adj.* Relating to any especially high final-drive gear ratio (see FREEWAY GEARS), a benefit to high-speed performance.

**long ram** (also **longhorn induction** or **longhorn cross ram**) *n.* Chrysler Corporation's high-performance, CROSS RAM induction system featuring exceptionally long 30-inch intake runners, which harnessed the intake charge's inherent pressure waves to create a "supercharging" effect and thereby increase MIDRANGE engine power. Produced from the 1960 through 1964 model years, LONG RAM INTAKES were featured on Plymouth, Dodge, DeSoto, and Chrysler PERFORMANCE cars.

**looks good goin' down the road** *adj.* Relating to a vehicle that is far from perfect in detail and finish but is nonetheless refined enough to be attractive from a reasonable distance. Example: "It won't be winning any trophies with the paint the way it is, but it still LOOKS GOOD GOIN' DOWN THE ROAD."

**lope** *n.* Any rough, thumping idle as produced by a high-performance camshaft (see CAM).

**loper** *n.* Any automotive camshaft (see CAM) featuring a rough, LOPEY idle.

**lopey** *adj.* Relating to a rough, thumping idle. Example: "A CAM that size is gonna have a real LOPEY idle to it."

**lose fire** *v.* To cease running or to "die" immediately prior to the outset of a DRAG RACE (said of any race vehicle). Typically, if the engine cannot be restarted within a prescribed time period the competitor is forced to forfeit the race.

**loud pedal** *n.* Any automotive accelerator pedal.

**louvered** *adj.* Punched with custom ventilating LOUVERS (said of any automotive body panel).

**louvers 1.** *n.* Any custom vents applied to automotive body panels (DECK LID, BELLY PAN, hood sides, etc.). Originally employed on DRAG and LAND-SPEED RACING vehicles to release heat and/or trapped air from a vehicle's interior spaces, LOUVERS were later adapted to STREET RODS and STREET MACHINES solely for aesthetic purposes. **2.** *n.* Any automotive rear-window treatment consisting of a series of horizontal visor-like slats employed to reduce visual glare and to enhance vehicle styling. While outside window LOUVERS were made available on a number of PERFORMANCE models from the late 1960s through the early 1970s, the type is perhaps most closely associated with the Boss-series SportsRoof Mustangs of 1969 and 1970. Larry Shinoda designed the LOUVERS (Ford referred to them as sport slats) as a part of the 1969 Boss 302 package.

**lowboy 1.** (also **lo-boy**) *n.* HOT ROD type featuring the essential characteristics of a HIGHBOY but with its body CHANNELED over its frame RAILS. **2.** *n.* Any STREET MACHINE featuring an exceptionally low RIDE HEIGHT, generally through radical suspension modifications. [Rare]

**low end** *n.* The lower-most part of any given engine's operational RPM range (as differentiated from MIDRANGE and TOP END).

**lowered lid** *n.* Any lowered vehicle roofline as accomplished through chopping (see CHOPPED).

**low 'n' slow** *adj.* Cruising style as typically practiced by the LOWRIDER CUSTOM CAR culture. Traditionally LOWRIDERS are driven slowly in an expression of cool, restrained elegance and style.

**lowrider 1.** (also **low**) *n.* Unique CUSTOM CAR type developed from, and closely related to, the Chicano (Mexican-American) culture of the American Southwest. LOWRIDERS are characterized by their extensive and ornate detailing, (traditionally) small tires and wheels, elaborate and exotic paint schemes, typically low RIDE HEIGHT, and frequent use of hydraulic

1964 CHEVROLET IMPALA **lowrider**[1]

suspension systems. Modern lowriding traces its roots to the 1930s and 1940s when Hispanics began lowering Chevrolet SEDANs through the conventional means of the time (cut or heated coil springs and sandbag-filled trunks). In 1959, builder Ron Aguirre installed the first hydraulically controlled suspension on his radical 1957 *X-Sonic* custom Corvette (see 'VETTE) allowing him to easily change the RIDE HEIGHT at any time. By the mid-1960s, Aguirre's breakthrough was being commercially adapted to LOWRIDERS, furthering their distinction from traditional Anglo-culture CUSTOM CARS. Throughout the 1960s and into the 1970s, the unique LOWRIDER style evolved and established itself within activity centers in Texas, New Mexico, and Arizona, as well as in Central and Southern California. At various times, heavy METALFLAKE, COBWEB, and LACE PAINTING flourished, as did twisted-metal grills, swivel BUCKET SEATS, and small-diameter steering wheels. In the 1970s, the five-spoke Cragar SS and Astro Supreme wheels favored in 1960s-era LOWRIDER applications gave way to AFTERMARKET wire RIMS (see WIRES), a wheel type that has remained dominant with LOWs to the present day. While full-size Chevrolet SEDANS have traditionally been the preferred LOWRIDER foundation, in recent years the style has been applied to a multitude of vehicle types, including minitrucks, American and European luxury SEDANS, PONY CARS, sports cars, light trucks, and Japanese import COUPES. **2.** *n.* Any individual involved in the building, driving, and/or showing of LOWRIDER CUSTOM CARS.

**Low Riser** (also **427 Low Riser**) *n.* High-performance 427-CID V8 engine produced by FoMoCo for 1963–1964 and again in 1968. The Low RISER was the first of several 427-CID Ford BIG-BLOCK engines and was directly evolved from the high-performance 390-CID and 406-CID engines that immediately preceded it. The name Low RISER commonly serves to differentiate the type from other 427-CID Ford engines produced during roughly the same time period (HIGH RISER, MEDIUM RISER, tunnel port, and CAMMER). When compared to these other motors the 427 LOW RISER featured a relatively low-profile intake manifold and head (see HEADS) intake-port design. The original solid-lifter 427 LOW RISER of 1963 and 1964 produced 410 BHP in single FOUR-BARREL form and 425 BHP with available DUAL QUADS. For 1968, the general 427 Low RISER design was re-released for use in Ford Mustang (see 'STANG) and Mercury Cougar PONY CARS. This engine differed from the earlier 427 Low RISERs in that it incorporated the improved SIDE-OILER cylinder block (see BLOCK). With its hydraulic camshaft (see CAM) and single FOUR-BARREL carburetor (see CARB), this more STREETABLE permutation of the Low RISER generated a still-respectable 390 BHP.

**low-tech** (also **lo-tech**) *adj.* HOT ROD or CUSTOM CAR style strongly based on tradition and relative simplicity. The LOW-TECH style is the antithesis (and, in part, the response to) the HIGH-TECH style of HOT ROD building popularized during the 1980s and 1990s. The RETRO ROD or RAT ROD movements of the 1990s and early twenty-first century typify the LOW-TECH style.

**LSR** (usually written, not spoken), see LAND-SPEED RACING

**lumpy cam**, see BIG CAM

**lumpy head** *n.* Any W Series BIG-BLOCK V8 engine as produced by Chevrolet for the 1958 through 1965 model years. Name is derived from the engine's unusual head (see HEADS) design, significantly featuring highly distinctive bulbous and scalloped valve covers. LUMPY HEADS were configured in 348 CID (1958 through early 1961), 409 (see '09) CID (late 1961 through mid-1965), and the ultrarare Z-11 427-CID race package (1963 only). Available in full-size passenger-car models, the W Series LUMPY HEADS carried the distinction of being Chevrolet's maximum-horsepower engines from their inception until their 1965 replacement by the Mark IV 396 BIG-BLOCK (see RAT).

1962 CHEVROLET 409
**lumpy head** VALVE COVER

**lumpy idle** *n.* Any rough idle as produced by a radical, high-performance camshaft (see CAM).

**lunch** *v.* To completely destroy any automotive mechanical part or component through demanding high-performance usage.

**lunchbox latches**, see TOOLBOX LATCHES

**lung 1.** *n.* Any single cylinder within an engine. **2.** see BLOWER

# M

**mag** *n.* Any automotive magneto ignition system comprising a permanent magnet generator producing its own consistent, reliable, and strong ignition spark. Since the late 1940s, magnetos have commonly been applied to a variety of DRAG and LAND-SPEED RACING applications.

**mags** (also **mag wheels** or **mag rims**) *n.* Custom wheels, generally constructed of cast or forged metals, employed to improve a vehicle's performance and/or appearance. The first MAG WHEELS were created exclusively for racing applications and produced in lightweight magnesium alloy (ultimately abbreviated to simply "mag"). Halibrand Engineering (see HALS) introduced the earliest magnesium racing wheels to circle-track competition during the late 1940s. The exotic magnesium wheels were slower to catch on at the DRAGS, but by the late 1950s most top-performing DRAG vehicles were running some form of custom or AFTERMARKET MAG RIMS. The mid-1960s witnessed the mass proliferation of a different type of mag wheel among virtually all street driving applications when HOT RODS, MUSCLE CARS, CUSTOMS, and STREET MACHINES of all types quickly made the switch from traditional steel RIMS to MAG WHEELS. These new STREET MAGS featured the popular look of true magnesium racing wheels but were produced in aluminum alloy or a combination of aluminum and steel. While neither as strong nor as light as their magnesium counterparts, aluminum wheels were less expensive to manufacture and much easier to care for (magnesium oxidizes and corrodes very quickly when exposed to natural airborne humidity or moisture). Aluminum construction remains the industry standard for custom and AFTERMARKET MAG WHEELS to the present day.

**mail-slot windows** (also **mail slots**) *n.* Any automotive window with its vertical height so drastically reduced by chopping (see CHOPPED) that it resembles a mere slit or "mail slot." Term most often used to describe the rear window of an early COUPE or SEDAN model.

**March Meet** *n.* The Bakersfield FUEL and Gas Championships, a DRAG racing event presented each March at the Famoso Raceway near Bakersfield, California. Beginning in 1959 and continuing through the mid-1960s, the MARCH MEET held great significance as a premier venue for FUEL DRAGSTER racing. Organized by the Smokers CAR CLUB, BAKERSFIELD helped keep FUEL racing alive during the infamous NHRA FUEL BAN (1957–1963). In more recent years, the Goodguys ROD & CUSTOM Association has promoted the annual Famoso MARCH MEET as a nostalgia DRAG racing, ROD RUN, and SWAP MEET event.

**mash it** (also **mash on the gas**) *v.* To aggressively and fully depress a vehicle's accelerator pedal.

**massage 1.** *v.* To subtly and artfully recontour any STOCK auto body component or panel to achieve a cleaner, more attractive appearance. **2.** *v.* To straighten damaged or distorted auto body panels, bringing a vehicle back to its FACTORY-original condition.

**match bash** *n.* Generally mid-1960s term for any DRAG MATCH RACE.

**match bash stocker** (also **match race stocker**) *n.* Mid-1960s term for any early, production vehicle-based FUNNY CAR. During the FUNNY CAR's formative years (1964–1966), the type's construction strayed dramatically from its Super STOCK roots, often leaving it without a clear class designation by DRAG racing's major sanctioning organizations. As a result, early FUNNYs were often relegated to exhibition or MATCH RACE-only status.

**matching numbers car**, see NUMBERS CAR

**match race** *n.* Any professional, sanctioned DRAG RACE wherein two vehicles are paid by promoters expressly to appear and compete against one another. While safety regulations are enforced, vehicles are often not held to established class restrictions, competing instead on a HEADS-UP, RUN WHAT YOU BRUNG basis. In a MATCH RACE, driver and/or car notoriety is expected to draw a large crowd of paying spectators. The MATCH RACE phenomenon experienced its greatest popularity from the mid-1960s through the early 1970s, most notably in America's Deep South, where it was common practice for spectators to bet cash on the outcome of races.

**Max Wedge** *n.* Chrysler Corporation's ultimate-performance, RB Series BIG-BLOCK engines (see WEDGE) as produced for the 1962 through 1964 model years. MAX WEDGE engines came in 413-CID form for 1962 and, with increased BORE, 426 CID during the 1963 and 1964 model years. The term MAX WEDGE was never officially employed by Chrysler Corporation, but was instead used by HOT RODDERS and DRAG racers on a colloquial basis.

**Mazooma!** (muh-ZOO-muh) *interj.* General exclamation as commonly expressed by Ed "Big Daddy" Roth's popular RAT FINK character. Term was created by Roth expressly for RAT FINK. Example: "Mazooma! Dem chrome GOODIES is shore lookin' fine!"

**meats** *n.* Any large vehicle tires, but especially the traction-enhancing tall and exceptionally wide rear tires as commonly featured on HOT RODS or DRAG racing vehicles.

**meats** ON 1934 CHEVROLET HOT ROD

**Medium Riser** (also **427 Medium Riser**) *n.* High-performance 427-CID V8 engine produced by FoMoCo for the 1965 through 1967 model years. Ford's 427 MEDIUM RISER included many of the same PERFORMANCE features as the 427 HIGH RISER that preceded it (cross-bolted main bearing caps, exceptionally large valves, solid-lifter camshaft [see CAM], etc.) but differed in its lower intake-port head (see HEADS) design. With its modified ports, the MEDIUM RISER's overall height was effectively reduced, eliminating the need for the hood scoops or TEARDROP HOODS required on the earlier HIGH RISER-powered cars. Additional MEDIUM RISER refinements included a forged steel crankshaft, (rather than the cast-iron CRANK used in the LOW RISER and HIGH RISER engines) and the introduction of the superior SIDE-OILER cylinder block (see BLOCK).

THE *HIROHATA* **Merc**[1]

**Merc** (MERK) **1.** *n.* Any automobile produced by the Mercury division of Ford Motor Company during the 1949 through 1951 model years. Often regarded as the most significant and popular CUSTOM CAR foundation of all time, Mercury's classic mid-century design achieved immediate favor through the work of CUSTOMIZERS like the Barris and Ayala brothers. The most celebrated of all custom MERCS was created for Bob Hirohata by Sam and George Barris in 1952. Hirohata's severely lowered 1951 COUPE included a CHOPPED roof, distinctive curved window frames, Buick side trim, SOMBRERO HUBCAPS, an OHV Cadillac V8 (see CADDY, Definition 2) , and signature two-tone green paint. The Hirohata MERC gained national attention when it was featured in the October 1953 issue of *Rod & Custom* magazine. Entitled "Kross Kountry in a KUSTOM—Mile After Mile In My Modified MERCILLAC," the feature described Hirohata's three-day road trip from Los Angeles to an Indianapolis, Indiana, car show. **2.** *n.* Any Mercury FLATHEAD V8 engine. MERC FLATHEADS were popular in 1940s and 1950s hot rodding applications for their larger displacement over their Ford counterparts. **3.** *n.* Any complete automobile or automotive component produced by the Mercury division of FoMoCo.

**Mercillac** (MERK-il-lack) *n.* Any Mercury automobile modified by the inclusion of a Cadillac (see CADDY, Definition 2) engine. Term was most commonly used during the 1950s, when the contemporary, large-displacement OHV Cadillac V8 engines were sometimes swapped into Mercury CUSTOM CARS for improved performance.

**metalfinish** *v.* To perform automotive body work without the use of any fillers whatsoever in the final finishing process. Requiring skill and patience, METALFINISHing may be variously accomplished by the stretching, shrinking, grinding, HAMMER-WELDing, filing, and/or sanding of body components. Regarded as the ultimate-quality method for the completion of custom bodywork.

**metalflake** (also **metalflake paint**) *n.* Custom paint style that employs exceptionally coarse flakes to achieve a highly distinctive glittery effect. The typical METALFLAKE PAINT treatment is applied in a series of layers. A base coat is covered by a clear layer that serves to suspend the actual polyester flake material. This flake layer, in turn, is covered by an additional clear layer to complete the process. Never featured in mainstream OEM paint schemes, the flashy METALFLAKE experienced its strongest popularity in 1960s custom paint applications. Period HOT RODS, CUSTOM CARS, and even DRAGSTERS were commonly treated to heavy 'FLAKE jobs. From the 1970s through the 1990s, the METALFLAKE style was applied almost exclusively to LOWRIDERS, but in the early twenty-first century its popularity has expanded considerably to include RETRO RODS and traditionally styled CUSTOMS. One popular modern CUSTOM CAR treatment restricts sparkling 'FLAKE paint to a vehicle's roof area, while utilizing a more conventional paint job on the remainder of its body.

**metallic paint** *n.* Common automotive paint type employing minute metal or metal-like particles to create a deep, richly glowing finish. While popular in many custom applications, METALLIC PAINTS have long been a part of OEM finishes as well. By the mid-1930s, various General Motors products were treated to factory METALLIC PAINT schemes.

**midnight auto supply** (also **midnight auto**) *n.* Auto parts source supplied by late-night theft from unattended vehicles. A euphemism for the stealing of parts.

**midrange** *n.* The middle or intermediate part of any given engine's operational RPM range (as differentiated from LOW END or TOP END).

**mile-an-hour** *n.* Slang term frequently used by DRAG racers in reference to a vehicle's recorded speed. Although a vehicle's terminal speed is irrelevant to the outcome of a DRAG RACE (barring disqualification, ET together with REACTION TIME determine the race's winner), recorded speeds can offer important insights into vehicle performance and assist in the process of engine and chassis tuning. Unlike the term "miles per hour," however, MILE-AN-HOUR is not typically modified by an empirical measurement. Example: "It's been runnin' consistent 12.30s all day, but for some reason the MILE-AN-HOUR has been off."

**mill** *n.* Any automotive engine, but especially one that is modified for improved performance. Term most commonly used by RODDERS during the 1950s and 1960s.

**Miss Golden Shifter** (also **Miss Hurst Golden Shifter**) *n.* Any of several promotional/public-relations representatives for Hurst Performance Products, but most often referring to the most popular and longest-tenured MISS GOLDEN SHIFTER, Linda Vaughn. Beginning in the early 1960s, Hurst began promoting its manual floor shifters by perching an attractive model on a platform mounted to a convertible's DECK LID. During racing intermissions, MISS GOLDEN SHIFTER rode standing on the platform alongside an 8-foot-tall, golden facsimile of a Hurst shift handle. Initially, a new MISS GOLDEN SHIFTER was named on a yearly basis with Jenene Walsh and Pat Flannery each holding the title. For

1966, a national contest was held in collaboration with *HOT ROD* magazine to determine the new MISS GOLDEN SHIFTER. Vaughn, a Georgia-born beauty queen, won the title and, due to her tremendous popularity and impeccable professionalism, maintained her position as MISS HURST GOLDEN SHIFTER for 13 consecutive years.

**mixer** *n.* Early HOT RODDER's expression for any automotive carburetor (see CARB). Describes the carburetor's function of mixing air with fuel.

**mod** *n.* Any automotive modification.

EARLY-1940S DRY LAKES
**modified**

**modified** *n.* Early LAND-SPEED RACING vehicle type similar to an open-wheeled STREAMLINER but differing in its omission of a streamlined tail piece. Most popular during the 1930s and 1940s, MODIFIEDS featured one-seat body structures generally derived from severely narrowed production ROADSTER bodies. The typical MODIFIED also included wire wheels, a streamlined GRILL SHELL, and a fuel tank mounted immediately behind its BOBTAILED body.

**Money talks, bullshit walks**. Traditional expression frequently used by serious street racers who compete for cash. Suggests that, "The time for talking is through. If you're serious about racing, show your money."

**monkey motion** *adj.* Relating to any overhead-valve system actuated by a single camshaft (see CAM) through a series of pushrods and rocker arms. The expression MONKEY MOTION was first popularized during the period of FLATHEAD engine dominance and is derived from the system's relatively complex, indirect nature. The MONKEY MOTION configuration has remained the standard for most HOT ROD and DRAG racing engines from its general inception (the late 1940s through the mid-1950s) to the present day.

**monochromatic** *adj.* Featuring an overall appearance characterized by a single color (said of any vehicle or vehicle component). The MONOCHROMATIC STREET ROD and STREET MACHINE fashion seeks to eliminate all chrome or brightwork finishes on trim, emblems, bumpers, etc., by painting components to match the vehicle's overall body color (most often soft pastel tones). Popular from the late 1980s through the mid-1990s, MONOCHROMATIC-styled vehicles were often embellished with complementary GRAPHICS.

**monster shirt**, see WEIRDO SHIRT

**Monte** (MAWN-tee) *n.* Any Chevrolet Monte Carlo. Introduced for the 1970 model year, the original Monte Carlo was deemed a "personal-luxury" COUPE and based on the intermediate General Motors G-body platform. An SS 454 option package was made available for 1970 and 1971 only. With 454-CID power and an upgraded suspension, these early Monte Carlo SS models exhibited genuine MUSCLE CAR performance. A new SS package was offered with the redesigned 1983 through 1988 Monte Carlo line. These rear-drive, V8-powered MONTES were largely inspired by the model's NASCAR racing successes and exhibited solid performance for their era. For 1986, a special Monte Carlo "Aerocoupe" was sold to the public to HOMOLOGATE its use in STOCK CAR racing. This rare model featured a dramatically sloping FASTBACK-style rear window and was popular enough to be re-released for 1987 and 1988, the end of the Monte Carlo's original production run. After a six-year absence, the Monte Carlo name was revived and assigned to the two-door version of the Chevrolet Lumina SEDAN. For the 2000 model year, the Monte Carlo was once again significantly redesigned, this time based on Chevrolet's new Impala (see IMPY) platform. While not a true MUSCLE CAR, this aerodynamic V6/front-drive Monte Carlo SS offers reasonable performance as well as the mystique of association with a NASCAR champion. The Monte Carlo, in its many iterations, holds the distinction of winning more NASCAR Winston Cup races than any other model in history.

**Moon discs 1.** *n.* Any custom, spun-aluminum wheel covers produced by the Moon Equipment Company (later Mooneyes USA, Inc.). MOON DISCS completely cover a wheel's outside surface, creating a smooth, flush extension to the tire's sidewall plane. Originally popularized during the 1950s in DRAG and LAND-SPEED RACING applications, MOON DISCS reduce turbulence around the wheels, thereby improving aerodynamics. MOON DISCS have also achieved moderate popularity in HOT ROD and CUSTOM CAR applications strictly for their CLEAN, racy look. **2.** *n.* Any spun-aluminum wheel discs produced in the style of the genuine Moon Equipment Company or Mooneyes USA products.

**Mooneyes** *n.* Popular logo associated with the Moon Equipment Company (later Mooneyes USA, Inc.). Dating to the 1950s, the MOONEYES logo has had several different iterations but consistently includes its namesake element of two stylized, canted eyeballs. Besides being variously featured on actual Moon speed equipment (MOON TANKS, gauges, breathers, etc.), the MOONEYES insignia has been successfully marketed in a multitude of accessory forms, including keychains, earrings, cigarette lighters, barstools, yo-yos, wrist watches, sunglasses, pocketknives, drinking glasses, and clothing.

EARLY-1960S **Mooneyes** LOGO

**Moon tank 1.** *n.* Any fuel tank as produced by Moon Equipment Company (or later Mooneyes USA, Inc.). MOON TANKS are cylindrical in shape, of aluminum construction, and generally possess only the very small capacity (several gallons) necessary for brief quarter-mile DRAG RACES. Especially popular in DRAG racing applications during the 1950s and 1960s, MOON TANKS have been more recently adapted to STREET RODS to evoke a traditional racy appearance. **2.** *n.* Any non-fuel tank (coolant recovery, oil, or vacuum) as produced by Moon Equipment Company or

3 1/2 GALLON **Moon tank**[1] ON 1932 FORD STREET ROD

Mooneyes USA, Inc. **3.** *n.* Any small cylindrical aluminum fuel tank as produced in the style of a true Moon Equipment or Mooneyes tank.

**MOPAR** (also **Mope**) (MOE-par) **1.** *n.* Any Chrysler Corporation or DaimlerChrysler product. Name is derived from Chrysler's traditional use of the term (a contraction of "motor parts") on their parts-division boxes. **2.** *n.* Chrysler Corporation or DaimlerChrysler.

**MOPAR** (MOE-par) **or no-car!** *interj.* Adamant endorsement of Chrysler Corporation vehicles.

**MOPAR** (MOE-par) **rules the dragstrip, Chevy rules the street, AMC rules the junkyard, and Ford beats the meat.** Highly biased commentary on the relative merits of American automotive manufacturers' products. (The expression "beats the meat" may relate to male masturbation or, in a more general sense, to a person or thing that is considered weak, ineffectual, mundane, or inept.)

**more-door** *n.* Any HOT ROD, STREET ROD, or STREET MACHINE based on a four-door body style. Term carries with it a slightly derogatory tone, reflecting the type's general lack of favor in the rodding community. In this case, "more" is generally perceived as being too much.

**motate** (MOE-tate), see HAUL

**motorhead**, see GEARHEAD

**motorvated**, see STOKED

**motorvation**, see PUSH

**mountain motor** *n.* Any high-performance V8 engine featuring an extremely large displacement. Most often employed in IHRA PRO STOCK DRAG racing applications, MOUNTAIN MOTORS commonly feature displacements in the 700-CID range, with some exceeding 800 CID.

**mouse** (also **mouse motor** or **mouse mill**) *n.* Any SMALL-BLOCK Chevrolet V8 engine, as produced from the 1955 model year to 2003. (Though retired from passenger-car duty during the 1990s, the traditional Chevrolet SMALL-BLOCK was used into the early 2000s in commercial vehicles.) The most popular engine in hot rodding history, the versatile SMALL-BLOCK CHEVY (see SBC) has been successfully employed in an incredibly broad range of applications. Since the mid-1950s, millions of STREET RODS, CUSTOM CARS, kits cars, and STREET MACHINES of all kinds have included the CHEVY SMALL-BLOCK V8 as their power source (the SBC is the all-time favorite choice for interbrand engine swapping). In addition, competition MOUSE MOTORS have powered DRAG cars, STOCK CARS, sprint cars, sports cars, Indy cars, circle-track modifieds, off-road, and LAND-SPEED

RACING vehicles. MOUSE MOTORS have also served in a wide variety of marine applications, and have even been adapted to power motorcycles, airboats, and at least one *competition chainsaw*. Chevrolet has manufactured its SMALL-BLOCK in displacements ranging from 262 to 400 CID, but resourceful HOT RODDERS have STROKED the engine to as large as 461 CID to improve its performance, and destroked it to as small as 183 CID to meet class-racing requirements. Additionally, exotic high-performance SBCs have been created in both three- and four-valve "pushrod" as well as single- and double-overhead CAM variations. The engine's incomparable popularity stems from its overall availability (MOUSE MOTORS were produced in the tens of millions), standardization of parts, small size and light weight, efficiency, response to PERFORMANCE modification, and an unparalleled legacy of relatively inexpensive AFTERMARKET PERFORMANCE parts. The SMALL-BLOCK CHEVY's nickname MOUSE was derived from its light weight and compact size when compared to other 1950s-era V8s, thus dating the term to the engine's early production years.

**Mr. Horsepower** *n.* Designated name for manufacturer Clay Smith Cams' product logo, a caricature of a crazed woodpecker with a cigar clenched in his beak. The MR. HORSEPOWER image achieved strong popularity as a cultural icon during the late 1950s and early 1960s, and again with the NOSTALGIA and RETRO ROD movements of the 1990s and early twenty-first century.

Mr. Horsepower

**M/Ts** (EM-TEES) *n.* Any diecast, finned-aluminum valve covers as produced by Mickey Thompson Equipment Company. M/Ts feature a distinctive tall, "boxy" style along with a finned top and trademark M/T logo. Initially produced during the mid-1960s, early M/Ts were often featured on full-competition DRAG racing vehicles (some early M/Ts were produced in then-exotic magnesium). From the late 1960s through the late 1970s, M/Ts experienced strong popularity in a wide variety of HOT ROD, MUSCLE CAR, and STREET MACHINE applications.

EARLY HEMI **M/T** VALVE COVER

**mud**, see BONDO

**muffs** *n.* Any automotive exhaust mufflers.

**mule** *n.* Any engine, automotive component, or complete vehicle that is used as a base for testing, experimentation, or research-and-development purposes.

**mural** *n.* Representational image or scene painted on the external body surfaces of a vehicle (usually by airbrush). Murals are unique in that they are most often presented on large, flat panels and consequently do not aspire to enhance a vehicle's overall form or body lines. Murals were especially popular on the customized vans of the 1970s (see the VAN CRAZE) and have maintained constant favor among LOWRIDERS from the 1970s to the present day.

**Muroc** *n.* MUROC dry lake (a.k.a. Rogers Dry Lake), a popular venue for lakes racing (see the LAKES) beginning during the early 1920s and continuing intermittently to the present day. MUROC was commandeered by the U.S. Army Air Corps in 1938, and the military allowed irregular lakes competition until 1942, after which all racing was suspended. LAND-SPEED RACING did not officially return to MUROC (now a part of Edwards Air Force Base) until 1996. The site's name was initiated by the Corum family that settled the area in the 1910s. When the U.S. Post Office deemed the name Corum unsuitable for a new stop (because of a similar pre-existing town name in California), the Corums simply reversed the spelling.

**muscle car 1.** *n.* Any mid-sized American passenger car produced from the mid-1960s through mid-1970s and equipped with a large-displacement V8 engine to provide exceptional straight-line performance. MUSCLE CARS were often treated to handling-oriented suspension upgrades, but acceleration remained the type's overriding focus. Jim Wangers, marketing executive for Pontiac, first coined the term MUSCLE CAR to promote the division's new-for-1964 PERFORMANCE model, the legendary GTO (see GOAT). Before the GTO, America's premier PERFORMANCE cars most often consisted of heavier, full-size SEDANS equipped with exotic, highly tuned race-style engines. The GTO provided similar performance by combining a milder V8 with a lighter, mid-sized body platform to create a less expensive, more STREETABLE package. The GTO's significant market success spawned an abundance of imitators from virtually all American manufacturers. These archetypal MUSCLE CARS were effectively killed off during the early to mid-1970s by skyrocketing insurance rates, the demise of high-octane leaded gasoline, and stringent new U.S. governmental emissions and safety standards. **2.** *n.* Any American automobile manufactured in the post-World War II period and featuring an engine with abundant horsepower and/or torque to produce outstanding vehicle performance. **3.** *n.* Any automobile equipped by its manufacturer with an exceptionally powerful and/or TORQUEY engine.

muscle truck[1]
2003 FORD LIGHTNING

**muscle truck 1.** *n.* Any light-duty pickup truck featuring the essential characteristics of a MUSCLE CAR (exceptionally powerful engine, along with upgraded running gear and suspension) to exhibit outstanding vehicle performance. MUSCLE TRUCKS came into vogue as a natural extension of American society's late-twentieth-century affinity with light pickup trucks. Notable examples of MUSCLE TRUCKS include: **a.** Dodge's "Li'l Red Express" short-bed stepside of 1978 and 1979, featuring a 225-BHP 360-CID engine; **b.** Chevrolet's 454 SS full-size, fleetside pickup of 1990 through 1993, with fuel-injected (up to 255 BHP) 454-CID BIG-BLOCK power; **c.** GMC's Syclone full-time all-wheel-drive compact pickup of 1991, equipped with a turbocharged (see TURBO), intercooled 4.3-liter V6 of 280 BHP; **d.** GMC's Typhoon compact SUV of 1992 and 1993, sharing common running gear with the earlier Syclone; **e.**

Chevrolet's extended-cab, short-bed Silverado SS of 2003 with full-time all-wheel drive and high-output 6.0-liter V8 producing 345 BHP; and **f.** Ford's SVT F-150 Lightning. Introduced as a 1993 model and continuing to the present day as the "world's fastest production pickup," recent Lightnings feature upgraded suspension and brakes and a supercharged (see BLOWER), intercooled 5.4-liter SOHC V8 engine producing 380 BHP. **2.** *n.* Any pickup truck/passenger car hybrid model (see CAMINO and 'CHERO) featuring the characteristics of a MUSCLE CAR.

**mystery motor** *n.* Any Mark IV BIG-BLOCK Chevrolet V8 (see RAT). A pre-production version of CHEVY's popular BIG-BLOCK debuted at 1963's Daytona 500 race but quickly disappeared from public view as a result of General Motors' post-1963 ban on all corporate-sponsored racing activity. In a May 1963 *HOT ROD* magazine article entitled "Chevrolet's 427 Mystery V8," technical editor Ray Brock explained that, "The most powerful high-performance engine at the 1963 Daytona 500 was a new V8 by Chevrolet. Unfortunately, these engines are not for sale." A strong air of mystery did, in fact, surround the powerful and innovative engine design until a 396-CID production version of the BBC was released during the 1965 model year. The BIG-BLOCK CHEVY's MYSTERY MOTOR name was most commonly used during the 1960s.

**Mystery Tiger** *n.* Fictitious character performing as the central figure in a successful 1966 Pontiac promotional program. The MYSTERY TIGER campaign featured two identically prepared Royal Bobcat 1966 GTOs (see GOAT) touring America's DRAG racing events along with a driver dressed in a complete tiger suit (including a full head mask obscuring the driver's identity). A challenger would be randomly selected from the audience by entry ticket number and offered a chance to DRAG RACE against the MYSTERY TIGER. Several different drivers actually played the tiger role during the course of the season, but as a program climax, George Hurst of Hurst Performance Products was unveiled and presented to the public as the one-and-only MYSTERY TIGER.

# N

**NA** (pronounced as separate letters), see NATURALLY ASPIRATED

**nailhead** (also **nailhead Buick**) *n.* Buick's first modern overhead-valve V8 engine as produced from the 1953 through 1966 model years. Term is derived from the engine's unconventional head (see HEADS)design featuring exceptionally small (nail-like) vertical valves. Despite its small-valve handicap, the NAILHEAD was widely used in high-performance applications during the 1950s and into the early 1960s. Period HOT RODDERS and racers successfully exploited the Buick's excellent torque properties and good LOW END to MIDRANGE horsepower levels. The pinnacle of FACTORY-produced NAILHEAD performance came in the form of the 401-CID with its 325-BHP version ably powering the Skylark-based Gran Sport MUSCLE CARS of 1965 and 1966, and the 425-CID engine with available DUAL QUADS and 360 BHP from 1964 through 1966. NAILHEADS are easily recognized by their vertical, upright valve cover placement.

**nail the throttle** (also **nail it**) *v.* To aggressively and fully depress a vehicle's accelerator pedal.

**nail-valve Buick** (also **nail-valve**) *n.* Early term for any VERTICAL-VALVE BUICK V8 (see NAILHEAD), specifically derived from the engine's exceptionally small exhaust valves, with their similarity in appearance to common framing nails. By the late 1950s, the type's early NAIL-VALVE name was effectively replaced by the current term NAILHEAD.

**NASCAR** (NASS-car) *n.* The National Association for Stock Car Auto Racing, since its late-1947 inception, the world's leading STOCK CAR racing organization. During the 1960s, NASCAR diversified to include a DRAG racing program, with a number of big-name STOCK CAR drivers (including "King" Richard Petty) briefly making the switch to straight-line competition.

**the Nationals** (also the **Nats**), see the BIG GO

**naturally aspirated** (ASS-per-ate-ed) *adj.* Relating to any engine that delivers its intake charge (air/fuel mixture) solely by means of the vacuum created during a cylinder's intake cycle. NATURALLY ASPIRATED engines differ from supercharged (see BLOWER) or turbocharged (see TURBO) engines, which instead mechanically force air/fuel mixture into their cylinders. Also NORMALLY ASPIRATED.

**necker knob** (also **necker's knob**) *n.* Alternative term for any steering wheel-mounted SUICIDE KNOB. Name derived from the concept that a steering-wheel spinner would free a driver's right hand or arm for "necking" with a passenger.

**negative rake** *n*. Any rearward incline or slant to a vehicle's body and suspended chassis assembly. Featured for solely aesthetic purposes on 1940s through early-1950s TAILDRAGGER CUSTOM CARS, and to provide a traction-enhancing rear-weight bias on 1960s-era DRAG RACE vehicles.

**nerf** *v*. Traditional circle-track racer's expression for any bumping or pushing between vehicles during the course of a race.

**nerf bars** (also **nerfs** or **nerfing bars**) **1.** *n*. Custom abbreviated protective bars replacing STOCK bumpers on a HOT ROD or sometimes acting as push bars at the rear of a DRAG racing vehicle. **2.** *n*. Any protective bars surrounding the nose, tail section, or tires of an open-wheeled race car.

**net horsepower** *n*. Horsepower rating system reflecting actual engine power levels with all relevant accessories in place (a complete engine as installed in a production vehicle). The alternative method of rating horsepower (GROSS HORSEPOWER) does not account for incidental accessories, thus resulting in inflated figures. The "net" horsepower rating method was adopted by most American manufacturers following the 1971 model year, causing a dramatic drop in advertised horsepower levels for 1972.

**neutral drop** *n*. In any automatic transmission-equipped vehicle, to free-REV an engine to a high RPM level with the gear selector in the neutral position followed by abruptly shifting to a forward gear. Typically practiced from a standing start to perform a BURNOUT (often in a vehicle that is incapable of burning out by any other means). NEUTRAL DROPS are extremely abusive and often destructive of transmission and driveline components. Example: "The kid was showing off by doing NEUTRAL DROPS in his mom's station wagon."

**newstalgia rod** *n*. Similar to the NOSTALGIA ROD type, NEWSTALGIA RODS are strongly based on the style and character of an earlier period in hot rodding's history. The NEWSTALGIA ROD deviates from the ultratraditional, however, by the subtle integration of modern technologies to improve the vehicle's overall DRIVEABILITY, ergonomics, reliability, or performance. The July 1977 issue of *HOT ROD* magazine included an early usage of the term "newstalgia." In it, automotive journalist Gray Baskerville titled a feature article "NEWSTALGIA" while showcasing builder Sam Foose's traditional, yet subtly refined, 1948 Ford CUSTOM.

**NHRA** (pronounced as separate letters) *n*. The National Hot Rod Association, the world's largest motorsports organization and DRAG racing's premier sanctioning body. Founded in 1951 largely through the work of its first president, Wally Parks (see WALLY), the NHRA held its first organized DRAG RACE in April 1953. From the time of its conception, the NHRA worked diligently to organize and standardize DRAG racing practices and, significantly, to improve the sport's safety. Through the NHRA's efforts, DRAG racing evolved and developed into the legitimate, professional sport it is today.

**niner**, see '09

**nitro** (NYE-troh) **1.** *n.* Nitromethane racing FUEL. Originally a commercial solvent type, nitromethane first fueled Vic Edelbrock's midget race cars in the late 1940s (see V8-60). During the early 1950s, RODDERS began to commonly run NITRO in both DRAG and LAND-SPEED RACING vehicles. Typically a percentage of the volatile FUEL was mixed with methanol (see ALKY) to produce the appropriate blend for a given application. Although NITRO offered the promise of tremendous performance increases, its successful burning required an extremely rich air/fuel mixture. Without adequate fuel delivery, many early NITRO-burning engines were damaged or destroyed. After the obstacle of sufficient fuel delivery was overcome by the introduction of efficient AFTERMARKET fuel-injection units, significantly higher percentages of NITRO were commonly used, producing tremendous power gains. Nitromethane-fueled vehicles (notably FUEL ALTEREDS, FUEL FUNNY CARS, and TOP FUEL DRAGSTERS) have historically and consistently achieved the ultimate in DRAGSTRIP performance, as well as spectator popularity. **2.** (also **nitro lacquer**) *n.* Any nitrocellulose lacquer automotive paint. Commonly used in early HOT ROD and CUSTOM CAR applications before its replacement by modern acrylic lacquers beginning in the 1950s.

**nitrous** (NYE-truss) *n.* Nitrous oxide, a mixture of nitrogen and oxygen that, when introduced (along with additional fuel) into a running engine, produces a dramatic increase in power. A street-driven vehicle equipped with nitrous oxide injection does not utilize the system during normal driving. Instead, it is activated only for brief periods when maximum power levels are desired. Automotive nitrous oxide systems were initially popularized during the mid-1970s and have since maintained strong favor in a broad variety of PERFORMANCE applications (see also GIGGLE GAS).

**no-name valve covers** *n.* Any AFTERMARKET valve covers with no manufacturer name or logo embossed or cast into their surfaces. In common usage since the mid-1960s, term has been used to describe a variety of chromed-steel or, more commonly, finned-aluminum custom valve covers.

**normally aspirated**, see NATURALLY ASPIRATED

**NOS 1.** (pronounced as separate letters) *adj.* New old stock. Relating to any automotive part or component produced by an automobile manufacturer but never installed on a new vehicle. NOS parts are instead stocked to be sold on a replacement basis. For restoration purposes, NOS components are the most coveted, as they are effectively new, precisely correct parts. **2.** (pronounced as separate letters or as NAWZ) *n.* Extremely popular brand of nitrous oxide injection system (see NITROUS) produced by NOS (Nitrous Oxide Systems, a division of Holley Performance Products, Inc.).

**nose 1.** *n.* The front-most portion of any vehicle's bodywork. **2.** *n.* In a HOT ROD application, the custom, streamlined replacement for a STOCK GRILL SHELL assembly (see TRACK NOSE). **3.** *v.* To remove STOCK hood emblems or ornamentation from an auto body followed by the filling of existing holes and refinishing to achieve a smoother, cleaner appearance.

**nose-bleeder** *n.* Any STREET MACHINE featuring an extremely high NOSE-BLEED RIDE HEIGHT.

**nose-bleed ride height** (also **nose-bleed stance**) *n.* Any extremely high vehicle RIDE HEIGHT (see JACKED-UP). Derived from a high altitude's perceived tendency to produce nose bleeds.

nose-bleed ride height
ON 1955 CHEVROLET

**nostalgia drags** (also **nostalgia drag races**) *n.* Any DRAG racing event focusing on vehicles, engines, or technology from an earlier period in DRAG history. As early as 1957, the term "nostalgia" was used to describe the NHRA's vintage four-cylinder (X designation) DRAG racing classes. During the 1960s, the Forever Four Club began running DRAG meets at various Southern California tracks to cater exclusively to vintage BANGER-motored vehicles. Interest in nostalgia-type racing was expanded during the 1970s as a number of significant historic DRAGSTERS (including Art Chrisman's *Hustler I* and Don Garlits' *Swamp Rat I*) were restored and made exhibition passes at major national DRAG events. The true catalyst for the modern nostaglia drag racing movement, however, came in the form of the Nostalgia Nationals held each year from 1981 through 1988 at Baylands Raceway (formerly Fremont DRAGSTRIP) in Fremont, California. Promoted by *STREET RODDER* magazine, the Nostalgia Nationals introduced the formation of nostalgia DRAG classes and the awarding of prize money for class wins, and, significantly, bred the formation of specific nostalgia-oriented DRAG racing sanctioning bodies. While modern nostalgia DRAG meets are often filled out with STREET RODS and 1960s-era MUSCLE CAR BRACKET RACING programs, a core of highly competitive nostalgia-inspired class racing still exists.

**nostalgia rod** *n.* Any HOT ROD designed and constructed to emulate the overall style and character of an earlier period in hot rodding's history.

**note** *n.* Any engine sound as emitted through a vehicle's exhaust system. A specific exhaust tone. Term derived from the more general concept of a musical note, a tone of definite pitch as made by a voice or musical instrument. Example: "That BIG CAM sure gives the thing a wicked NOTE at idle."

**NSRA** *n.* The National Street Rod Association. Formed in 1970, the NSRA played a significant role in the street rodding hobby's growth and has remained a popular and influential organization to the present day.

**numbers car** *n.* Any automobile featuring original, correct, and appropriately matching serial numbers throughout its body and chassis components. FACTORY VIN (vehicle identification number) and individual stamped or cast part numbers serve to authenticate and legitimize a rare (often high-performance) model car. Correct numbers, in turn, tend to greatly increase a vehicle's worth.

# O

**Oakland Roadster Show** (also **Oakland**) *n.* Traditional term for the GRAND NATIONAL ROADSTER SHOW (GNRS), arguably the world's most prestigious HOT ROD and CUSTOM CAR show and the oldest continuous event of its kind (see also the GRANDDADDY OF THEM ALL). Though OAKLAND's first 1949 show featured a variety of principally new automobiles, a small group of HOT ROD ROADSTERS was also invited to participate. The popularity of these modified vehicles led to the first exclusively HOT ROD OAKLAND show in 1950. Over time, GNRS has grown to include CUSTOM CARS, STREET MACHINES, MUSCLE CARS, hot boats, and motorcycles. The show's highlight comes with the annual presentation of the AMBR (America's Most Beautiful ROADSTER) award, along with its 9-foot-tall trophy (see the BIG TROPHY). Historically held in Oakland, California, the GNRS was presented at a variety of San Francisco Bay Area venues from 1998 through 2003, followed by a move to the Los Angeles County Fairplex in Pomona in 2004.

**oats** *n.* Power. Horsepower or torque as produced by any engine.

**OCIR** (pronounced as separate letters) *n.* Orange County International Raceway (see the COUNTY).

**odd rod** *n.* Any vehicle bearing the exaggerated, outrageous characteristics featured in artwork for the ODD RODS bubblegum card series. Expression may also be used in reference to any ROD or CUSTOM based on a highly unusual or atypical vehicle type.

**Odd Rods** *n.* Bubblegum card series produced by The Donruss Company from 1969 through 1973, featuring grotesque HOT ROD/monster caricatures. Subseries include: ODD RODS, Odder ODD RODS, Oddest ODD RODS, Fabulous ODD RODS, Fantastic ODD RODS, ODD ROD All Stars, Fiends and Machines, and Silly Cycles.

**odd swap** *n.* Any highly unusual or unconventional SWAP procedure, oftentimes involving the combining of products from entirely unrelated manufacturers and sometimes components from different technological eras. Example: "Talk about your ODD SWAPS . . . I knew a guy who stuffed a Ford FLATHEAD into an early Corvette [see 'VETTE]."

**OEM** (pronounced as separate letters) *adj.* STOCK, as produced by an original automobile manufacturer and differentiated from any AFTERMARKET product. Abbreviation derived from the term "original equipment manufacturer."

**off**, see BLOW SOMEONE'S DOORS OFF

**off the line** *adj.* Relating to the first moments of a DRAG RACE. The instant that participants leave their stationary positions on the starting line.

**off the trailer** *adj.* Describes the condition of a race vehicle precisely as transported on a trailer to a race course and run "as-is" with no tuning procedures yet performed. Example: "We're running 9.60s OFF THE TRAILER. Just wait 'til we get things dialed in."

**OHC** (usually written, not spoken) *adj.* Relating to any engine featuring an overhead camshaft (see CAM) configuration.

**Ohio flames** ON
CUSTOM "SPEEDSTAR" COUPE

**Ohio flames** *n.* Unique graphic treatment characterized by a narrow, flowing, and highly elongated adaptation of the traditional CRAB-CLAW FLAME style. A single highly prolific team of Ohio ROD builders and painters is credited with establishing and popularizing this distinct version of a classic theme. Beginning in the late 1990s, the work of Wade Hughes, Bill "Short & Round" Roell, and Jim "Dauber" Farr was introduced to a broad audience through appearances on numerous magazine feature and cover cars. The term OHIO FLAMES was coined by noted automotive journalist Pat Ganahl.

**OHV** (also **OH**) (usually written, not spoken) *adj.* An abbreviation for overhead-valve, which describes an engine configuration wherein all intake and exhaust valves are positioned *above* an engine's cylinders rather than beside them, as is the case with the archaic SIDEVALVE or FLATHEAD design. Though more complex, overhead-valve engines are inherently more efficient than their SIDEVALVE counterparts. Variations on the OHV design have been the automotive industry standards from the 1950s to the present day.

**oil down** *n.* In DRAG racing, any significant oil spill on a track's surface as a result of a competing vehicle's mechanical failure. Term dates to at least the 1950s.

**Olds** *n.* Any complete automobile or automotive component produced by the Oldsmobile division of General Motors.

**one legger** *n.* Alternative, slang term for any OPEN REAREND. Term is derived from the type's tendency to spin or smoke only one tire under hard acceleration or while performing a BURNOUT.

**on kill** *adj.* Relating to a highly aggressive, ultimate-performance state of engine, drivetrain, and/or chassis tune (fuel mixture, timing, BLOWER boost, clutch, etc.). When a DRAG racing vehicle is set ON KILL, it is pushing the envelope of its performance capabilities, producing absolute maximum power levels but in imminent danger of traction loss or mechanical failure. Example: "We had the thing set ON KILL, but it still wasn't enough to win in the finals."

**on one** *adj.* Experiencing an exceptionally strong DRAG racing PASS. Example: "Too bad the BLOWER belt let go 'cause it felt like it was really ON ONE."

**on the bottle** *adj.* Equipped with and running a nitrous oxide injection system (see NITROUS). The term's bottle reference describes the steel canister or "bottle" that contains nitrous oxide prior to being introduced into a running engine. Obviously derived from the more common slang term for a person on an alcoholic binge.

**on the bubble** *adj.* Possessing the slowest recorded time during the course of a DRAG RACE qualifying session. A racer who is ON THE BUBBLE is qualified to race but holds the lowest position in a fixed-number field of competitors. Until the full qualifying session is complete, this racer is in imminent danger of being bumped with no chance to race during actual competition.

**on the clock** *adj.* A reference to the measure of actual miles a vehicle has been driven, as recorded by the in-dash odometer gauge. Example: "He found a CLEAN '66 Chevelle in the want ads with only 60,000 miles ON THE CLOCK. Some grandma had been using it as her GROCERY GETTER."

**on the juice** *adj.* Equipped with a nitrous oxide injection system (see NITROUS). Like ON THE BOTTLE, derived from the more common slang term for a person on an alcoholic binge.

**on the motor** (also **on the engine**) *adj.* Relating to the running of any DRAG racing engine in its normal configuration, differentiated from running with the additional performance benefit of nitrous oxide injection. Example: "It'll run mid-tens ON THE MOTOR alone . . . better ON THE BOTTLE."

**open rearend** (also **open diff**) *n.* Any automotive REAREND incorporating a full and constant differential action. In traction-impaired situations, an OPEN REAREND always transfers power to the wheel experiencing the *least* amount of traction, seriously compromising vehicle performance in many cases. Not providing the traction of LIMITED SLIP (see POSI) or LOCKED REAREND types, OPEN REARENDS are generally considered less desirable in hot rodding and DRAG racing applications.

**O-ring tires** *n.* Any modern, high-performance radial tires featuring a large outside diameter and extremely short sidewall area. When mounted to necessarily large diameter wheels, the narrow sidewall accounts for an appearance somewhat similar to a rubber O-ring seal.

**orphan** *n.* Any HOT ROD, STREET ROD, or CUSTOM CAR based on a vehicle whose original manufacturer is no longer in business (Studebaker [see STUDE], Hudson, Kaiser, etc.).

**ought-nine**, see '09

**outfit**, see HOT IRON

**out of shape** *adj.* Out of control. Term describes the condition of a vehicle either partially or fully losing control during the course of a race. Example: "He got OUT OF SHAPE and crossed the centerline."

**out of the hole** (also **out of the chute** or **out of the gate**), see OFF THE LINE

**outrigger tubes** *n.* The exceptionally long intake runner tubes as featured on Chrysler Corporation's LONG RAM and SHORT RAM (Definition 1) induction systems. Being of extreme length, OUTRIGGER TUBES place the engine's dual FOUR-BARREL carburetors (see CARB) fully outboard or *beside* the motor rather than above it, as would be normal in most dual-QUAD applications.

**over-detail** *v.* To modify any vehicle with a perceived excess of ornamentation or ornate detail work. Negative attitudes toward over-detailing stem from the school of thought that a simple, CLEAN appearance is of paramount importance and that "more" is not necessarily better. Over-detailing may occur in the form of gold-plated and/or elaborately engraved underhood components, an excess of chrome-plated suspension (or even body) parts, custom-etched widow glass, upholstered wheelwells, etc. While a broad spectrum of SHOW-oriented HOT RODS and CUSTOM CARS exhibited extravagant detailing from the late 1950s through the mid-1970s, the style has been most associated with LOWRIDER CUSTOMS in more recent years.

**overhead 1.** *n.* Any engine featuring an overhead-valve configuration (see OHV). Term most often used during hot rodding's early years (pre-1960s), when overhead valves were the high-performance exception rather than the norm that they are today. Example: "By the end of the '50s, modern OVERHEADS had pretty much finished off the old FLATHEAD Ford." **2.** *adj.* Relating to any overhead-valve equipped engine (OVERHEAD Chevy, OVERHEAD V8, etc.).

**over-restore** *v.* When restoring any vehicle to a STOCK condition, to include subtle changes or improvements beyond what would have existed in a SHOWROOM STOCKER. To make a car "nicer" or "better" than it was when new. Examples of over-restoring may include painting (or powder coating) chassis components when components were left in a bare-metal state during original manufacture, painting on original-style body GRAPHICS that were FACTORY-furnished in decal form, and replacing STOCK imitation wood grain interior appliqués with genuine wood veneer. The term OVER-RESTORE often carries with it a negative connotation, implying that vintage PERFORMANCE vehicles should be restored to an absolutely original, historically correct state.

**oversquare** *adj.* Relating to any engine with a cylinder BORE diameter larger than its STROKE length, the standard configuration for most modern V8 engines. When compared with their UNDERSQUARE counterparts, OVERSQUARE engines offer the advantages of longer engine life and greater horsepower potential (through inherent shorter-STROKE REVving capacity).

**over-the-counter** *adj.* Relating to any part or component that is sold by an automotive manufacturer on a retail basis, with the purchaser accepting responsibility for installation. Term serves to draw a distinction from a component that may be purchased already built into a vehicle as a FACTORY-production option.

# P

**packs** (also **pacs**) *n.* Any exhaust mufflers featuring a GLASS-PACK or STEEL-PACK "straight-through" design.

**pancaked** *adj.* Modified through the radical body alteration of significantly flattening. Term is most often associated with the practice of reducing the high crown of an early-model (generally 1940s through 1950s) vehicle hood. Pancaking is accomplished through an extensive cutting, sectioning, and refinishing process and is often executed in concert with other radical body modifications (chopping, channeling, overall body sectioning, etc.).

**panel delivery** (also **panel** or **panel truck**) *n.* Vintage (generally 1920s through 1960s) automotive body style based on a commercial truck platform and serving to allow fully enclosed cargo hauling. Similar in principle to the contemporary SEDAN DELIVERY (commercial vehicle with sheetmetal rear body sides), a PANEL DELIVERY differs by its true truck foundation and somewhat larger size and is also commonly distinguished by dual rear freight-access doors. Though never achieving the popularity of its SEDAN DELIVERY counterparts, the PANEL DELIVERY has nonetheless experienced moderate favor in street rodding applications.

panel paint job ON
LARRY WATSON'S 1958 THUNDERBIRD

**panel paint job** (also **panel job**) *n.* Custom multicolored automotive paint treatment consisting of an overall base color partially covered by an accenting second color. With a PANEL JOB, the accent color serves to define and delineate a vehicle's individual body panel shapes as determined by STOCK body character lines and/or ornamental trim pieces. The PANEL JOB style was introduced by famed custom painter Larry Watson during the late 1950s. Customized from SHOWROOM-new, Watson's personal candy-burgundy-over-silver-PEARL 1958 Ford Thunderbird (see SQUAREBIRD) is considered to have been the very first recipient of a PANEL PAINT JOB.

**part out** (also **part**) *v.* To partially or fully disassemble a vehicle (or sometimes major vehicle component), disperse all worthwhile parts, and scrap anything deemed useless or unmarketable. To permanently reduce a vehicle to its various parts. Example: "The thing's got some real serious CANCER goin' on. I'm just gonna grab whatever I can use and PART OUT what's left."

**parts car** *n.* Any vehicle valued only for parts or components needed to complete a different automotive project. After the PARTS CAR has been stripped of everything useful, whatever remains is sold off or scrapped.

**Paso** (PASS-oh) *n.* The Cruisin' Nationals, a popular HOT ROD and CUSTOM CAR gathering held each Memorial Day weekend in the Central

California town of Paso Robles. Presented by the West Coast Customs organization since 1981, PASO was initially conceived as a get-together for traditional CUSTOM CARS (many of which were excluded from STREET ROD gatherings of the time by "pre-1949 only" restrictions). While a broader variety of vehicle types now participate in the event, the Cruisin' Nationals still remain a mecca for the ultratraditional HOT ROD and CUSTOM CAR.

**pass** *n.* Any singular DRAG or land-speed race as executed by an individual vehicle (differentiated from the many races typically occurring at an organized racing meet or event). May relate to side-by-side competition or to a solo run against the clock. Example: "If we can put together another PASS like that, we stand a good chance of making the program."

**patch out**, see LAY RUBBER

**pavement polisher 1.** *n.* Any HOT ROD or CUSTOM CAR featuring an extremely low RIDE HEIGHT. **2.** *n.* Any high-performance HOT ROD or STREET MACHINE capable of burning rubber with ease.

**pavement pounder** (also **pavement ripper**) *n.* Any radical, race-type HOT ROD, but especially one that is street-driven.

**peaked** *adj.* Modified through a custom alteration in which one or more body panels are adorned with a subtle, straight "bead" or "rib" to enhance factory-original shape or lines. A peak, for example, may be worked into the centerline of a vehicle's hood, fenders, DECK LID, or, very commonly, to the top of a FILLED 1932 Ford GRILL SHELL.

**peaky** *adj.* Possessing a narrow, generally high-RPM POWER BAND (said of a complete engine or engine component). Term most often relates to a race-style engine producing abundant power, but only when consistently revved to a high and limited RPM range. Outside this range, horsepower and/or torque levels fall off abruptly. Because of its implied limitations, the term PEAKY usually carries with it a negative connotation.

**peanut-slot mags** (also **peanut slots** or **peanut-slot Halibrands**) *n.* Alternative and colloquial expression for any small-window Halibrand DRAG racing wheels (see KIDNEY BEAN MAGS). Name derived from the unique shape of its surface windows.

**pearl** (also **pearlescent**) *n.* Popular custom paint type featuring the luminous, iridescent qualities of an actual pearl. As with a real pearl, light striking a PEARLESCENT paint finish has the effect of softly yet distinctly changing the color of light-saturated areas. In rodding and CUSTOM CAR applications, PEARL finishes were first popularized during the mid- to late 1950s on high-end CUSTOMS and SHOW RODS. The 1950s- and 1960s-era

Murano-brand PEARL paints were renowned for their brilliant shimmering qualities but were discontinued during the 1970s due to their toxic lead content. Modern PEARLS are achieved by infusing paint with minute mica particles.

**pedal the throttle** (also **pedal it**), see BACK-PEDAL

**peel out** (also **peel** or **peel off**), see LAY RUBBER

peep mirror

**peep mirror** *n.* Any small, round automotive sideview mirror featuring a short and curved mounting arm. Popular in many STREET rodding applications, the simple, CLEAN, and compact PEEP MIRRORS are typically clamped to the leading or upper edge of a vintage auto's door frame.

**peg legger** (also **peg leg**), see ONE LEGGER

**pencil tip** *n.* Type of chromed, custom exhaust system tip featuring an open end that is rolled tightly in on itself to create a smooth, finished appearance.

CHRYSLER'S **pentastar** EMBLEM

**pentastar** (PEN-tuh-star) *adj.* Relating to any Chrysler Corporation or DaimlerChrysler product. Term refers to the manufacturer's logo featuring a five-pointed star within a pentagon that was first introduced in 1963 and has been in intermittent use to the present day. A small PENTASTAR emblem was affixed to the lower right area of front fenders on most Chrysler Corporation production cars during the 1960s and early-1970s MUSCLE CAR era.

**perfect light** *n.* A DRAG racing REACTION TIME in which a racing vehicle begins moving virtually simultaneously with the CHRISTMAS TREE's green "go" signal. Although the concept of a perfect REACTION TIME is, by nature, only theoretical, it is possible for a driver to achieve a PERFECT LIGHT to the measured standard of one one-thousandth of a second.

**perforated**, see LOUVERED

**performance** *adj.* High-performance.

1932 FORD **phaeton** STREET ROD

**phaeton** (FAY-eh-tun) *n.* Vintage (generally 1900s through 1930s era) body style featuring front and rear full-width bench seats and a folding, convertible soft top. Typically including fully detachable windshield structures and removable side curtains, PHAETONS may be thought of as the four-passenger equivalents to early ROADSTER models. While PHAETONS have experienced marginal popularity in PERFORMANCE-oriented hot rodding applications, their greater favor has come in the role of the FULL-FENDERED, mild-mannered STREET ROD.

**phantom** *n.* STREET ROD type wherein a unique custom body style is created from an OEM production model of the past. A PHANTOM is thus a highly distinctive, one-off model that was never commercially produced in an earlier time but "might have been" had market and manufacturing circumstances been different. PHANTOM construction is typically accomplished through the modifying, adapting, and/or combining of original VINTAGE TIN auto bodies. Examples of PHANTOMS might include: **a.** A 1937 Ford THREE-WINDOW COUPE (Ford originally produced THREE-WINDOWS only from 1932 through 1936, with 1937 COUPES being offered solely in a FIVE-WINDOW style); **b.** A 1948 Chevrolet extended-cab pickup truck (modern-style crew or extended-cab options were not made available to late-1940s light pickup truck buyers); or **c.** A 1933 Ford "C400" convertible SEDAN (Ford's early convertible SEDANS were produced only as 1931 A400 and 1932 B400 models). The term PHANTOM and its building style were initially popularized during the 1980s and have maintained strong favor into the twenty-first century.

1948 CHEVROLET
EXTENDED-CAB **phantom**

**phone booth** *n.* Any HOT ROD with its primary body structure loosely bearing the vertical boxy shape and proportions of a traditional telephone booth. Term is most often used to describe STOCK-bodied Model T Ford (see T-BONE) COUPES, but may be used in reference to virtually any HOT ROD or STREET ROD with a substantially tall, narrow, and rectangular body. HOT ROD builder Carl Casper capitalized on the popular 1960s-era PHONE BOOTH term and style by creating a parody for the show circuit. Named *Phone Booth*, Casper's T-chassis, EARLY HEMI-powered 1964 SHOW ROD featured an actual glass telephone booth, complete with a pay phone, as its main body structure. The *Phone Booth* was also released as a 1/25th-scale MPC plastic model kit.

**phone booth**
1928 FORD PICKUP

**phone booth T** *n.* Any Model T Ford-based (see T-BONE) HOT ROD featuring a PHONE BOOTH-type body.

**pick 'em up** *n.* Any light-duty open truck (an adaptation of the mainstream expressions "pickup" or "pickup truck"). Beginning in the 1970s and continuing to the present day, all major American manufacturers have produced high-performance models based on their light-truck series (see MUSCLE TRUCK). Pickups have also traditionally been a popular foundation for HOT ROD, CUSTOM, and STREET MACHINE modification.

**pie-crust slicks** *n.* Early DRAG SLICK type distinguished by a uniform series of ribs or scallops on the outer edge of its sidewalls. Popular from the late 1950s through the mid-1960s, the term PIE-CRUST SLICKS is derived from the tires' similarity in appearance to the outer rim of a pie crust.

**pie plates** (also **pie plate caps** or **pie plate hubcaps**) *n.* Any simple, elemental automotive hubcaps bearing a resemblance to metallic pie plates (see POVERTY CAPS).

**pie wagon** *n.* Alternative expression for any C-CAB-type HOT ROD. The term PIE WAGON dates to the early part of the twentieth century, when enclosed C-CAB vehicles were used to deliver pies and other baked goods. In 1968, designer Tom Daniel created an ultramodern interpretation of a C-CAB SHOW ROD in the form of a 1/24th-scale Monogram model kit. Named *Pie Wagon*, Daniel's vision included the signature C-CAB elements of arched roof and C-shaped cab openings, but featured a freeform style for the remainder of the body design. An opening rear door revealed racks of pies, while exterior decals featured a "Mother's Pies" logo. Box art exclaimed, "It's CHERRY!"

**pig**, see PUMPKIN

**pinched** *v.* Relating to any automotive frame with its two parallel frame RAILS moved closer together than would be normal in a STOCK application. Early-vintage HOT ROD frames are sometimes PINCHED to conform more closely to stock body lines. Example: "To my eye, the '29 A HIGHBOY on DEUCE RAILS just doesn't look right unless the frame is PINCHED at the cowl."

**pink slip** (also **pink**) *n.* A vehicle's ownership certificate or, more formally, certificate of title. Derived from the overall pink color of many such title cards. When a pink slip is transferred between owners it may be considered an actual changing of vehicle ownership.

**'pins**, see HAIRPINS and HOOD PINS

**pipes** *n.* Highly general term relating to virtually any automotive exhaust pipes.

**piss wind** (WINED) *v.* To REV an engine to an exceptionally high RPM level.

pistol grip
SHIFTER

**pistol grip** (also **pistol grip shifter**) *n.* Unique manual transmission shift handle provided as standard equipment on all Dodge and Plymouth B-BODY and E-BODY four-speed cars from the 1970 through 1974 model years. (PISTOL GRIPS were not available with MOPAR's A-BODY and C-BODY offerings.) The PISTOL GRIP SHIFTER consists of a floor-mounted Hurst four-speed linkage topped with an unusual vertical handle in place of the more conventional spherical shift knob. When shifting, the PISTOL GRIP is grasped in a partial fist similar to the grip used when firing a handgun or pistol.

**pit tootsie** *n.* Generally demeaning or sexist term for any female member of a DRAG racing pit crew or female visitor to a DRAG racing team. A PIT TOOTSIE is most valued for her appearance. Example: "Do yourself a favor . . . get over and check out Scott's latest PIT TOOTSIE."

**pizza cutters** *n.* Any exceptionally narrow front tire/wheel combinations as commonly featured on purpose-built DRAGSTERS.

Name derived from a similarity in appearance to a roller-style pizza-cutting tool.

**'plant** *n.* POWERPLANT. Any automotive engine.

**plant it** *v.* To aggressively and fully depress a vehicle's accelerator pedal.

**plastic 1.** *n.* Somewhat derogatory term for any fiberglass (see 'GLASS) automotive body or body component. **2.** *n.* Any polyester-based auto body filler, such as the popular BONDO brand. Term often carries a pejorative tone when used by bodymen who prefer METALFINISH work or lead filler.

**plugs 1.** *n.* Any automotive sparkplugs **2.** see LAKES PLUGS

**pocket rocket** *n.* Any vehicle of small physical size and possessing outstanding performance.

**poked**, see BORED

**poked 'n' stroked** *adj.* Both BORED and STROKED to increase DISPLACEMENT (said of an engine).

**polished 1.** *adj.* Shined and/or buffed to a high luster for aesthetic purposes (said of any non-ferrous-metal automotive components, generally aluminum or magnesium). **2.** *adj.* Relating to any internal engine components (intake ports, exhaust ports, combustion chambers, etc.) that are thoroughly smoothed to improve engine performance.

**Poncho** (PAWN-cho) *n.* Any complete automobile or automotive component produced by the Pontiac division of General Motors.

**ponies** *n.* Horsepower, as produced by an engine.

**pony**, see 'STANG

**pony car** *n.* Any of several lightweight, nimble "personal cars" initially produced during the mid-1960s largely as a result of the immensely popular Ford Mustang (see 'STANG), the inspiration for the type's PONY CAR name. Among its many distinctive features, the Mustang's revolutionary long-hood/short-DECK styling influenced all PONY CARS to follow. Although most PONY CARS historically have been FACTORY-equipped with mild small-displacement V8 engines (making for capable yet somewhat uninspired performance), manufacturers have consistently provided a wide variety of high-performance PONY CAR options and submodels. Important examples of PERFORMANCE-oriented PONY CARS include: **a.** Ford's Shelby, Mach 1, Boss, SVO, and Cobra R Mustangs; **b.** Mercury's GTE and Eliminator Cougars;

**pony car**
1968 MERCURY COUGAR GTE

**c.** Chevrolet's Z-28 (see Z), SS 396, COPO, and IROC Camaros; **d.** Pontiac's Trans Am (see T/A), Formula, SD 455, and RAM AIR Firebirds (see 'BIRD); **e.** Dodge's R/T and T/A Challengers; **f.** Plymouth's Formula S, 'CUDA , and AAR 'CUDA Barracudas; and **g.** American Motors' Javelin-based AMX (see JAV). While seldom adhering to the explicit MUSCLE CAR canon (intermediate-bodied SEDAN powered by large-displacement V8 engine), PONY CARS are sometimes considered MUSCLE CARS as well, representing an overlapping of genres and terminologies. PONY CARS are perceived to be MUSCLE CARS when treated to significant high-performance options or option packages and especially when FACTORY-equipped with BIG-BLOCK V8 engines.

**poop deck** *n.* Alternative and relatively rare expression for any early automotive TURTLE DECK trunk assembly.

**pop 1.** *n.* Any nitromethane racing fuel (see NITRO). Term may be derived from "soda pop" or "popskull," a term for raw, inferior whiskey. **2.** *n.* Any specialized racing fuel, excluding gasoline.

**pop a wheelie** *v.* In any vehicle, to perform or experience a WHEELSTAND.

**pop the chute,** see HANG OUT THE LAUNDRY

**pop the clutch** *v.* To abruptly engage the clutch of a manual-transmission vehicle, generally to perform a BURNOUT or to effect a positive vehicle LAUNCH.

**pop-top,** see FLIP-TOP

**porcupine** (also **porcupine motor** or **porcupine mill**) *n.* Early term (generally 1960s era) for Chevrolet's Mark IV RAT MOTOR. Name is derived from the BIG-BLOCK CHEVY's unique canted SEMI-HEMI valve arrangement. With valve covers removed, valves appear splayed at peculiar angles (26 degrees for intakes and 16 degrees for exhausts) reminiscent of a porcupine's quills.

**ported** *adj.* Modified by having intake or exhaust ports enlarged, reshaped, or matched for improved performance (said of any relevant engine component).

**portholes 1.** *n.* A signature design element of 1950s-era Buick passenger cars. Officially designated "Ventiports" by Buick, PORTHOLES were first introduced with the manufacturer's 1949 offerings. Sets of either three or four (depending on specific model) chromed round or oval ports were fitted to each front fender, easily distinguishing the marque from all other vehicles. Buick PORTHOLES from the 1950s have traditionally been adapted to CUSTOM CARS in a variety of applications, variously serving as custom taillight bezels, imitation or functional through-body exhaust outlets, and SUNKEN ANTENNA bezels. **2.** *n.* The small, round "quarter windows" as featured in Ford Thunderbird (see T-BIRD) removable HARDTOPS during the 1956–1957 (PORTHOLES were not available in 1955) and 2002–2003 model years. PORTHOLE windows of this type were also produced in AFTERMARKET form and commonly featured in the side panels of 1970s-era customized vans (see VAN CRAZE).

portholes² ON
1957 THUNDERBIRD

**posi** (PAW-zee) **1.** *n.* Any LIMITED SLIP differential system functioning within a driven automotive axle assembly. As with a standard OPEN REAREND's differential mechanism, POSI units allow for full differential action (see REAREND) under normal driving conditions. POSIS differ, however, by their ability to direct appropriate and efficient power to *both* rear wheels in traction-limited situations. While promoted by manufacturers as a safety feature, POSI units are more renowned for their quality of enhancing vehicle performance under hard acceleration. LIMITED SLIP-type differentials were introduced by a variety of manufacturers during the late 1950s and have remained a standard or optional feature on high-performance models since. Though all serve the same function, LIMITED SLIP units have been assigned various names by their respective makers (FoMoCo's Traction-Lok, Chrysler's Sure-Grip, AMC's Twin-Grip, etc.). Chevrolet dubbed their LIMITED SLIP units "Positraction." In its full "positraction" and shortened "POSI" forms, CHEVY's terminology has become a generic, commonly used reference to LIMITED SLIP units of any manufacture. **2.** (also **posi rearend**) *n.* Any complete automotive REAREND featuring a LIMITED SLIP or "positraction" feature.

**positive rake** *n.* Any forward incline or slant to a vehicle's body and suspended chassis assembly. A POSITIVE RAKE is a traditional and very common element in HOT ROD aesthetics.

**post** *n.* Any true SEDAN model automobile as manufactured in the POSTWAR period. Term is most often used to describe 1950s and 1960s "pillared" SEDANS, distinguishing the type from concurrently produced HARDTOP models. The term POST is specifically derived from the fixed B-PILLAR and solid door-window frames present on all SEDAN models. While perceived as less glamorous than their HARDTOP counterparts, two-door POSTS have traditionally been popular foundations for STREET MACHINE and DRAG RACE modification. From the mid-1950s through the 1960s, in particular, POST models were often preferred in maximum-performance applications for their inherent advantages of relative lightness and structural rigidity.

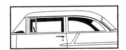

1957 CHEVROLET 150-SERIES
post

**postwar** *adj.* After World War II. All domestic automobile production was curtailed during the Second World War, with manufacturers engaged instead in various military contracts. Production for the civilian market resumed in late 1945, with 1946 model cars being essentially repackaged

1942 (PREWAR) models. The term POSTWAR most often refers to the first fully redesigned automobiles produced after the war, commonly released as 1949 models. In street rodding applications, the PREWAR/POSTWAR distinction holds significant relevance. Traditionally (especially during the 1970s and 1980s), many STREET ROD organizations and events accepted only pre-1949 model vehicles, deliberately excluding later-vintage STREET MACHINES, CUSTOMS, and MUSCLE CARS. In more recent years, these restrictions have often been relaxed, with 1950s and even early-1960s era vehicles typically being allowed to participate.

**pot**, see JUG

**poverty caps** (also **poverty hubcaps**) *n.* Any automotive hubcaps featuring a stark, elemental, "bare-bones" style. Term most often represents the least expensive wheel cover FACTORY-available on a given automobile model. From the late 1950s through the early 1970s MUSCLE CAR era, POVERTY CAPS were sometimes provided as a part of a stripped-down, no-frills PERFORMANCE car package.

**powderpuff** (also **powder puff**) **1.** *adj.* Relating to any organized DRAG racing class or program exclusively for female drivers. The POWDERPUFF term and class distinctions were most common during the 1950s and 1960s, after which female competitors were typically integrated into mainstream DRAG competition. **2.** *n.* Any female driver participating in a POWDERPUFF DRAG racing class or event.

**power adder** *n.* Any of several systems employed by hot rodders and DRAG racers to dramatically increase a given engine's performance. Popularized during the late 1990s and into the twenty-first century, the term may be used to describe a supercharger (see BLOWER), turbocharger (see TURBO), or nitrous oxide injection (see NITROUS).

**power park** *v.* To park any vehicle (generally a high-end STREET ROD) in a prominent place so as to be easily admired by spectators or the general public. Vehicles are most often POWER PARKed at outdoor car shows or ROD RUNS. The term POWER PARK sometimes carries with it a slightly derogatory tone, suggesting that a vehicle's main intended purpose is that of a static display.

**powerplant** *n.* Any automotive engine.

**powershift** (also **power shift**) *v.* To maintain full throttle while upshifting a manual transmission's gears. Often practiced in all-out DRAG racing competition.

**powerslide**, see SLIP 'N' SLIDE

**powerstand**, see WHEELSTAND

**prewar** *adj.* Before World War II. Relating to any vehicle manufactured prior to the American automobile industry's shift to wartime military production (generally 1942 or earlier model year).

**projectile-bird**, see BULLETBIRD

**Pro Stock 1.** *n.* DRAG racing class with competing vehicles loosely based on current or near-current American COUPE and SEDAN production cars. Modern PRO STOCK DRAG cars commonly include OEM-inspired body structures, manual transmissions, and gasoline-burning NATURALLY ASPIRATED engines. In part because of strong manufacturer brand identities, the NHRA's PRO STOCK class has maintained exceptional popularity from its 1970 origin to the present day. **2.** (also **Pro Stocker**) *n.* Any individual vehicle competing in a PRO STOCK DRAG racing class.

EARLY-2000S
CHEVROLET CAVALIER
**Pro Stock**

**Pro Street 1.** *adj.* Relating to a street-legal DRAG RACE vehicle (or a vehicle with such an appearance) that is loosely based on a full-bodied PRO STOCK DRAG racing car, but equipped with all legally required STREET equipment. In addition to roll cages, fuel cells, and WHEELIE BARS, the signature element of the PRO STREET style is a radically narrowed REAREND working in conjunction with immense rear tires and WHEEL TUBS. The PRO STREET type was conceived in the late 1970s and experienced extreme popularity throughout the 1980s. From the late 1990s to the present day, PRO STREET has evolved to place greater emphasis on DRIVEABILITY and true performance (traditionally, PRO STREET performance has often fallen short of the type's aggressive look). **2.** *v.* To modify any vehicle or vehicle system in a PRO STREET style.

**Pro Touring** *adj.* Relating to a style of custom-built vehicle that is capable of excellent all-around road performance and good real-world DRIVEABILITY. A PRO TOURING vehicle goes beyond the requisite hot rodding demand for outstanding straight-line acceleration, placing an emphasis on such performance aspects as handling, TOP END speed, and braking. The PRO TOURING vehicle type has gained an initial and strong popularity in the early twenty-first century.

**Pro Tree**, see CHRISTMAS TREE

**prune** someone *v.* To soundly beat an opponent in a DRAG RACE. Generally 1950s-era usage.

**pruned by a stocker**, see CHOPPED BY A STOCKER

**puffer**, see BLOWER

**puking chicken**, see SCREAMING CHICKEN

**pull** someone *v.* To establish or increase a lead during the course of a DRAG RACE. To "pull" ahead or away from a competitor. Example: "In Top Stock Eliminations, Mozer PULLed Eckstrand at half track and held on for the win."

**pull the frontend** (also **pull a wheelie** or **pull the wheels**) *v.* In any vehicle, to perform or experience a WHEELSTAND.

**pump** (also **pumper**), see BLOWER

**pumped up** *adj.* Highly modified for improved performance (said of either a complete vehicle or an individual vehicle component, most often an engine).

**pump gas** *n.* Any gasoline of the type purchased directly from a public service station's pumps (as differentiated from specialized high-octane racing gasoline).

**pumpkin** *n.* Any rear-wheel-drive automotive third member of the Hotchkiss (removable, front-loading) type. In a Hotchkiss REAREND, the PUMPKIN comprises the "drop-out" assembly, including gear case, carrier, pinion support, and yoke. Term is inspired by the unit's similarity in shape and size to the actual fruit.

**pumpkin seed** (also **pumpkin seed streamliner**) *n.* Any LAND-SPEED RACING STREAMLINER featuring the overall "flattened teardrop" shape of a pumpkin seed. The first 'LINER to employ the style (nicknamed *The Pumpkin Seed*) was constructed by the prolific and innovative RODDER Bill Burke. At BONNEVILLE in 1960, the tiny Ford six-cylinder-powered machine shattered the existing Class D (122 to 183 CID) record by running over 205 miles per hour. A collaboration with celebrated racer Mickey Thompson followed for 1961, providing *The Pumpkin Seed* with an M/T-prepared BLOWN Pontiac Tempest four-cylinder engine. Thompson's potent FOUR BANGER pushed the little STREAMLINER to over 264 miles per hour before it succumbed to mechanical failure.

**pump salt**, see SHOOT THE SALT

**punch 1.** *n.* Any hard, intense acceleration as exhibited by a PERFORMANCE vehicle. **2.** *n.* Power. Horsepower or torque as produced by any engine.

**punched 1.** (also **punched out**) see BORED **2.** see LOUVERED

**punch it** *v.* To aggressively and fully depress a vehicle's accelerator pedal.

**push** *n.* Any power source functioning to propel a vehicle. An indirect reference to a vehicle's engine. Example: "With a 394 OLDS for PUSH, that little HIGHBOY oughta HAUL ASS!"

**pussy-foot rearend** (also **pussy-foot suspension**) *n.* Any independent REAREND assembly (see WIGGLY REAREND). Most often refers to the JAG REAREND, hence, the "cat" association.

**put** someone **down** *v.* Generally 1950s and 1960s expression for defeating an opponent in a DRAG RACE.

**put** someone **in the box** *v.* A more modern adaptation of the traditional expression, PUT someone ON THE TRAILER. "In the box" refers to the now-popular enclosed trailer, as differentiated from the open trailers more commonly used in the past.

**put** someone **on the trailer** *v.* In organized DRAG racing, to defeat an opponent during the elimination ROUNDs of competition. When a competitor loses a single-elimination ROUND, he or she is generally through racing for the remainder of the event. Because most serious race vehicles are trailered, it is possible to PUT someone ON THE TRAILER, out of competition and ready for the ride home after a loss in a single ROUND. Example: "He definitely had the stronger running car, but we managed to PUT him ON THE TRAILER in the semis."

**put the power to the ground** *v.* In any DRAG racing application, to achieve full driven-wheel traction under hard acceleration. To make practical use of all horsepower and/or torque produced by an engine.

# Q

**Q-jet** *n.* Any Rochester-brand Quadrajet FOUR-BARREL carburetor (see CARB). The spreadbore Q-JET was commonly featured as original equipment on moderate- to high-performance General Motors (as well as some FoMoCo) MUSCLE CARs during the 1960s and early 1970s.

**quad 1.** *n.* Any FOUR-BARREL carburetor (see CARB). **2.** (also **quad manifold** or **quad setup**) *n.* Any high-performance induction system featuring four TWO-BARREL carburetors.

**quad headlights** ON EARLY-1960S CUSTOM ROD

**quad headlights** *n.* Any automotive headlight system featuring four separate and individual lamps for styling and/or improved illumination. American manufacturers began adding a second pair of headlights to their upscale luxury cars in 1957, and by 1958 QUADS had become the industry standard. Although positioning varied among models (side-by-side, vertically stacked [see STACKED HEADLIGHTS], or diagonally canted [see CANTED HEADLIGHTS]), QUAD HEADLIGHTS were prominently featured on most 1960s and 1970s high-performance cars and MUSCLE CARS. Significantly, many CUSTOM CARS and even some early-model HOT RODS were fitted with elaborate QUAD HEADLIGHT treatments during the late 1950s and early 1960s.

**Quadrajunk** *n.* Any Rochester-brand Quadrajet (see Q-JET) FOUR-BARREL carburetor (see CARB). The derogatory term QUADRAJUNK name is derived from the perception that the Q-JET is less than capable in true high-performance applications. Despite the fact that great advances have been made in Quadrajet modification and performance, it has historically been common practice to replace OEM Q-JETs with various AFTERMARKET carburetors.

**quads,** see DUAL QUADS and QUAD HEADLIGHTS

**the quarter** *n.* The quarter-mile (or 1,320 feet), the most common official length of a DRAG RACE course. Though variations have been used throughout organized DRAG racing's history, the quarter-mile has consistently remained the most popular track format. One popular theory suggests the distance was originally inspired by quarter-horse racing's similar course length. Example: "What'll it do in the QUARTER?"

**quarter-pounder** *n.* Any especially powerful or QUICK DRAG racing vehicle. Term derived from DRAG racing's common quarter-mile course length combined with a reference to the popular McDonald's restaurant hamburger sandwich of the same name.

**quick** *adj.* Capable of exceptional or outstanding acceleration. Differentiated from the term FAST, which may relate to acceleration, but most often describes a high TOP END speed.

**quickchange** (also **quickchange rearend** or **quickie**) *n.* Any automotive REAREND featuring a capability to quickly access and change final-drive ratio gear sets. Popular for its unique tuning potential in early (especially 1950s era) DRAG, ROUNDY-ROUND, and LAND-SPEED RACING, the QUICKCHANGE has more recently experienced favor in street rodding applications strictly for its traditional, racy appearance.

# R

**R's**, see RPM

**race for pinks** (also **race for pink slips** or **race for slips**) *v.* To engage in a DRAG RACE in which the winner receives the loser's vehicle in reward (see PINK SLIP).

**race Hemi** (HEM-ee) **1.** *n.* Any 426-CID LATE HEMI engine produced expressly for the purpose of NASCAR or DRAG competition. Introduced in 1964, the 426 RACE HEMI predated the milder STREET HEMI by a full two years (the STREET HEMI was initially conceived only to HOMOLOGATE the more powerful RACE HEMI to NASCAR regulations). The highly successful Dodge and Plymouth RACE HEMIS differed from their STREET HEMI cousins by their higher compression ratios (see SQUEEZE), exotic induction systems (variously including aluminum or magnesium CROSS RAM INTAKES or even Hilborn fuel injection), more radical valve timing, tubular steel exhaust HEADERS, and sometimes aluminum HEADS and water pumps. **2.** *n.* Any complete Dodge or Plymouth automobile featuring a 426-CID RACE HEMI engine as original equipment.

**radius** *v.* To cut away material in a circular or semicircular fashion. In HOT ROD or DRAG racing applications, the term is most often used to describe the enlarging of auto body wheel openings to provide additional clearance for oversized tires. Radiused wheel openings are cut slightly larger than corresponding tire diameters, allowing the tires to extend beyond the vehicle's outermost body panels. By the 1980s, the popularity of severely narrowed REARENDS (working in conjunction with WHEEL TUBS) all but put an end to the practice of radiusing wheel openings.

**rag rod**, see RAT ROD

**ragtop** (also **rag**) *n.* Any automobile featuring a convertible soft top.

**rail** (also **rail job** or **rail dragster**) *n.* Any maximum-performance DRAGSTER featuring only the very minimal bodywork necessary to enhance safety and performance. Term originally popularized during the 1950s when the first true purpose-built DRAGSTERS were stripped of all unnecessary weight, often leaving little more than a pair of bare automotive frame RAILS, running gear, and a driver's seat.

**railbirds** *n.* At any organized DRAG racing event, the line of spectators standing along the crowd-control fence immediately adjacent to the actual DRAGSTRIP. RAILBIRDS choose to get as close to the racing action as the general public is allowed.

**rails** *n.* Any automotive frame rails. The two parallel steel rails defining the longitudinal perimeters of any early automotive frame. Example: "As far as I'm concerned, it's not a HIGHBOY without DEUCE RAILS."

**rake 1.** *n.* Any incline or slant to a vehicle's body and suspended chassis assembly. Term most often refers to a lower front/higher rear body attitude (POSITIVE RAKE) but may also describe a low rear bias (NEGATIVE RAKE). RAKES have long provided a fundamental element to traditional HOT ROD and CUSTOM CAR aesthetics. **2.** *n.* Any incline or slant incorporated into a vehicle component or part. Example: "Before I even think about putting a top on it, I plan on giving the windshield a serious RAKE."

rake[1] ON 1957 CHEVROLET CAMEO CARRIER PICKUP

**rally wheels** (also **rallye wheels**) **1.** *n.* Any of a large number of OEM FACTORY MAGS produced by major American manufacturers and featured as standard or optional equipment on high-performance vehicles. Although widely varying in styles, RALLY WHEELS all serve to enhance vehicle appearance with some form of stylized steel center (generally a slot or spoke design) and distinctive ornamental center cap. From the mid-1960s through the mid-1970s MUSCLE CAR era, General Motors, Chrysler Corporation, FoMoCo, and AMC all produced FACTORY MAGS dubbed RALLY WHEELS through corporate marketing and/or public recognition. **2.** *n.* Any AFTERMARKET wheels produced in the style of OEM RALLY WHEELS and referred to as RALLY WHEELS by their manufacturer.

CHEVROLET **rally wheel**[1]

**ram air** *n.* Any fresh-air induction system employed to increase engine performance levels. Because fresh, cold air carries a denser air/fuel mixture to an engine's combustion chambers than does warm underhood air (equating to improved engine performance), virtually all major American manufacturers provided some form of fresh-air induction to enhance their respective MUSCLE CARS' performance during the late 1960s and early 1970s. In the typical OEM RAM AIR system, a hood scoop is equipped with some form of driver-actuated control allowing either underhood air or fresh external air to be directed to the engine's carburetor (see CARB), depending on weather conditions and/or performance needs.

**Ram Air** *n.* Any of a series of high-performance 400-CID engines produced by Pontiac from 1967 through 1970. Pontiac's RAM AIR series was named for the functional, fresh-air induction systems that accompanied the engines in their Firebird (see 'BIRD) and GTO (see GOAT) installations. The specialized, high-performance RAM AIR engines were numbered in various subseries (RAM AIR I through RAM AIR V) as they evolved in sophistication and power output.

**ram horns** (also **ram's horns**) **1.** *n.* Any cast-iron exhaust manifolds featuring a symmetrical, dual-arch design so as to resemble the horns of

1957 CHEVROLET
**ram horn**[1] MANIFOLD

an actual ram. The relatively efficient RAM HORNS were most notably featured as original equipment on early SMALL-BLOCK Chevrolet V8 engines (see MOUSE). Introduced in late 1956, CHEVY'S RAM HORNS were commonly employed on FACTORY SBCs throughout the 1960s and into the 1970s. Chevrolet RAM HORNS have long been a popular choice in tight-chassis street rodding applications for their compact, BLOCK-hugging design. **2.** *n.* Any of the graceful individual-tubed, cast-iron HEADERS as featured on 1962 through 1964 Chrysler Corporation MAX WEDGE engines. MAX WEDGE RAM HORNS sweep *upward* from exhaust ports and arch rearward to terminate at a down-facing flange near the back of the cylinder block (see BLOCK).

**Rancho,** see 'CHERO

**rap the pipes** (also **rap the mufflers**) *v.* With driveline disengaged, to briefly REV a vehicle's engine, creating a loud and impressive noise through the exhaust system. Term most popular during the 1940s and 1950s.

**rat** (also **rat motor** or **rat mill**) **1.** *n.* Any Mark IV BIG-BLOCK Chevrolet V8 production engine. Chevrolet applied its powerful BIG-BLOCK to passenger-car applications from the 1965 through 1976 model years (specific engine displacements included 396, 402, 427, and 454 cubic inches). Available in many significant high-performance iterations, the RAT MOTOR established a strong PERFORMANCE legacy while powering CHEVY's mid- and full-size SEDANS, as well as Corvette (see 'VETTE) models. Beyond its production car usages, the BIG-BLOCK CHEVY has achieved extreme popularity in myriad hot rodding and racing applications for its cost effectiveness, parts interchangeability, and outstanding performance potential. The engine's RAT name was established by the mid-1960s and is derived from its relationship to the smaller, pre-existing Chevrolet MOUSE MOTOR. **2.** *n.* Any of the highly popular GM CRATE MOTOR and/or AFTERMARKET BIG-BLOCK Chevrolet derivatives of the original Mark IV production BIG-BLOCK.

**ratchet jaw** *n.* Derogatory expression for any person who is perceived to talk too much. A HOT RODDER who talks incessantly or constantly boasts of his own accomplishments. Term compares the action of an individual's jaw to the quick reciprocating motion of a common ratchet tool and was most commonly used during the 1960s.

© Ed "Big Daddy" Roth, 1984

**Rat Fink**

**Rat Fink** *n.* The most celebrated of Ed "Big Daddy" Roth's many WEIRDO CHARACTERS. RAT FINK is depicted as an upright, jagged-toothed, bug-eyed rodent in overalls with the initials RF emblazoned across his potbelly. In the book *Confessions of a Rat Fink,* "Big Daddy" relates that RAT FINK was conceived as a pencil drawing on a fast-food restaurant napkin "in the '50s." When Roth (1932–2001) recognized the potential of his caricature, he transferred the image to his shop refrigerator door with an overhead projector. After approaching an engraver to produce a T-shirt silkscreen for the image, the engraver informed Roth that he would need a suitable black-and-white illustration to work from. With the only acceptable RAT FINK likeness being painted on his refrigerator, Roth was forced to remove the entire door and bring it to the engraver. Roth claimed to have used this original artwork through 1984. During the early and mid-1960s, RAT FINK achieved an unprecedented level of popularity and was marketed in a vast array of mediums. Closely tied to the 1960s-era DRAG and hot rodding cultures, RAT FINK was sometimes painted on race vehicles and often adorned car windows in decal form. Like other 1960s-era icons, RAT FINK'S popularity diminished somewhat in the following decades but has enjoyed a strong resurgence during the 1990s and into the twenty-first century. As of 2004, RAT FINK'S likeness had been made available in T-shirt, key ring, sticker, figurine, pendant, drink coaster, poster, wristwatch, comic book, plush toy, antenna topper, air freshener, and even electric guitar and amplifier forms, among others. The name RAT FINK itself may have been inspired by the popular comedian and television talk-show host Steve Allen, who was known to commonly use the expression during the time of RAT FINK'S creation.

**rat rod** *n.* Retro-styled HOT ROD bearing an unfinished, often relatively crude appearance and constructed from genuine vintage parts. The use of old parts and components gives RAT RODS an air of authenticity and frequently provides a patina that is considered desirable to the type. (So popular is the aged, well-worn look that some rodders painstakingly re-create it with various modern techniques.) It is often noted, in defense of the RAT ROD genre, that an imperfect or rough style is an integral aspect of the type's authenticity; the unfinished appearance of RAT RODS very accurately mirrors the true period style of the cars that they are built to replicate. In this respect, these vehicles are "finished" to a state of perfection, accurately expressing the spirit and character of an earlier time. Like the term RETRO ROD, the term RAT ROD has been in common usage in the 1990s and into the twenty-first century.

**reacher** *n.* STREET ROD type with a strong focus on reliability, economy of operation, and driving comfort. A ROD that may be safely and reasonably driven on long trips. Term and style were most popular from the late 1970s through the mid-1980s.

**reaction time** *n.* At the outset of a DRAG RACE, the time that it takes a driver to put his vehicle in motion after being signaled to start. Typically measured to the thousandths of a second, REACTION TIME is a critical factor in determining the outcome of any DRAG RACE.

**Real Street 1.** *adj.* Relating to a PERFORMANCE vehicle type derived from the PRO STREET movement but differing in its practical DRIVEABILITY. A style of vehicle that is very QUICK or FAST but may still be reasonably driven in true STREET applications. With 1980s-era PRO STREET vehicles being treated to evermore impractical, race-oriented elements, their originally intended STREET MACHINE character and function was essentially lost over time. The REAL STREET term was popularized during the 1990s. **2.** *n.* Any of several sanctioned DRAG racing classes named REAL STREET and adhering to the spirit of the REAL STREET vehicle type. The popular NMRA (National Mustang [see 'STANG] Racers Association) REAL STREET class, for example, features STOCK-based 1979 and newer V8 Ford Mustangs. With manual transmissions and single POWER ADDERS (either supercharger [see BLOWER] or nitrous oxide injection [see NITROUS]) NMRA REAL STREET Mustangs attain WHEELSTANDing, 10-second RUNS.

**rearend** (also **rear**) *n.* In any front-engine/rear-wheel-drive vehicle, the rear axle assembly that receives the rotational movement of a driveshaft (as produced by engine and transmission) and redirects it, in a perpendicular fashion, to turn the vehicle's rear wheels. This redirection is accomplished by means of a ring-and-pinion gear set that also serves to reduce actual wheel speed, in relation to driveshaft speed, by a given ratio (final-drive ratio). REARENDS most often incorporate a coupling that provides for a "differential" in rotating speeds between the two driven wheels as is appropriate for cornering, surface, or traction demands. Because of this differential feature, complete rear axle assemblies are sometimes referred to as "differentials" or, in slang terms, DIFFS.

**rearend gears** *n.* Any automotive rear axle's final-drive ratio gear set (see REAREND).

the **red eye** *n.* Alternate term for any DRAG racing REDLIGHT start.

**redlight** (also **red light**) **1.** *n.* In organized DRAG racing, any foul start occurring when a driver leaves his stationary starting position before being signaled to go (see CHRISTMAS TREE). When an early start takes place, the TREE's lowermost bulb glows red, signaling the violating participant's immediate loss. **2.** *v.* To commit a foul or REDLIGHT start while DRAG racing.

**redline 1.** *n.* The highest effective RPM level of any given engine beyond which power levels decline or mechanical failure may occur due to over-revving. Derived from the red area commonly marking the upper RPM limit on a vehicle's tachometer. **2.** *v.* To REV an engine to its maximum practical RPM level.

**redlines** (also **redline tires**) *n.* Any automotive tires featuring a narrow red sidewall stripe. REDLINES were featured in many OEM 1960s-era MUSCLE CAR applications, but perhaps most notably as standard equipment on early Pontiac GTO models (see GOAT). The introductory 1964 GTOs were offered with $7^1/_2$x14-inch, U.S. Royal "Tiger Paw" (Super Safety 800) REDLINES as standard equipment.

**reel** someone **in** *v.* To gain on or catch up to an opponent during the course of a DRAG RACE. Example: "He pulled a GATE JOB on me, but I managed to REEL him IN by the thousand-foot mark."

**repro** (REE-pro) (also **repop**) *adj.* Reproduction. Term generally refers to new AFTERMARKET replacement parts for vintage vehicles.

**repro rod** (REE-pro) (also **repop rod**) **1.** *n.* Any HOT ROD or STREET ROD constructed entirely of new, AFTERMARKET parts and components. **2.** *n.* Any CLONE of a significant pre-existing HOT ROD.

**resin**, see ROSIN

**resto** (REST-oh) *n.* Restoration, as relating to any vehicle or vehicle component. Example: "How's the Camaro RESTO coming along?"

**resto racer** (REST-oh) **1.** *n.* Type of DRAG RACE vehicle that is appreciably restored to FACTORY-original condition but deviates from STOCK by the inclusion of all necessary performance modifications (updated high-performance running gear, suspension MODS, etc.) to create a competitive race car. **2.** *n.* Any historically significant DRAG RACE vehicle restored to its original period race configuration.

**resto rod** (REST-oh) *n.* STREET ROD type featuring an appreciably STOCK, restored outward appearance but incorporating modern or updated running gear, suspension, etc., for improved comfort and DRIVEABILITY. Significantly differing in style from traditional HOT RODS and especially from ultra-CLEAN HIGH-TECH STREET RODS, RESTO RODS often feature all original trim and many STOCK accessories. The RESTO ROD style experienced its strongest popularity during the 1970s.

1926 FORD SEDAN **resto rod**

**restyling** (also **re-styling**) *n.* Alternative expression for any automotive customizing. The more formal RESTYLING term experienced its strongest popularity from the late 1940s through the early 1960s and was more often used in printed text than in spoken language. During the late 1950s and early 1960s, Universal Publishing and Distributing Corporation produced a small-format magazine (see the LITTLE PAGES) titled *Rodding and Re-styling*. The magazine's March 1959 issue included a special section on "Jig-Saw Customizing: The Quick Way to Radical Styling."

**retro rod** *n.* Type of ultratraditional NOSTALGIA ROD, constructed to very accurately emulate the HOT RODS of an earlier era (most often the 1940s through early 1960s). RETRO RODS are usually owner-built from genuine vintage parts in the authentic manner of the early HOT RODDER. Individual craftsmanship and ingenuity are stressed while professional labor and the purchasing of new "cookie-cutter" AFTERMARKET components are avoided whenever possible. Practitioners of the RETRO ROD style oftentimes expand on the pure, unadulterated character of their cars to include an entire subculture or lifestyle including vintage-inspired dress, music, etc. The RETRO ROD movement has gained strong popularity during the 1990s and early twenty-first century, in part, as a backlash to high-dollar, professionally constructed HIGH-TECH HOT RODS.

**rev** (also **rev up**) an engine *v.* To increase an engine's speed as measured in RPM.

**revival rod**, see RETRO ROD

**revs**, see RPM

**RF** (pronounced as separate letters), see RAT FINK

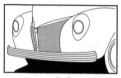

1937 DESOTO
**ribbed bumper**[1]

**ribbed bumper 1.** *n.* Unique bumper type featured as original equipment exclusively on 1937 DeSoto automobiles. An extremely popular addition to late-1930s through early-1950s era CUSTOMS, the classic DeSoto RIBBED BUMPERS were constructed in a simple "blade" style with five distinct horizontal ribs running across the full width of their face. It may be noted that, in order for the DeSoto front bumpers to fit properly on the Ford and Mercury FAT-FENDER CUSTOMS, they were necessarily narrowed by removing a section from their center, followed by welding or bolting the two ends back together. Also, the 1937 DeSoto rear bumpers were less popular in CUSTOM applications due to their undesirable, deeply arched shape. **2.** *n.* Plymouth bumper from 1949 featuring a bulky "channel" construction and three large horizontal ribs. The 1949 Plymouth bumpers achieved some popularity in CUSTOM CAR applications but not nearly approaching that of the 1937 DeSoto's bumpers. **3.** *n.* Any AFTERMARKET bumper produced in the classic ribbed style.

**rice boy** *n.* Derogatory term sometimes used by HOT RODDERs for high-performance import (see RICE ROCKET) builders or drivers.

**rice rocket** (also **rice grinder**, **ricer**, or **rice burner**) *n.* Any custom-modified or STOCK high-performance Japanese import automobile as significantly popularized during the 1990s and early twenty-first century.

**ride 1.** *n.* Any automobile. **2.** *n.* Any professional race-driving job. Example: "I'm still trying to find myself a RIDE for next season."

**ride bitch** *v.* To ride in the center position of a (three-across configured) automobile bench seat. Term most often refers to the front-center bench seat location, between the driver and "shotgun" (see RIDE SHOTGUN) positions. The term RIDE BITCH is derived from the notion that the middle seat position is most often occupied by a female passenger. Though generally perceived as coarse, vulgar, and/or derogatory, the slang term "bitch" is sometimes used to describe any "girl" or woman.

**ride height** *n.* The relative height of any vehicle's suspended body/chassis assembly. In hot rodding, DRAG racing, and CUSTOM CAR applications, a vehicle's RIDE HEIGHT is commonly adjusted (raised or lowered) from what would be considered normal in a STOCK production vehicle. During hot rodding's long history, every conceivable variation in RIDE HEIGHT has been popularized in the interests of either improved performance or aesthetics.

**ride shotgun** (also **ride shot**) *v.* To ride in the "shotgun" (front passenger seat) position of an automobile, generally perceived as the most desirable by riding passengers. Term derived from America's Old West, when stagecoach companies employed shotgun-carrying guards to ride alongside stage drivers. The expression RIDE SHOTGUN is especially relevant when cruising.

**ride the clutch,** see SLIP THE CLUTCH

the **Ridler** *n.* The Don Ridler Memorial Award, the highest award presented each year at the prestigious Detroit Autorama car show. Named for Don Ridler, the show's producer from the mid-1950s through 1961, the RIDLER was first awarded in 1964 (the year after Don's untimely death). In order to qualify for the trophy, the Autorama must be the competing vehicle's first public showing.

**rig,** see HOT IRON

**rims** *n.* Any automotive wheels. Although this slang term is commonly used to describe entire wheels, in correct usage RIMS refers only to the outer ring portion of a (generally OEM and steel) wheel, which is mated to a wheel "center" to produce a complete wheel.

**rip,** see HAUL

**ripple bumper** *n.* Modern (1990s and early-twenty-first century) expression for any traditionally styled CUSTOM CAR RIBBED BUMPER.

**ripplewalls,** see WRINKLEWALLS

**Riv** (also **Rivi**) *n.* Any Buick Riviera as produced from the 1963 through 1993 or 1995 through 1999 model years (no 1994-designated Rivieras were made available). As conceived, the distinctive personal-luxury Riviera was originally slated for Cadillac production but was instead offered to Buick to meet the division's more pressing market needs. The

**171**

1963 through 1965 first-generation RIVI COUPES featured crisp, angular styling and were powered by either 401-CID or 425-CID NAILHEADS of up to 360 BHP. A Gran Sport PERFORMANCE package was optional on the Riviera in 1965, and included a 360-HORSE dual-QUAD NAILHEAD, performance-modified automatic transmission, larger dual exhaust, 3.42-geared Positraction (see POSI) REAREND, and unique wheel covers. The 1966 model year brought a complete redesign with a more streamlined long-hood, semi-FASTBACK body style. Though the 360-HORSE NAILHEAD was still its top engine option, the RIVI's available Gran Sport package was abbreviated to simply GS, variations of which were available to the Riviera through 1975. From 1967 through 1969, all Rivieras were powered by Buick's new single-QUAD 430-CID engine of 360 BHP. For 1970, the 430 was BORED to 455 CID, providing an increased 370 BHP. The 1971 through 1973 model years offered the controversial BOATTAIL RIVIERAS and waning power from the model's 455 engines. As a last vestige of MUSCLE CAR performance, the 1974 Riviera's "Stage 1" 455 option provided a meager 245 NET HORSEPOWER. Following the 1973 model year, the Riviera was significantly restyled, losing much of its distinctive personal/PERFORMANCE car character. While subsequent RIVIS established a niche in the mainstream marketplace, none are considered historically important or collectable. Early Rivieras, however, have long experienced popularity in various STREET MACHINE and CUSTOM CAR applications. The 1963–1965 RIVS, in particular, are highly desirable foundations for mild custom and LOWRIDER modification. Note: Buick also used the Riviera name to denote its many HARDTOP-configured production cars during the late 1940s through early 1960s, with the designation being attached to a variety of more general series (Special Riviera, Super Riviera, Roadmaster Riviera, etc.). These early Rivieras are less often modified in a STREET MACHINE or CUSTOM CAR style and are seldom referred to as RIVS or RIVIS.

**roach coach** (also **roach**) *n.* Any old, substantially dilapidated vehicle.

**roach rod**, see RAT ROD

**road burner** *n.* Any especially FAST or QUICK street-driven automobile, but especially one that is capable of easily burning rubber. Term experienced its greatest popularity during the 1960s.

**roadster 1.** *n.* Vintage (generally 1930s or earlier) automobile body style configured as an open, two-door passenger car with a two-person seating capacity (not including optional RUMBLE SEAT). Early ROADSTER models are distinguished by their convertible soft tops, lack of roll-up glass side windows (snap-in transparent side curtains could be installed in case of inclement weather), and fully detachable windshield assemblies. The traditional ROADSTERS were typically the least expensive and lightest models produced by any given manufacturer. Besides their accessibility and performance-enhancing light weight, ROADSTER models were also highly valued among early RODDERS for their sleek, elemental appearance; during hot rodding's formative years, the ROADSTER was the overwhelmingly favorite body style with a very strong popularity continuing to the present day. Although original ROADSTER production numbers were relatively high, the availability of true VINTAGE TIN bodies has significantly decreased over time. Today, the vast majority of ROADSTER HOT RODS are constructed with new reproduction bodies of either fiberglass (see 'GLASS) or steel. **2.** *n.* Any open, two-passenger sports or PERFORMANCE model produced after and/or without the signature elements of the true vintage ROADSTER. Notable examples of this type include the Chevrolet Corvette (see 'VETTE), Ford-powered AC Cobra, and Dodge Viper ROADSTER models. **3.** *n.* Early (generally 1940s and 1950s) term, specifically for a ROADSTER model modified in a HOT ROD style. Because the term HOT ROD often carried with it negative connotations (shoddy vehicle workmanship, reckless or irresponsible drivers, etc.) during this period, modified ROADSTER owners sometimes distanced themselves from these stigmas by referring to their vehicles simply as ROADSTERS.

1967 AC COBRA **roadster**[2]

**roadster pickup** *n.* Early vehicle type combining the essential characteristics of both ROADSTER and pickup truck models. ROADSTER PICKUPS feature the small narrow-box pickup beds common to their period of manufacture and a two-person open cab with available ROADSTER-like soft top. Variations on the ROADSTER PICKUP theme date to the very early part of the twentieth century, when many such vehicles were home-crafted or otherwise converted from conventional ROADSTER and runabout models. The ROADSTER PICKUPS most often modified in a HOT ROD or STREET ROD style, however, were FACTORY-produced from the mid-1920s through the mid-1930s. Although historically ROADSTER PICKUPS have been used in a variety of racing applications (TRACK ROADSTER, LAND-SPEED RACING, DRAG racing, etc.), since the 1960s the type has been more commonly associated with street rodding.

1928 FORD
**roadster pickup**
STREET ROD

**roaring roadsters** *n.* Expressive name for the ROADSTER-based competition vehicles commonly raced on circle-tracks from the late 1940s through the early 1950s (see TRACK ROADSTER).

**rock crusher** *n.* Any Muncie M-22 close-ratio four-speed manual transmission. The high-performance M-22 was provided in General Motors vehicles for the 1965 through 1972 model years. While most manual-transmissioned GM MUSCLE CARS received either the lower-performance M-20 or M-21 four-speeds, the durable M-22 was reserved for ultimate-performance and race-car applications. The M-22 featured relatively coarse-pitch helical gears for additional strength. These strong but noisy gears were the inspiration for the type's ROCK CRUSHER name.

**rockerhead** *n.* Any engine featuring an overhead-valve configuration (see OHV) actuated by a system of pushrods and

**173**

rocker arms. The ROCKERHEAD term was most commonly used during and prior to the 1950s.

**rocket engine** (also **rocket motor** or **rocket**) *n.* Any Oldsmobile "Rocket V-8" engine, an essentially conventional (albeit innovative) internal-combustion engine introduced by Oldsmobile for the 1949 model year (see KETTERING V8). The new motor's "Rocket" designation proved highly effective, associating the marque with futuristic high performance in the public's mind. In racing applications, ROCKET-powered OLDS SEDANS achieved outstanding success on the 1950s-era STOCK CAR circuit. Rocket V-8s were also an extremely popular addition to HOT RODS and DRAG vehicles during the 1950s and early 1960s.

**rod**, see HOT ROD

**rodder**, see HOT RODDER

**rodney** *n.* Alternative and rarely used term for any HOT ROD.

**rod run 1.** *n.* Any organized road tour as practiced with a group of HOT RODS or STREET RODS. **2.** *n.* Any HOT ROD or STREET ROD social gathering at a single, predetermined destination point.

**rods** *n.* Any automotive piston engine's connecting rods. Connecting rods serve to convert the pistons' reciprocating (back-and-forth) motion to a rotating motion of the engine's crankshaft (see CRANK).

**rod shop** *n.* Any shop or facility specializing in the professional, contracted construction of HOT RODS or, especially, STREET RODS. The ROD SHOP phenomenon was generally initiated along with the STREET ROD movement of the 1970s and steadily gained in popularity until reaching its peak with the economic boom of the 1990s.

**roll and pleat** (also **roll 'n' pleat**), see TUCK 'N' ROLL

**rolled pan** ON
1929 FORD ROADSTER

**rolled pan** (also **roll pan**) *n.* Custom body panel serving to cleanly and continuously integrate a vehicle's STOCK body components with its front or rear chassis area. Typically, a ROLLED PAN begins at the lowermost portion of a vehicle's front or rear OEM body panels, then arches or "rolls" downward and inward toward the vehicle's underside. The ROLLED PAN "finishes" the body by fully extending its lines to an area not normally visible. When ROLLED PANS are fitted to vehicles, STOCK bumpers are commonly replaced with custom units or omitted entirely. Traditionally, ROLLED PANS have been individually fabricated from sheet steel or aluminum, but more recently have been mass-produced in fiberglass and ABS plastic to fit modern and standardized production vehicles. In hot rodding applications, ROLLED PANS date to at least the 1940s, when they were sometimes used in conjunction with BELLY PANS to create streamlined LAND-SPEED RACING body envelopes.

**rolled rear pan**, see ROLLED PAN

**roller 1.** *n.* Any incomplete automobile chassis in its developmental or formative stages, but advanced to the point of resting on wheels. **2.** see ROLLER CAM

**roller cam** (also **roller**) *n.* Any high-performance camshaft (see CAM) working in conjunction with special, roller-tipped valve lifters. A ROLLER CAM configuration serves to reduce friction and facilitate the use of more radical CAM profiles. HOT RODDER Chet Herbert adapted Harley-Davidson motorcycle roller-tappet technology to American V8 engine designs, with his innovative and influential ROLLER CAMS being first popularized during the early 1950s.

**roller motor** *n.* Any high-performance engine equipped with a ROLLER CAM and, most often, roller rocker arms.

**rollers** *n.* Any automotive wheels.

**rolling stock 1.** *n.* General expression relating to any complete tire/wheel set as featured on an individual vehicle. Term most often describes custom or AFTERMARKET components. Example: "Yeah, I know they look pretty bitchin', but it's kinda hard for me to justify spending more on ROLLING STOCK than I paid for the car." **2.** *n.* Any grouping or collection of vehicles. [Rare]

**rolling toy box** *n.* Any enclosed trailer used by a DRAG racing team to transport race vehicles, tools, and related equipment. ROLLING TOY BOXES are sometimes elaborately appointed with complete mobile work/machine shops and even lounge or living areas.

**roll off** (also **roll out of**) *v.* To release a throttle pedal in a relatively slow, consistent, and gentle manner. Example: "In that situation, just ROLL OFF the throttle 'til the FRONTEND settles back in."

**roll on** (also **roll into**) *v.* To depress a throttle pedal in a relatively slow, consistent, and gentle manner. Example: "The only way that I can get this thing OUT OF THE HOLE is to gradually ROLL ON the gas."

**romp on it** *v.* To aggressively and fully depress a vehicle's accelerator pedal.

**roots rod**, see RETRO ROD

**Rosamond** *n.* ROSAMOND dry lake, a racing location used intermittently from the mid-1920s through 1948. ROSAMOND was not as popular as other lakes locations (see the LAKES) due to its relatively small usable area and inferior surface.

**rosin** *n.* Powdery substance spread over a DRAGSTRIP's surface to enhance the traction properties of racing vehicles. Typically employed from the mid- to late 1960s, powdered ROSIN was poured from a canister and then usually spread and evened with a push broom over a short segment of track surface. During a pre-race ritual, BURNOUTS were performed through the ROSIN, forming a sticky traction-enhancing substance on the vehicles' tire surfaces. Long, wet BURNOUTS effectively replaced the use of ROSIN during the 1970s.

**round** *n.* Any singular, individual DRAG RACE occurring within a greater formal DRAG RACING event.

**roundy-round** *adj.* Traditional expression relating to virtually any automotive oval-track racing.

**row gears** (also **row a tranny** or **row a four-speed**, etc.) *v.* To shift gears in any manual-transmission vehicle. The term ROW is adapted from the more common usage, meaning to propel a boat over water with oars.

**RPM** (pronounced as separate letters) *n.* Revolutions per minute, the common measure of an engine's speed.

**RPO** (pronounced as separate letters) *n.* Regular Production Option. Abbreviation used by General Motors to indicate an automotive option or package as mass-produced on a regular vehicle assembly line (distinguished from a limited edition or special-order option). The term RPO followed by a representative number is frequently used to describe a high-performance option produced by General Motors during the 1960s through 1970s MUSCLE CAR era.

**rubber** *n.* Any automotive tires.

**rubber band** TIRE

**rubber bands** (also **rubber band tires**) *n.* Any modern low-profile, high-performance radial tires featuring a large outside diameter and extremely short sidewall area (see also O-RING TIRES). When mounted on necessarily large diameter wheels, the type's narrow sidewall accounts for an appearance vaguely similar to an actual rubber band.

**rubber rake** *n.* Any vehicle RAKE resulting solely from the running of relatively tall rear tires together with relatively short front tires and no chassis or body modifications.

**rumble seat** *n.* Any open-air auxiliary seat as featured on generally late-1920s through late-1930s era production automobiles. A RUMBLE SEAT takes the place of a conventional trunk on what would normally be a two-passenger model (COUPE, ROADSTER, CABRIOLET, etc.). Opening rearward, a RUMBLE SEAT lid's inside panel is upholstered to form the seat's back rest. When not in use, a RUMBLE SEAT may be folded shut to form an uninterrupted rear body surface. RUMBLE SEATS have long experienced moderate popularity in street rodding applications.

**rumpity-rump** (also **rumpy** or **rumpity**) *adj.* Relating to any rough, "thumping" engine idle or any radical, high-performance camshaft (see CAM) producing such an idle. Example: "With that size CAM you're definitely gonna have to contend with a RUMPITY-RUMP idle."

**run 1.** see PASS **2.** *v.* To perform very strongly, with abundant power (said of an engine or vehicle). Example: "Yeah, I know it looks impressive with the TUNNEL RAM and all, but the thing just doesn't RUN." **3.** *v.* To DRAG RACE. **4.** see ROD RUN

**run** someone **down**, see REEL someone IN

**run for pinks**, see RACE FOR PINKS

**run for tin** *v.* At an organized DRAG event, to race exclusively for trophies (as differentiated from competing for money or other prizes).

**run like a raped ape** (also **run like a scalded dog**) *v.* To run very strongly, producing abundant power (said of an engine or vehicle). Example: "When the NITROUS kicks in, the thing RUNS LIKE A RAPED APE."

**runner** *n.* Any vehicle capable of or exhibiting strong, competitive performance.

**'Runner** *n.* Any Plymouth Road Runner model (see BIRD).

**runout area**, see SHUT-DOWN AREA

**run out of power** *v.* To surpass the upper limits of an engine's practical RPM range, resulting in a decreased power level. Example: "The Buick's got great LOW END, but it'll RUN OUT OF POWER long before it ever sees six GRAND."

**run** a vehicle **out the back door** *v.* To race a vehicle fully and aggressively through the finish line area, or BIG END, of a DRAGSTRIP (distinguished from the practice of limiting TOP END performance, as may occur during a TEST AND TUNE session or when BRACKET RACING).

**run the number** *v.* In DRAG racing, to record a strong and competitive elapsed time (see ET) in a given class or situation.

**run what you brung** (also **run what ya brung**) *adj.* Relating to legal, sanctioned DRAG racing on an organized DRAGSTRIP, but with no regard to class designation or equipment rulings other than mandatory safety requirements. "Anything goes," HEADS-UP racing. Example: "Back in those days things were a lot simpler . . . strictly RUN WHAT YA BRUNG."

**rusto rod** *n.* Any HOT ROD or STREET ROD featuring a significantly rusted or corroded body structure. Used in parody of the more conventional expression RESTO ROD.

# S

**sack o' walnuts** *n.* Any very rough and irregular steel auto body or auto body panel, often resulting from amateurish attempts at straightening dents. Name derived from the irregular, bumpy shape of an actual sack of walnuts.

**sail panels** *n.* Any broad, deeply trailing automotive rear-roof pillars featured in conjunction with a recessed, more vertical BACKLIGHT. The resulting "tunneled" rear-window effect creates the impression of slender "fins" or "sails" extending rearward from the window's location. SAIL PANELS were featured on a number of significant 1960s-era MUSCLE CAR models but perhaps most notably as a common styling cue on all General Motors intermediate HARDTOPS produced during 1966 and 1967.

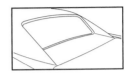

**sail panels** ON
1966 CHEVELLE SS 396

**salt car** (also **salt shaker**, **salt pounder**, or **saltster**) *n.* Any high-performance automobile created exclusively for the purpose of LAND-SPEED RACING on the BONNEVILLE Salt Flats.

**saltliner** *n.* Any high-speed STREAMLINER created exclusively for the purpose of LAND-SPEED RACING on the BONNEVILLE Salt Flats.

**sanitary** (also **sano** [SAN-oh]), see CLEAN (Definition 2)

**Santa Banana** *n.* The Santa Ana DRAGS, an early and highly renowned series of DRAG racing events presented on a vacant runway at Southern California's Santa Ana Airport (later Orange County Airport and currently John Wayne International Airport). Founders C. J. "Pappy" Hart, Frank Stilwell, and Creighton Hunter staged the STRIP's first event on June 19, 1950, charging 50 cents for admission and clocking performance with rudimentary timing equipment. Quickly gaining in popularity and sophistication, the Santa Ana DRAGS are widely regarded as the first professional, commercially viable DRAG races. Hart remained the manager of the STRIP's operations until its 1959 closure.

**sauce** *n.* Power. Horsepower or torque as produced by any engine.

**saw** someone **off** *v.* To soundly beat an opponent in a DRAG RACE.

**SBC** (usually written, not spoken) *n.* SMALL-BLOCK CHEVY (see MOUSE).

**scallops** *n.* Custom, multicolored automotive paint scheme featuring a series or pattern of elongated "spear" shapes. SCALLOPS may be employed in widely varying styles and forms to accentuate overall vehicle body lines or to complement individual panel shapes. In their most popular application, however, a uniformly spaced series of SCALLOPS trail rearward from a vehicle's leading edges, implying a sense

**scallops** ON
1932 FORD CABRIOLET

of motion or speed. SCALLOPS achieved their greatest popularity from the late 1950s through the early 1960s, but have gained renewed favor during the 1990s and early twenty-first century.

**scarfer** *n.* Any exceptionally QUICK or FAST vehicle. Term most popular during the 1950s and 1960s.

**scattershield** *n.* Safety device (most often of a die-stamped steel construction) replacing a STOCK, cast-iron, or aluminum bellhousing unit and functioning to contain dangerous debris or shrapnel in the event of a clutch explosion. SCATTERSHIELDS were significantly popularized during the 1960s and have remained a standard fixture on DRAG cars to the present. In the 1950s, a lesser level of clutch protection was often achieved by affixing a section of $1/4$-inch steel plate above a DRAG vehicle's bellhousing.

**SCJ** (usually written, not spoken) *n.* Any Super Cobra Jet engine or any vehicle powered by a Super Cobra Jet engine (see CJ).

**scoot 1.** *n.* Strong performance characteristics as exhibited by any engine or complete vehicle. **2.** *v.* To demonstrate exceptional vehicle performance. Example: "Those new Power-Pack CHEVYS really SCOOT."

**scratch** *n.* Any rubber-burning traction loss resulting from the overpowering of a vehicle's tires (see BURN RUBBER). Term pertains especially to the generally short period of traction loss experienced while upshifting during hard acceleration. Example: "It gets third-gear SCRATCH no problem with the new ASS-END gears."

**scratch mark** *n.* The dark mark or stripe of solidified rubber left behind on a paved surface as evidence of a vehicle's BURNOUT.

**scratch out,** see LAY RUBBER

**screamer 1.** *n.* Any very QUICK or FAST vehicle, but especially one featuring a high-RPM, race-type engine. **2.** *n.* Any engine producing its peak horsepower at an exceptionally high RPM level.

**screaming chicken** *n.* Large graphic decal consisting of a highly stylized fire-breathing bird with broadly spread wings featured as a hood adornment on 1973 through 1981 Pontiac Trans Am (see T/A) models. Although available only as an extra-cost option, the SCREAMING CHICKEN was nonetheless selected by most T/A buyers during the period of its availability.

1973 **screaming chicken**

**screw** *n.* Any automotive rear axle's final-drive ratio gear set (see REAREND).

**SCTA** (pronounced as separate letters) *n.* Southern California Timing Association, the longest-lived and most influential of all American LAND-SPEED RACING organizations. In November 1937, five Southern California CAR CLUBS met to establish a greater association to organize dry lakes (see the LAKES) racing events. After presenting their first lakes meets in mid-1938, the SCTA expanded rapidly by incorporating the majority of the region's CAR CLUBS into a viable, popular, and even larger organization. Though SCTA activity was suspended during World War II, racing resumed in April 1946, and the late 1940s witnessed the high mark in dry lakes racing as well as SCTA popularity. (In 1948, the SCTA experienced its largest size with more than 500 active members and 31 affiliate CAR CLUBS.) Lakes racing and SCTA popularity waned substantially during the 1950s, largely due to the introduction of localized DRAG racing and the shifting of LAND-SPEED RACING's focus to BONNEVILLE. In modern times, the SCTA continues to hold lakes meets at both EL MIRAGE and MUROC.

**sculptured** *adj.* Molded or blended in a smooth, flowing integrated style (said of a CUSTOM CAR or CUSTOM ROD's body styling). Term is most often used to describe the styling of the exotic SHOW-type RODS and CUSTOMS of the late 1950s and early 1960s.

**seat time** *n.* Any practical, hands-on race-car driving experience. Time behind the wheel of a race vehicle in actual competition. Term most commonly used in reference to drivers who are novices or beginners in a particular type or class of racing.

**seaweed flames** *n.* Custom flame paint treatment (see FLAMES) featuring an elongated, highly sinuous seaweed-like style. Introduced by renowned painter Larry Watson in the late 1950s.

**seaweed flames** ON 1955 CHEVROLET

**sectioned** *adj.* Modified through the radical body alteration of removing a central horizontal strip or "section" from a vehicle's overall body length, followed by reattaching the remaining upper and lower portions. The effect is a vertical shortening of the entire body structure. Differs from CHOPPED, which describes modification by the removal of a horizontal cross-section specifically from the vehicle's GREENHOUSE area. While most often applied to overall body modifications, the term SECTIONED may also relate to ancillary body panels (hood, GRILL SHELL, fenders, etc.).

**sectioned** 1950 OLDSMOBILE

**sedan 1.** *n.* Vintage (generally 1930s and earlier) automobile body style configured as a closed two- or four-door passenger car with a four-person seating capacity. The traditional SEDAN's roof is much longer than that of a contemporary COUPE model, extending fully to the rear of the vehicle while covering the passenger compartment's two full-width bench seats. Though never achieving the immense popularity of COUPE or ROADSTER models, two-door SEDANs in particular have experienced moderate favor

1929 FORD **sedan**[1] HOT ROD

as foundations for HOT RODS, competition vehicles, and especially STREET RODS. **2.** *n.* 1940s and later two- or four-door closed automobile featuring both front and rear seats and a capacity of four to six passengers. After the 1930s, the typical SEDAN's roof no longer extended to the vehicle's rear. Instead, the type's passenger compartment was followed by a separate and pronounced trunk area. During the 1950s, a distinction also arose between what was referred to as a HARDTOP model and a true SEDAN. While very similar in overall configuration, the SEDAN fundamentally differs from the HARDTOP by its retention of fixed B-PILLARS. A HARDTOP model tends also to display a slightly sleeker, shorter overall roof than a comparable SEDAN. In true racing applications, the "pillared" SEDAN is generally preferred over the HARDTOP for its slightly lighter weight and greater overall vehicle rigidity.

1940 FORD
**sedan delivery**
STREET ROD

**sedan delivery** *n.* Vintage (generally 1920s through 1960s) automotive body style significantly based on a contemporary SEDAN or station wagon but differing in its intended light-commercial usage. Early examples (roughly 1920s through 1940s) were configured as passenger SEDANs with integrated sheetmetal body panels replacing all side window glass behind the front seat positions. Typically, a single side-opening rear door served to access the early SEDAN DELIVERY's enclosed rear cargo area. Though similar in principle to their predecessors (light commercial haulers with fully sheetmetal rear body sides), 1950s and later versions were usually based on station wagon models and most often featured tailgate-style rear cargo access. A relatively rare type, the SEDAN DELIVERY has long experienced moderate to strong popularity as foundations for STREET RODS. Station wagon-based (especially TRI-FIVE CHEVY) models have traditionally been favored in STOCK class DRAG competition as well.

**semi-hemi** (SEM-ee-HEM-ee) *n.* Any engine featuring a canted valve layout producing "modified hemispherical" or near-hemispherical combustion chambers. In PERFORMANCE applications, the SEMI-HEMI design is highly regarded for its free-breathing efficiency. Although a number of traditional high-performance V8 engine types have featured canted valve configurations (notably including FoMoCo's 351C and Boss 302 [see Boss]), the term SEMI-HEMI is most often used in reference to the BIG-BLOCK Chevrolet RAT.

**set of wheels** *n.* Any automobile. Expression achieved its strongest popularity from the 1940s through the 1960s, when it was often used to describe HOT RODS and STREET MACHINE-type vehicles.

**setup 1.** *n.* Any PERFORMANCE-oriented induction system (either a fuel-injection unit or carburetor(s) [see CARB], along with intake manifold and related hardware). Term most often used during the 1940s and 1950s to describe a high-performance, multiple-carburetor system. **2.** *n.* General term for virtually any automotive mechanical system or assemblage.

**shadetree mechanics** *n.* Any non-professional or hobby-oriented mechanical tinkering as practiced in the outdoors, under the canopy of a shade tree. Term oftentimes carries with it an air of idyllic, Rockwell-esque American mythology.

**shaft,** see CRANK or CAM

**shaker hood** (also **shaker scoop** or **shaker**) *n.* Any OEM high-performance, fresh-air induction system featuring an intake scoop mounted directly to the vehicle's engine. With a SHAKER system, a large hood opening allows for the engine-mounted scoop to protrude through the hood (a rubber seal surrounding the scoop prevents water from entering the engine compartment in wet weather). Functional SHAKER systems also feature a driver-actuated control to select external fresh air or underhood air, depending on driving conditions and/or performance needs. The system's name is derived from the fact that a SHAKER SCOOP "shakes" or generally moves with the vehicle's engine (including lateral torquing motion) and independent of the surrounding body panels. SHAKER systems were available on Chrysler, FoMoCo, and Pontiac PERFORMANCE models during the early 1970s (Pontiac continued production of its SHAKER on Trans Am [see T/A] models through 1981, but after 1972 the systems were non-functional).

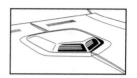

shaker hood ON
1970 PLYMOUTH 'CUDA

**shave 1.** *v.* To remove STOCK trim, emblems, and/or accessories from an automotive body (followed by the filling of existing holes and refinishing) to achieve a smoother, cleaner appearance. **2.** *v.* To resurface a mechanical component (cylinder block [see BLOCK] deck surfaces, cylinder heads [see HEADS], etc.) through machining.

**shaved bumpers** *n.* Any automotive bumpers smoothed in appearance by the removal of all external-surface mounting hardware, a popular CUSTOM CAR modification. Typically, mounting through-bolts are welded to the bumpers and their heads ground flush with the bumper's outside surface. Following alterations, bumpers are most often replated in chrome.

**shave 'n' a haircut** *n.* General expression for the overall cleaning of a vehicle's exterior appearance though the removal of STOCK trim, ornamentation, and accessories. Derived and extended from the term SHAVE, the expression SHAVE 'N' A HAIRCUT suggests a more comprehensive exterior treatment. Example: "I know it looks kinda frumpy now, but I'm thinkin' a SHAVE 'N' A HAIRCUT will do wonders on this one."

**shell 1.** see GRILL SHELL **2.** *n.* Any automotive body stripped of running gear and/or other major components. Sometimes a bare body with no chassis whatsoever.

shillelagh

**shillelagh** (shi-LAY-lee) *n.* Any manual transmission floor-shift lever that is unusually long or exaggerated in style (a type especially popular in 1950s through early-1960s hot rodding applications). Although in large part inspired by aesthetics, extended SHILLELAGHS were sometimes thought to provide additional leverage, in turn facilitating faster, more positive shifts. The term SHILLELAGH is derived from the Irish word for a wooden club or cudgel.

**shit all over itself** (also **shit on itself**) *v.* To stumble, falter, or generally perform very poorly (said of an engine or vehicle). Derived from the reaction of some animals when subjected to frightening or otherwise unpleasant situations.

**shoe 1.** *n.* Any automobile driver, but especially referring to a professional race-car driver. **2.** *v.* To drive a race car in actual competition. Example: "Who are you gonna find to SHOE for you on Sunday?"

**shoebox** *n.* Any HOT ROD, STREET MACHINE, CUSTOM CAR, or DRAG racing vehicle based on a production automobile with large, "boxy" overall styling. Often used to describe TRI-FIVE CHEVYS, the term SHOEBOX may relate to any late-1940s, 1950s, or sometimes 1960s production car.

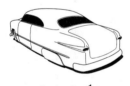

shoebox Ford[1]
1949 FORD CUSTOM

**shoebox Ford 1.** *n.* Any Ford COUPE or SEDAN as produced during the 1949 through 1951 model years. Term is derived from the type's decidedly "boxy" SLAB-SIDED overall styling. Since its introduction, the SHOEBOX FORD has experienced relatively strong popularity as a foundation for HOT ROD, STREET MACHINE, and CUSTOM CAR modification. **2.** *n.* Any post-1951 Ford automobile produced with an exceptionally "boxy" style. [Rare]

**shoes** *n.* Any automotive tires.

**shoot fire** *v.* To shoot flames from a vehicle's exhaust with a FLAMETHROWER device.

**shootin' ducks** *adj.* Relating to any loud series of misfires as heard through a DRAG racing engine's exhaust system. Expression is derived from the sounds commonly produced by a duck hunter's shotgun. Example: "You've definitely got yourself an ignition problem. You were SHOOTIN' DUCKS big time IN THE LIGHTS."

**shoot the salt** *v.* To land-speed race on the BONNEVILLE Salt Flats.

**short** *n.* Generally pre-1960s expression for virtually any car, but oftentimes describing a high-performance HOT ROD or STREET MACHINE. Term was first used in reference to city streetcars because their runs were "short" compared to those of trains. Later, the expression evolved to include automobiles.

**shortblock** *n.* Partial engine assembly including cylinder block (see BLOCK) and all components housed *within* the cylinder block, but excluding cylinder heads (see HEADS) and all other external engine components. Term generally refers to a new or remanufactured unit.

**short ram 1.** *n.* Chrysler Corporation high-performance CROSS RAM induction system featuring the same overall characteristics as a LONG RAM, but significantly distinguished by its shorter internal runner length. While providing exceptional MIDRANGE performance, Chrysler's LONG RAM intake hampered upper-RPM power levels. The SHORT RAM was tailored to higher-RPM usage by cutting the LONG RAM's internal runner length by half (down to 15 inches). As with the LONG RAM, Chrysler's hotter SHORT RAM was produced from the 1960 through 1964 model years. **2.** *n.* Any Chrysler Corporation maximum-performance CROSS RAM induction system as featured on 1962 through 1964 MAX WEDGE engines as well as 1964, 1965, and 1968 RACE HEMI engines. Though sharing the SHORT RAM name with Chrysler's higher-performance OUTRIGGER TUBES, the MAX WEDGE and HEMI engine SHORT RAMS featured a radically different design with much shorter overall runners. A true racing induction system, this MOPAR CROSS RAM iteration was designed to provide ultimate high-RPM DRAGSTRIP performance.

**short-shift** *v.* To manually upshift a transmission at a relatively low engine RPM level. Sometimes an advantage in specific high-performance applications.

**short time** *n.* In organized DRAG racing, any measured "60-foot time." Commonly provided to racers by DRAGSTRIP timing equipment, a SHORT TIME is the precise time (as measured to the thousandth of a second) that it takes for a vehicle to cover the first 60 feet of a DRAG RACE course. SHORT TIMES can be an invaluable aid in performance-tuning a DRAG vehicle.

**shot** *n.* Any individual, singular DRAG RACE, but with the added implication of very strong performance. Example: "He took home the GOLD with a solid 7.40 SHOT."

**shotgun motor** *n.* Any Boss 429 high-performance engine produced by Ford Motor Company for the 1969 and 1970 model years (see Boss).

**shot rod** *n.* Derogatory 1950s term for any crudely constructed and often unsafe home-built HOT ROD.

**show** *adj.* Relating to any complete vehicle or vehicle component created with a strong emphasis on a custom, exotic, or highly refined appearance. A car or part that is worthy of presentation in a car show. Term sometimes carries the implication of mediocre performance and draws a distinction between vehicles that are "go"

(PERFORMANCE) oriented and those with a greater emphasis on "SHOW" or appearance.

**show 'n' shine** (also **show and shine**) *n*. Any informal ROD and CUSTOM show as generally presented at an outdoor venue. Term typically relates to a low-key social gathering rather than to a seriously competitive SHOW car exhibition.

**showroom** *adj*. Relating to a vehicle condition that is perfect and pristine in every way, as well as absolutely STOCK. Describes a vehicle as if it were a truly new car, not yet sold by its original manufacturer and resting in an automotive dealership's sales showroom.

**shred tread**, SEE BURN RUBBER

shrouded lakes pipes

**shrouded lakes pipes** (also **shrouded lakers** or **shrouded side pipes**) *n*. Unique CUSTOM CAR styling treatment wherein conventional outside-body LAKES PIPES are partially covered or "shrouded" with a segment of integrated, semi-tubular bodywork. SHROUDED LAKES PIPES achieved their strongest popularity in early-1960s CUSTOM CAR applications.

**shut down** (also **shutdown**) *n*. The act of defeating an opponent in a DRAG RACE. Term dates to at least the late-1950s and experienced its strongest popularity during the 1960s.

***Shut Down*** *n*. Capitol Records compilation album featuring HOT ROD MUSIC from a variety of artists. Released in the summer of 1963, *SHUT DOWN* includes songs by the Beach Boys, Robert Mitchum, the Cheers, and the Super Stocks. In 1964, Capitol followed up with an album entitled *SHUT DOWN, Volume 2*, this time with exclusive Beach Boys content (significantly including the song "Shut Down," released the previous year as a single ).

**shut** someone **down** *v*. To defeat an opponent in a DRAG RACE.

**shut-down area** *n*. On any DRAGSTRIP, the area of the track extending beyond the finish line. A long SHUT-DOWN AREA is typically provided to allow race vehicles ample room to slow from high terminal speeds.

**siamesed** (SIGH-ah-meased) *adj*. Relating to any pair of engine cylinders, ports, etc., that are atypically joined in some fashion. Example: "The 400-CID SMALL-BLOCK CHEVY's cylinders are SIAMESED, allowing for no coolant circulation between bores."

**side-oiler** (also **427 side-oiler**) *n*. FoMoCo-produced 427-CID V8 engine type featuring a unique, free-flowing oiling system. The superior 427 SIDE-OILER features its main oil-gallery on the lower left side of its cylinder block (see BLOCK), providing direct lubrication to the engine's main bearings. All FoMoCo 427-CID engines produced during the 1965 through 1968 period (including LOW RISER, MEDIUM RISER, tunnel port, and CAMMER configurations) were of the SIDE-OILER design.

**side pipes** (also **sidepipes**) *n.* Any automotive exhaust pipes positioned beside a vehicle's lower body panels between the front and rear wheels. Functional SIDE PIPES typically feature mufflers or exhaust baffles and end in "turn-outs" immediately in front of the rear tires. Many SIDE PIPES also include some form of external metallic heat shielding. SIDE PIPES have been made optionally available on a number of FACTORY PERFORMANCE cars, significantly including mid- to late-1960s Corvettes (see 'VETTE). In AFTERMARKET form, SIDE PIPES experienced their greatest popularity during the 1970s when commonly fitted to STREET MACHINES and customized vans (see the VAN CRAZE). The LAKES PIPES used in late-1950s through early-1960s CUSTOM CAR applications may be considered a type of SIDE PIPES.

**sidevalve** (also **side-valve**) *n.* Any FLATHEAD engine. The FLATHEAD's more formal SIDEVALVE name refers to the type's intake and exhaust valve positioning within the BLOCK and *beside* the cylinder bores. A SIDEVALVE configuration differs from an overhead-valve system (see OHV), in which valves are positioned above each cylinder.

**sidewinder 1.** *n.* Any DRAG racing vehicle with its engine mounted in a transverse manner as opposed to the more conventional inline-with-chassis layout. Such configurations have been attempted sporadically in DRAGSTER design from as early as the 1950s but never with appreciable success. One theoretical advantage of the SIDEWINDER layout is the harnessing of a running engine's lateral torquing motion to enhance vehicle traction. Notable examples of the SIDEWINDER design include *The Sidewinder*, a BLOWN HEMI-powered mid-engine creation of 1959 featuring a massive chain-drive system (campaigned by Chuck Jones, Joe Mailliard and Jack Chrisman), as well as Jones' 1961 *Magwinder*; similar in layout to *The Sidewinder* but featuring a cutting-edge custom chassis by renowned builder Kent Fuller and a highly streamlined custom body envelope. The car's magnesium body panels and frame construction accounted for its *Magwinder* name. **2.** *adj.* Relating to any transversely mounted engine layout.

sidewinder[2]
THE *MAGWINDER*

**sin bin** *n.* Any customized van featuring amenities such as a built-in bed, bar, exotic lighting, mirrors, and/or heavily padded floor and walls, all to provide a suitable environment for romantic or sexual encounters. Term and style were both popular during the 1970s VAN CRAZE.

**single-bar flippers,** see FLIPPERS

**single stick** *adj.* Relating to any single-overhead camshaft (see CAM) engine configuration. Term most popular during or prior to the 1950s.

**sit bitch**, see RIDE BITCH

**sit on a rake** *v.* To feature an incline or slant (said of a vehicle's body and suspended chassis assembly [see RAKE]). Example: "With the new FRONT CLIP installed I'm hoping that it'll SIT ON A nice RAKE."

**six banger** (also **six**, **six holer**, **six lunger** [LUNG-er], or **six shooter**) *n.* Any six-cylinder automotive engine.

**six-barrel 1.** *n.* Any high-performance induction system featuring three TWO-BARREL carburetors (see CARB). The Plymouth division of Chrysler Corporation applied the term SIX-BARREL to its FACTORY-produced 440-CID (1969 through early-1972) and 340-CID (1970 only) PERFORMANCE engines. Likewise, Ford used the term for its high-performance 406-CID engine's induction system in 1962 advertising. **2.** *adj.* Relating to any POWERPLANT mounting a high-performance induction system featuring three TWO-BARREL carburetors (see CARB).

**Six in a row can go.** (also **Six in a row does go.** or **Six in a row will go.**) Popular expression affirming the PERFORMANCE potential of any inline six-cylinder engine.

**six pack** (also **six pac** or **six pak**) *n.* Any high-performance, induction system featuring three TWO-BARREL carburetors (see CARB). The Dodge division of Chrysler Corporation applied the term (alternately SIX PACK or SIX PAK) to their FACTORY-produced 440-CID (1969 through early-1972) and 340-CID (1970 only) PERFORMANCE engines (see also SIX-BARREL).

**skinnies** *n.* Any exceptionally narrow tire/wheel combination. Commonly featured as front ROLLING STOCK on HOT RODS and DRAG racing vehicles for their practical advantages of reduced rolling resistance and light weight, or for purely aesthetic reasons.

**skinny whites** *n.* Any whitewall tires featuring relatively thin white sidewall bands. Commonly featured on 1960s-era BELLFLOWER CRUISER CUSTOM CARS and have been a popular addition to LOWRIDER CUSTOMS from the 1960s to the present.

**skins 1.** (also **skin**) *n.* Early HOT RODDER's expression for any automotive tires. Term most popular from the 1940s through the 1960s. **2.** *n.* Any vehicle's interior upholstery material.

**skirts**, see FENDER SKIRTS

**Skylark wires** (also **Skylark wheels** or **Skylarks**) *n.* Any of the exotic, chrome-plated Kelsey-Hayes wire wheels (see KELSEYS) of the type featured on the limited-edition 1953 and 1954 Buick Skylark production cars. The exclusive SKYLARK WIRES have long been a prestigious addition to STREET and SHOW CUSTOM CARS.

**slab-side** (also **slab-sided**) *adj.* Relating to any automotive body style with smooth, integrated body sides forming a single consistent plane from the front to the rear of the vehicle. Term most commonly used to describe the first POSTWAR automobiles produced by major American manufacturers (generally released as 1949 models). Although the SLAB-SIDE style has dominated the automotive industry for more than 50 years, its late-1940s introduction was then considered highly innovative and progressive.

**slam** *v.* To drop a vehicle's RIDE HEIGHT to an extremely low level, generally through radical suspension modifications. Example: "I'm gonna SLAM the thing right into the pavement."

**'slammer,** see DOORSLAMMER

**slantback** (also **slantback sedan**) **1.** *n.* Any SEDAN produced by Ford Motor Company for the 1935 through 1937 model years and featuring a smooth, uninterrupted "slant" to its rear body structure (distinctly differing from Ford's concurrently produced "humpback" SEDAN models). In street rodding applications, the SLANTBACK is strongly preferred over the humpback for its more elegant, free-flowing style. **2.** *n.* Any non-Ford SEDAN produced during the 1930s and featuring a smooth, sloping rear body style.

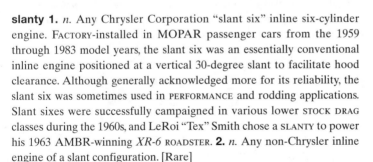
1937 FORD **slantback**[1]
STREET ROD

**slanty 1.** *n.* Any Chrysler Corporation "slant six" inline six-cylinder engine. FACTORY-installed in MOPAR passenger cars from the 1959 through 1983 model years, the slant six was an essentially conventional inline engine positioned at a vertical 30-degree slant to facilitate hood clearance. Although generally acknowledged more for its reliability, the slant six was sometimes used in PERFORMANCE and rodding applications. Slant sixes were successfully campaigned in various lower STOCK DRAG classes during the 1960s, and LeRoi "Tex" Smith chose a SLANTY to power his 1963 AMBR-winning *XR-6* ROADSTER. **2.** *n.* Any non-Chrysler inline engine of a slant configuration. [Rare]

**slats,** see LOUVERS (Definition 2)

**sled,** see LEAD SLED

**sleeper** *n.* Any vehicle with a STOCK, conservative, and/or mundane external appearance that belies a very strong PERFORMANCE potential. A car that looks slow but is, in fact, very FAST. A SLEEPER's appearance may present a distinct advantage when racers CHOOSE OFF.

**slice 'n' dice** *v*. To extensively alter any complete vehicle or vehicle component through a combination of radical body modifications (chopping, channeling, sectioning, etc.).

**slicks** *n*. Any high-performance DRAG racing tires featuring an absolutely smooth, treadless contact surface. DRAG SLICKS' design provides maximum traction on clean, dry racing surfaces. Popularized in DRAG applications by the early 1950s, the first DRAG SLICKS consisted of recapped conventional tires with rigid sidewalls and relatively hard rubber compounds. During the 1960s, custom PIE-CRUST SLICKS and later soft compound WRINKLEWALL SLICKS replaced the earlier recap types, bringing about tremendous performance increases.

MID-1960S **slingshot** DRAGSTER

**slingshot** (also **slingshot dragster**) *n*. Early RAIL DRAGSTER configuration featuring a narrow (typically elongated) chassis, its engine mounted immediately forward of the rear axle, and the driver positioned low and behind the rear axle assembly. The SLINGSHOT type dominated DRAGSTER design from the mid-1950s through the early 1970s when, in the interest of improved driver safety, it was eclipsed by the modern rear-engine DRAGSTER. The first successful SLINGSHOT DRAGSTER was constructed in late 1954 by motorsports renaissance man Mickey Thompson. When fellow HOT RODDER Leroy Neumeyer witnessed the car at the Santa Ana DRAGS (see SANTA BANANA) he commented to Thompson that its configuration reminded him of a slingshot, giving birth to the popular name.

**slip 'n' slide** (also **slip 'n' slide Powerglide**) *n*. Any Chevrolet Powerglide two-speed automatic transmission. The Powerglide was introduced in 1950 as CHEVY's first fully automatic transmission and remained in production through 1977. During its manufacturing run, the Powerglide was often derided by HOT RODDERS for its poor performance, and the transmission's early nicknames described the STOCK unit's tendency to slip (not positively transfer engine power) under load. Ironically, from the late 1970s to the present day, modified Powerglides have become favorites in a variety of DRAG racing applications.

**slippery** *adj*. Streamlined. Possessing favorable aerodynamics.

**slippery Stude**
1953 STUDEBAKER
STARLIGHT COUPE

**slippery Stude** (STEW-dee) *n*. Any of the exceptionally streamlined Studebaker Starlight (pillared COUPE) or Starliner (pillarless COUPE) models produced from 1953 through 1955. The SLIPPERY STUDE's design was largely the work of Robert Bourke from the firm of renowned industrial designer Raymond Loewy (accounting for the model's alternative LOEWY COUPE nickname). Studebaker originally contracted with Raymond Loewy Associates for a show car design but was so enamored with the results that they rushed the model into actual production. Notable and innovative SLIPPERY STUDE features include a low overall profile, a relatively long WHEELBASE, restrained use of decorative ornamentation, and a long, sloping hood. SLIPPERY STUDES found almost immediate favor in LAND-SPEED RACING (and to a lesser degree in DRAG racing) applications, where their wind-cheating design was of obvious benefit. The March 1955 issue of *HOT ROD* magazine featured an article on a 167-mile-per-hour 1953 Starlight COUPE powered by an INJECTED, NITRO-burning Ardun-MERC, referring to the car as a "production-line STREAMLINER." Titled "SLIPPERY STUDE," the feature indicates that the expression dates to at least that time period.

**slip the clutch** *v.* During the course of a DRAG RACE, to partially disengage a manual transmission's clutch by lightly depressing the clutch pedal, thus slightly reducing the power directed to the vehicle's driven wheels (improving traction), while simultaneously maintaining engine RPM.

**sloper** (also **slope back**) *n.* Any Australian two-door COUPE/SEDAN hybrid model, as produced from the mid-1930s through the early 1940s. SLOPERS are distinguished by their highly unique roof line, which forms a graceful unbroken curve from windshield to rear bumper (much in the style of latter-decade FASTBACK models). Sporty and practical, SLOPERS were originally popular with families and, oftentimes, traveling salesmen.

1939 FORD **sloper** STREET ROD

A broad range of manufacturers produced SLOPERS, most significantly the Australian divisions of Chevrolet, Buick, Oldsmobile, Pontiac, Plymouth, Dodge, and Ford. The SLOPER's mixed COUPE/SEDAN identity is clearly evidenced by its original manufacturer's model designations. General Motors products were named "All-Enclosed COUPES," while Ford referred to its versions as "TUDORS" (a name shared with Ford's conventional two-door SEDANS of American manufacture). Along with Australia's other significant and completely unique model, the COUPE utility (see UTE), SLOPERS have long been a part of that country's considerable hot rodding tradition.

**slot mags** (also **slotted mags** or **slots**) **1.** *n.* Any AFTERMARKET custom MAG WHEELS featuring an overall "dished" shape and a series of generally rectangular or oval openings in their surface for the purpose of lightening, brake cooling, and/or aesthetics. While Halibrand Engineering (see HALS), American Racing Equipment, and E-T Wheels have all produced significant true-racing, slot-style MAG WHEELS, the SLOT MAGS term is more often applied to aluminum STREET wheels. Especially popular during the 1960s and 1970s, STREET-oriented SLOT MAGS were manufactured by Ansen Automotive (the notable "Ansen Sprint" wheel as introduced in 1963), Cragar, Fenton, Mickey Thompson, Superior, and US Indy. **2.** *n.* Any OEM steel FACTORY MAGS featuring the general style and characteristics of AFTERMARKET SLOT MAG wheels. [Rare]

**slugs** *n.* Any automotive pistons. Fitted closely to an engine's cylinders, pistons are moved by the force of the burning air/fuel mixture. The piston's reciprocating (back-and-forth) motion is in turn converted, via connecting rods (see RODS), to rotate an engine's crankshaft (see CRANK). In the typical four-stroke automotive engine, pistons also serve to draw unburnt air/fuel mixture into cylinders, compress the air/fuel mixture, and expel burnt exhaust gasses on respective engine cycles.

**slush box** (also **slushbox**) *n*. Derogatory expression for any automotive automatic transmission. Term most popular from the 1950s through the early 1960s period, when manual transmissions were strongly favored in high-performance applications. "Slush" describes the hydraulic fluid-actuated drive system employed by most automatic transmissions.

**small-block** *n*. Any V8 engine featuring a relatively small physical size and internal displacement (generally between 250 and 350-CID). Term most often used to draw a distinction between various engine series produced by a single manufacturer. For example, Ford Motor Company's "90-degree" series engines produced in 221-CID through 351-CID form are referred to as SMALL-BLOCKS, while Ford's concurrently produced FE Series engines in 332-CID through 428-CID variations are considered BIG-BLOCKS.

**small Chevy** *n*. Any SMALL-BLOCK Chevrolet V8 engine (see also MOUSE and SBC).

**Smithy's** (SMIT-ees) *n*. The most renowned and longest-lived of all STRAIGHT-THROUGH MUFFLER types. Known for their unique, rich EXHAUST NOTE and blue hammertone finish, SMITHY's-brand mufflers experienced strong popularity during the 1940s and 1950s in a variety of CUSTOM CAR, HOT ROD, and STREET MACHINE applications. Billed as "The Original SMITHY's since 1920," SMITHY's have gained renewed favor with the 1990s and early-twenty-first-century RETRO ROD and traditional CUSTOM CAR movements.

**smoke** someone (also **smoke** someone **off**), see DUST someone

**smoke 'em**, see BURN RUBBER

**smokey** (also **smoky** or **smokie**) *n*. Any intense BURNOUT producing abundant tire smoke.

**smooth 1.** *v*. To subtly change the shape, contours, or configuration of any overall auto body or body component to achieve a cleaner, more streamlined custom appearance. Such modifications may include nosing, decking, frenching, filling body seams, altering or completely removing STOCK body beads, etc. **2.** *v*. To straighten damaged or distorted auto body panels, bringing a vehicle back to its FACTORY-original condition.

**smoothie** (also **smoothy**) *n*. Any STREET ROD or CUSTOM CAR featuring an extremely CLEAN streamlined appearance. Term is most often associated with the ultra HIGH-TECH, high-dollar RODS and CUSTOMS of the 1990s to present.

**smoothies** (also **smoothie caps**) *n.* General term for any custom hubcaps featuring a smooth, unadorned, and generally convex shape.

**sneeze a blower** *v.* To experience a slight or negligible engine backfire within a high-performance supercharger (see BLOWER). Most often occurs during engine startup and generally does not damage components.

**sock motor 1.** *n.* Any FoMoCo-produced single-overhead CAM (see SOHC) 427-CID engine (see CAMMER). Name is a result of its phonetic similarity to the SOHC abbreviation. **2.** *n.* Any engine featuring a single-overhead camshaft configuration.

**SOHC** (usually written, not spoken) *n.* Single-overhead camshaft (see CAM).

**solids**, see STEELIES

**sombreros** (also **sombrero hubcaps**) (som-BRARE-ohs) **1.** *n.* Original-equipment wheel covers as featured on various 1947 through 1952 Cadillac production models. Experienced strong popularity in late-1940s and early-1950s era CUSTOM CAR applications for their simple, smooth, and elegant style. The type's name is derived from its distinctive, deeply sculptured shape resembling a Mexican sombrero hat. **2.** *n.* Any original-equipment or AFTERMARKET hubcaps produced in the overall style of genuine Cadillac SOMBREROS.

sombrero[1] HUBCAP

**soup job** *n.* Early term for any vehicle modified for improved performance. Since the early 1960s, the term has effectively been replaced with HOT ROD.

**soup up 1.** (also **soup**) *v.* To modify any vehicle for improved performance (generally 1960 and earlier usage). **2.** see SOUP JOB

**spaghetti** (also **spaghetti wiring**) *n.* Automotive electrical wiring done in a crude, amateurish, and disorderly manner so as to resemble a dish of spaghetti.

**spaghetti headers** (also **spaghetti pipes**) *n.* Any automotive HEADERS or exhaust pipes constructed from AFTERMARKET flexible exhaust tubing. Commonly featured on home-built HOT RODS and DRAG vehicles of the 1950s.

**spank** *v.* Traditionally, an East Coast variation of the expression DECK (to remove STOCK rear DECK emblems, ornamentation, or handles from an auto body, followed by the filling of existing holes and refinishing to achieve a smoother, cleaner appearance).

**speed knob**, see SUICIDE KNOB

**speedo** *n.* Any automotive speedometer.

**speed shift**, see POWERSHIFT

**speed shop** *n.* Any business specializing in the retail sale of PERFORMANCE-oriented auto parts. Early dry lakes (see the LAKES) competitor and PERFORMANCE parts merchant Karl Orr is widely credited with originating this term as proprietor of the 1940s-era Karl Orr Speed Shop.

LATE-1910S MODEL T
**speedster**

**speedster** *n.* Seminal American PERFORMANCE vehicle type that was, in many ways, the forerunner of what we know today as the HOT ROD. Usually home-built, the typical SPEEDSTER consisted of a production automobile chassis (most often provided by a Model T Ford [see T-BONE]) mounting a radically stripped-down body and hopped-up motor. While SPEEDSTERS were constructed in later years, the type's popularity peaked during the Model T era of the 1910s and 1920s. Typical SPEEDSTER modifications included the removal of much of the existing body or the replacing of STOCK body panels with streamlined custom sheetmetal, the souping up of the original engine (oftentimes with the addition of an AFTERMARKET OHV or OHC HEAD), and the replacing of heavy STOCK wheels with AFTERMARKET wire RIMS.

**Speed Week** *n.* The Bonneville Nationals, hot rodding's weeklong, premier LAND-SPEED RACING event held on the world-famous BONNEVILLE Salt Flats. SPEED WEEK is presented during the second week of August each year by Bonneville Nationals, Inc., an affiliate of the SCTA.

**spin a wrench**, see TURN A WRENCH

**spin donuts** *v.* To perform multiple DONUT maneuvers in a vehicle.

**spinners** (also **spinner caps** or **spinner hubcaps**) *n.* Alternative term for any FLIPPER-style hubcaps as commonly featured on 1940s through early-1960s CUSTOM CARS.

**split manifold** *n.* AFTERMARKET exhaust manifold system as traditionally applied to high-performance inline six-cylinder engines. While a conventional inline six-cylinder's manifold funnels exhaust from all cylinders into a single exhaust pipe, a SPLIT MANIFOLD divides the engine's exhaust into two groupings of three. Each manifold grouping then feeds into a separate exhaust pipe, creating a free-breathing dual exhaust system.

**splitters** *n.* Appearance-enhancing, chrome-plated exhaust tailpipe "split" tip. Most often employed in dual exhaust applications, SPLITTERS are fitted to the end of each tailpipe, dividing the single pipe into two distinct tips. SPLITTERS typically exit a vehicle's underside at a point beneath each rear quarter panel. In STOCK applications, Pontiac is most noted for offering exhaust SPLITTERS on their GTO (see GOAT) and Trans Am (see TA) PERFORMANCE models.

**split window 1.** (also **split**) *n.* Any 1963 Chevrolet Corvette (see 'VETTE) Sport COUPE model. This first of the Sting Ray series Corvette COUPES featured a unique two-piece or "split" rear window and ranks among the most coveted of all Corvettes for its first-of-series status, unique one-year-only window treatment, and exceptional all-around performance (1963 marked the introduction of the first fully independent Corvette suspension, while the potent 327-CID engine boasting up to 360 fuel-injected horsepower was carried over from the 1962 Corvette line). **2.** *n.* Any automobile featuring a two-piece or "split" BACKLIGHT.

**split window**[1]
1963 CORVETTE SPORT COUPE

**split wishbones** (also **split 'bones**) *n.* Any STOCK WISHBONE radius-rod assembly modified by "splitting" its single, centrally located chassis mounting point and relocating individual radius-rod ends outward on a vehicle's chassis. Most popular during the 1940s through the 1960s, SPLIT WISHBONES were commonly employed to provide additional clearances for swapped-in later model engine/transmission combinations. Since the 1970s, OEM WISHBONE suspensions have more frequently been replaced altogether with custom and AFTERMARKET systems within street rodding applications.

**spoiler** *n.* Any airfoil or similar GROUND EFFECTS device affixed to, or integrated into, a vehicle to enhance high-speed driveability and/or vehicle appearance. Beginning during the late-1960s MUSCLE CAR era and continuing to the present day, front and rear SPOILERS have commonly been provided as standard or optional equipment on FACTORY-produced PERFORMANCE vehicles. At high vehicle speeds, properly designed and tuned SPOILERS exert downforce on a vehicle, improving stability and driver control, but in most STREET applications the presence of SPOILERS is purely aesthetic. Front SPOILERS sometimes also serve to direct air toward a vehicle's radiator, thereby improving engine cooling.

REAR-DECK **spoiler** ON
1969 GTO JUDGE

**Spoiler** *n.* Any Mercury Cyclone SPOILER model as produced from 1969 through 1971. Based on Mercury's intermediate Montego line, Cyclone SPOILERS were made available with potent 428 and 429 Cobra Jet (see CJ) engines, heavy-duty running gear, and suspension upgrades, all making for exceptional STREET performance. The Cyclone SPOILER II was produced for 1969 only, sharing its aerodynamic nose with Ford's Torino Talladega (see DROOP-SNOOT). All SPOILERS came equipped with their namesake rear DECK SPOILER.

**spongies** *n.* Any large, soft compound WRINKLEWALL DRAG racing slicks. Term most popular during the 1960s.

**spoon pedal** *n.* Simple, compact accelerator pedal type with the overall appearance of an actual teaspoon. The type's clean, stylish appearance and small size have made it a consistent favorite in a variety of street rodding applications. Currently available in AFTERMARKET reproduction form, original SPOON PEDALS were featured as original equipment on Ford passenger cars during the 1932 through 1934 model years.

**Sportsman Tree**, see CHRISTMAS TREE

CHEVROLET SUBURBAN-BASED
**sport truck**[1]

**sport truck 1.** *n.* Any light-duty commercial vehicle (pickup, van, or SUV) custom-modified in such a way as to improve its performance and/or appearance. Although the road performance (acceleration, handling, etc.) of SPORT TRUCKS is generally enhanced, their originally intended functions of passenger and/or freight hauling are often impaired or eliminated. Custom SPORT TRUCKS are most often based on late-model (1980s through early twenty-first century) vehicles and commonly feature: **a.** Severe lowering through suspension modifications; **b.** Large-diameter BILLET custom wheels; **c.** Mild body modifications (shaved doorhandles, recessed license plates, LOUVERS, etc.); **d.** Exotic custom paint treatments (often including GRAPHICS); **e.** GROUND EFFECTS in the form of SPOILERS, AIR DAMS, or WINGS; **f.** Mildly modified engines and running gear; and **g.** Powerful custom sound systems. **2.** *n.* Any STOCK, FACTORY-production commercial vehicle produced with an emphasis on a distinctive personalized appearance or character, improved road (or off-road) performance, and a diminished consideration for practical hauling or work capabilities.

**spot** ON
1949 MERCURY CUSTOM

**spots** *n.* Any accessory spotlights as commonly affixed to the lower A-PILLARS of traditional CUSTOM CARS. A near-requisite addition to 1940s through early-1960s era CUSTOMS, spotlights were employed more for aesthetic purposes than practical function (as evidenced by the fact that many vintage SPOTS were of a non-functional or "dummy" type). As a design element, the inclusion of brightly plated spotlights was perceived by some to "visually lower" a vehicle. The most celebrated of all traditional spotlight types were the Series-112 produced by the Appleton Corporation. With their positioning controlled by an internal handle, spotlights are always left in their resting or "turned-down" position when maximizing their visual appeal.

**spray 1.** (also **spray job**) *n.* Any exterior automotive paint finish. Example: "What really makes the car is its KANDY magenta SPRAY." **2.** see NITROUS

**spreader bars** *n.* Round tubular bars functioning to connect a generally early-1930s vintage auto frame's RAILS. SPREADER BARS are attached between the tips of front or rear FRAME HORNS, lending strength and rigidity to the extreme ends of the frame. In hot rodding applications,

STOCK SPREADER BARS are often replaced with custom units or even removed altogether.

**sprinkler system** *n.* Early expression for any overhead-valve (see OHV) system featured on an automotive engine. Term most often used during or prior to the 1950s as a reference to the type's then-unique operation.

**sprint car nose** *n.* Alternative expression for any HOT ROD TRACK NOSE. Name is a reference to its common usage on contemporary circle-track racing sprint cars.

**Squarebird** *n.* Any Ford Thunderbird (see T-BIRD) as produced from 1958 through 1960 model years. Nicknamed SQUAREBIRD for their squareish roofline and overall rectangular appearance, these second-generation Thunderbirds have long been popular bases for CUSTOM CAR modification. Standard SQUAREBIRD power came in the form of Ford's FE Series 352-CID BIG-BLOCK with 300 BHP or an optionally available MEL-series 430-CID V8 producing 350 BHP (for 1959 and 1960).

**squat** *v.* At the outset of a DRAG RACE, to experience a pronounced lowering or dipping to the rear portion of a vehicle as a result of WEIGHT TRANSFER.

**squeeze** (also **squeeze factor**) *n.* Compression ratio. Within any engine cylinder, the ratio between the cylinder's maximum volume (piston at its lowest or "bottom dead center" position) and minimum volume (piston at its highest or "top dead center" position). Higher compression ratios inherently produce greater horsepower and torque in an engine. Increasing compression ratios by various means has traditionally been a popular method among hot rodders to improve engine performance.

**squirrel** *n.* Early and derogatory term for any young and exceptionally reckless or dangerous driver. A SQUIRREL often owned a crude, inferior HOT ROD but tried to impress others with his perceived courage, skill, and "coolness" in driving. Term experienced its greatest popularity during the 1940s and 1950s.

**squirrel cage** *n.* Any extensive or elaborate protective roll cage. Term most popular during the 1950s and 1960s.

**squirrel knob**, see SUICIDE KNOB and NECKER KNOB

**squirt brakes**, see JUICE BRAKES

**squirter** *n.* Early HOT RODDER's expression for any automotive carburetor (see CARB).

**squirt job** *n.* Any automotive exterior paint job.

**stab 'n' steer** *n.* Drag racing driving style consisting of merely depressing an accelerator pedal and steering, as necessary, to keep the vehicle headed in a straight line. Racing as experienced (most often) with an automatic transmission, requiring no shifting or clutch pedal finesse. Example: "I can't see the fun in driving an automatic. It's nothing but stab 'n' steer."

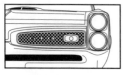

stacked headlights ON 1967 Pontiac GTO

**stacked headlights** *n.* Any quad headlight treatment configured in a vertically stacked manner. Stacked headlights were a signature design element of most FoMoCo and Pontiac muscle cars during the mid-1960s.

**stacks 1.** see velocity stacks **2.** *n.* Any custom, high-performance exhaust pipes consisting of a series of short steel tubes extending from individual engine exhaust ports.

**stage** *v.* Immediately prior to the actual running of a drag race, to maneuver a participating vehicle into the precise, stationary starting position. Photoelectric light beams running perpendicular to the track's axis are broken by the racer's front wheel, lighting a signal on the Christmas Tree when the driver's position is correct.

**staging lanes** *n.* Series of parallel, marked lanes leading to the starting end of a dragstrip. Organized and segregated by class, vehicles wait in the staging lanes for their turn to race.

**staging war**, see burndown

**stance** *n.* The general attitude of a vehicle's body and chassis assembly relative to a horizontal axis (see positive or negative rake) combined with its overall ride height. How a vehicle "sits." Though varying widely through historical trends and movements, stance has always been a fundamental element of hot rod and custom car aesthetics.

**stand on it** *v.* To aggressively and fully depress a vehicle's accelerator pedal.

'Stang
2000 Mustang Cobra R

**'Stang** *n.* Any Ford Mustang. Introduced on April 15, 1964, as a 1964 1/2 model, the first Mustangs offered affordable price, a sporty feel (with the practicality of seating for four), and, perhaps most importantly, exceptional styling. The early Mustang's outstanding market success established the widespread popularity of the pony car concept, while its name provided the direct inspiration for the term pony car. Performance-oriented Mustang submodels and factory HP options have continually served to further the original pony car's considerable legacy. Mustang performance standouts include: **a.** The small-block-powered

Shelby GT 350s of 1965 through 1970 and BIG-BLOCK-powered Shelby GT 500s of 1967 through 1970 (originally modified for Ford by racer Carroll Shelby's firm, Shelby Mustangs were treated to various engine, chassis/suspension, and appearance upgrades); **b.** The potent 428 Cobra Jet-powered Mustangs of 1968 through 1970 (see CJ); **c.** The various Boss-series Mustangs produced from 1969 through 1971 (see Boss); **d.** The Mustang SVOs of 1984 through 1986 (with intercooled, turbocharged [see TURBO] 2.3-liter four-cylinders and a strong emphasis on handling and agility); and **e.** The limited-edition Mustang Cobra Rs of the 1990s and year 2000 period. FACTORY-built for racing (the inspiration for the type's "R" designation), all Cobra Rs featured significant engine, drivetrain, and chassis upgrades. The remarkable 2000 edition included a 385-BHP 5.4-liter DOHC V8, 6-speed manual transmission, rear-seat delete, prominently bulged hood, and a 12-second quarter-mile capability. While few Cobra Rs were ever formally raced, the Mustang model has, in fact, experienced a long history of racing successes. Mustangs won the coveted SCCA Trans-Am road-racing series in 1966, 1967, and 1970. Early Mustangs also fared well on the DRAGSTRIP, with CAMMER-powered FASTBACKS dominating in mid-1960s A/FX competition, and 428 Cobra Jet cars frequently taking Super Stock honors during the late 1960s. SLIPPERY FASTBACK Mustang bodies were also favored in late-1960s GASSER and FUNNY CAR applications. More recently, the Mustang's strong DRAG racing popularity resulted in the formation of the NMRA (National Mustang Racers Association), a major organization catering to generally late-model Mustang DRAG competition.

**Starfires** (also **Starfire caps** or **Starfire flippers**) **1.** *n.* Distinctive tri-bar hubcaps as originally featured on 1956 Oldsmobile Starfire production models. While similar to their Fiesta predecessors, STARFIRES differed by their absence of a central emblem or crest and instead included three small ringed-globe logos between each of their three decorative bars. **2.** *n.* Any AFTERMARKET hubcaps featuring the essential tri-bar style of true production STARFIRE CAPS. During the late 1950s and early 1960s, both OEM Oldsmobile Starfire and AFTERMARKET Starfire-style caps experienced strong popularity in CUSTOM CAR, HOT ROD, and STREET MACHINE applications.

1956 OLDSMOBILE
**Starfire**[1] CAP

**Starwars air cleaner** *n.* Original-equipment, dual-snorkel air cleaner assembly featured exclusively on 400-CID and 430-CID V8-powered Buick PERFORMANCE cars during the 1967 model year. The unusual red-plastic (glass-filled polyester) air cleaner came as standard equipment on all Riviera- and Skylark-based GS models and was optionally available on Wildcat, Electra 225, and standard Rivieras. The type's name was coined retroactively in response to director George Lucas' popular 1977 science-fiction film *Star Wars.*

**Starwars air cleaner**

**steam** *n.* Power. Horsepower or torque as produced by any engine.

**steamroller meats** (also **steamroller tires**) *n.* Any of the especially massive (and, significantly, wide) rear tires as commonly featured on high-performance STREET MACHINES, HOT RODS, or DRAG racing vehicles. Term was largely popularized in association with the PRO STREET movement of the 1980s and derives from a similarity in appearance to an actual steamroller's roller unit.

**steel** *n.* Any automotive body panel or complete body, but most often referring to original, vintage sheetmetal components as utilized in STREET ROD buildups. Example: "Even marginal '32 STEEL is getting absurdly expensive these days."

**steelies** (also **steels**) *n.* Any solid (as differentiated from wire-type) steel automotive wheels. Term most often refers to the OEM steel wheels popularized in hot rodding applications during the late 1940s and the 1950s. STEELIES are often adorned with CAPS 'N' RINGS to enhance their appearance.

**Steel is real.** Traditional STREET RODDER's expression of preference for original steel auto bodies over modern fiberglass (see 'GLASS) reproductions. Interestingly, with the advent of steel reproduction bodies in the 1990s, STEEL is not necessarily "real" (true VINTAGE TIN) any longer.

**steel-packs** (also **steel-pacs**) *n.* Any high-performance, free-flowing exhaust mufflers wherein exhaust gasses pass directly through a ventilated tube surrounded by tightly packed fibrous steel. STEEL-PACKS function essentially in the same manner as their GLASS-PACK counterparts, differing only by their actual packing material.

**steep gears** (also **steep gearing**) *n.* Any relatively high (numerically low) automotive final-drive ratio (see REAREND).

**stick 1.** see STICKSHIFT **2.** *n.* Any automotive engine's camshaft (see CAM). Derived from the camshaft's long stick-like shape (also may be considered a contraction of the slang term for a camshaft, BUMPSTICK).

**stickshift 1.** *n.* Any manual automotive transmission. **2.** *n.* Any vehicle equipped with a manual transmission.

**stick** an engine **with a cam** *v.* To replace a STOCK, OEM-type camshaft (see CAM) with an AFTERMARKET or high-performance model. Example: "In the next phase, I'll STICK it WITH A CAM and bolt on a set of HEADERS. Those changes oughta easily put me in the high twelves."

**stiff gears** (also **stiff gearing**) *n.* Any rear axle gear set (final-drive ratio) featuring a relatively low (numerically high) gear ratio.

**stir gears** *v.* To shift a manual transmission's gears (generally refers to a floor shift application).

**stir soup** *v.* To shift a manual transmission through a sloppy or imprecise shift linkage.

**stock 1.** *adj.* Unmodified. As produced by an original automotive manufacturer (said of any automotive component or complete vehicle). **2.** *n.* Any unmodified vehicle, but especially one that is high-performance in nature. [Rare]

**stock car** *n.* Any circle-track racing vehicle essentially based on a late-model American production SEDAN or COUPE.

**stocker 1.** *n.* Any unmodified vehicle as produced by its original manufacturer. **2.** *n.* Any race car configured in a pure STOCK or near-STOCK manner. **3.** *n.* Any individual vehicle part or component that is FACTORY-original or OEM in nature.

**stoked** *adj.* Powered. Term typically follows a specific engine type, indicating what POWERPLANT is used to motivate a given vehicle. Example: "Nothing says '50s like a FLATHEAD-STOKED DEUCE COUPE."

**stomped**, see CHOPPED

**stomp on it** *v.* To aggressively and fully depress a vehicle's accelerator pedal.

**'Stones** *n.* Any tires produced by Firestone (Bridgestone/Firestone, Inc.).

**stoplight grand prix** *n.* Alternative term for street racing. Any spontaneous, illegal DRAG racing on city streets as practiced from stoplight to stoplight.

**stormer** *n.* Any very QUICK or FAST vehicle.

**stovebolt 1.** (also **stovebolt six**) *n.* Any Chevrolet inline six-cylinder engine, but especially relating to the early-model OHV six-cylinders introduced during the 1929 model year. The engine's STOVEBOLT name is derived from its $1/4$-20 slotted-head bolts, resembling those of an antique stove. The term STOVEBOLT was most commonly used during and prior to the 1960s. **2.** *n.* Any complete Chevrolet automobile, but especially one powered by, or produced during the time of, the STOVEBOLT six-cylinder.

**straightaway racing**, see LAND-SPEED RACING

**straight axle 1.** *n.* Any tubular-steel front axle with virtually no bend or curvature to its overall shape. STRAIGHT AXLES were initially popularized in 1960s-era DRAG racing applications where they provided the high centers of gravity advantageous to WEIGHT TRANSFER. In subsequent

straight axle[1] ON
1956 CHEVROLET SEDAN

decades, STRAIGHT AXLES have sometimes been fitted to STREET MACHINES solely to furnish a racy, 1960s-era look or STANCE. **2.** *n.* General expression for any solid automotive front axle (as differentiated from a non-rigid system employing independent suspension).

**straight eight** *n.* Any inline eight-cylinder automotive engine. While the STRAIGHT EIGHT is generally considered a poor configuration for high-performance applications, early RODDERS nonetheless modified the type with some success (particularly in dry lakes [see the LAKES] competition). While Buick, Oldsmobile, Chrysler, and Hudson all produced inline eight-cylinder engines, the advent of the 1950s-era overhead-valve V8 effectively put an end to the STRAIGHT EIGHT's production.

**straight six** *n.* Any inline six-cylinder automotive engine. Through largely overshadowed by their V8 counterparts, STRAIGHT SIXES have long experienced moderate popularity in hot rodding and street rodding applications, and have also proven competitive in DRAG and LAND-SPEED RACING, especially in circumstances where engine displacement is restricted by class limitations. Historically, the most popular and successful use of STRAIGHT SIXES for PERFORMANCE applications occurred from the late 1940s through the mid-1950s when Chevrolet and GMC SIXES were SOUPED UP and run head-to-head against Ford's FLATHEAD V8s. With their relatively large displacements and overhead-valve configuration, CHEVY and JIMMY STRAIGHT SIXES managed very competitive power levels. Ultimately, both the STRAIGHT SIXES and FLATHEAD V8s were eclipsed by the then-revolutionary overhead-valve V8 engine types.

**straight-through mufflers** (also **straight-thru mufflers**) *n.* Any high-performance exhaust mufflers wherein exhaust gasses pass directly through a ventilated tube surrounded by tightly packed fiberglass (GLASS-PACKS) or fibrous steel (STEEL-PACKS). STRAIGHT-THROUGH MUFFLERS are differentiated from the more conventional "baffle" mufflers that deaden sound by deflecting exhaust through internal chambers.

MID-1950S **streamliner**[1]

**streamliner 1.** *n.* Any LAND-SPEED RACING vehicle featuring a custom, purpose-built streamlined body enveloping its entire chassis, including the wheels (post-1948 usage). **2.** *n.* Any LAND-SPEED RACING vehicle featuring a custom, purpose-built streamlined body but maintaining an open-wheel configuration (pre-1949 usage; after 1948, this type became known as a LAKESTER). **3.** *n.* Any purpose-built DRAGSTER featuring bodywork enveloping the full chassis (including front and rear wheels) to provide high-speed streamlining.

**street** *adj.* Relating to any complete vehicle or vehicle component designed for, and reasonably compatible with, everyday street or highway driving. Example: "Three-seventy-threes are a good, all-around STREET gear."

**streetable** *adj.* Capable of being operated in a reasonably comfortable, safe, and reliable manner in normal street or highway driving applications. Term may describe either a complete vehicle or an individual vehicle component (engine, camshaft [see CAM], induction system, etc.) and serves to distinguish such a vehicle or component from any impractical, temperamental, race-only counterpart. Example: "There's no way you're gonna convince me that a TUNNEL RAM with twin 1150 Dominators is any kind of STREETABLE SETUP."

**street freak 1.** (also **freak**) *n.* Custom STREET MACHINE type featuring showy, outrageous, or sometimes eccentric modifications in order to garner attention while boulevard cruising, or simply to stand out from the crowd. Most popular during the 1970s, the STREET FREAK style often featured unconventional makes or models as foundations, ultrawild paint schemes, bizarre interbrand engine swaps, outlandish GROUND EFFECTS, NOSE-BLEED RIDE HEIGHTS, superchargers (see BLOWER), and/or lavish crushed-velvet interiors. Some 1970s-era STREET FREAKS went so far as to include radical ENGINE SETBACKS, FLIP-TOP bodies, altered WHEELBASES (see AWB), multiple engines, and/or DRAG CHUTES. **2.** *n.* Any individual displaying an intense interest in and dedication to creating, driving, and/or cruising custom STREET MACHINES. Term experienced its greatest popularity during the 1970s.

AMC GREMLIN **street freak**[1]

**street Hemi** (HEM-ee) **1.** *n.* High-performance HEMI-HEAD V8 engine as produced by Chrysler Corporation from the 1966 through 1971 model years. Very conservatively rated at 425 BHP, the STREET HEMI was a de-tuned version of the competition-only 426-CID RACE HEMI. STREET HEMI-equipped cars have proven to be among the quickest and fastest true production vehicles ever released by a major American manufacturer. **2.** *n.* Any complete Dodge or Plymouth automobile featuring a 426-CID STREET HEMI engine as original equipment.

**Street is neat**. General expression of favor for STREET RODS and/or street rodding. Term experienced its strongest popularity during the 1970s.

**street machine** *n.* Any relatively modern-era production vehicle that has been custom modified for improved appearance and/or performance. The highly general STREET MACHINE term serves to distinguish the type from traditional early-model HOT RODS or STREET RODS. While similar in principle to their vintage-bodied counterparts, STREET MACHINES are based on newer production era (generally 1950s or later) vehicle foundations. In 1963, disc jockey (and noted HOT ROD MUSIC composer) Roger Christian of Los Angeles radio station KFWB recorded a single entitled "Little Street Machine." Performing as "Hot Rod Rog," Christian's track dates the STREET MACHINE expression to at least that time.

**street race 1.** *n.* In its hot rodding context, most often refers to an illegal, on-highway DRAG RACE (as differentiated from other forms of racing [cross-country rallies, etc.] that may be practiced on public streets). **2.** *v.* To engage in any illegal on-highway DRAG RACE.

**street rod 1.** *n.* Modern term for any early-bodied modified vehicle similar to a traditional HOT ROD but differing in its focus on safety, comfort, and DRIVEABILITY. During the 1960s, the popularity of traditional HOT RODS faltered significantly, but by the early 1970s a new version of the classic HOT ROD style began to emerge. In the October 1971 debut issue of *STREET ROD* magazine, editor Bruce Miller wrote, "From Maine to California, street rodding is fast becoming a favorite family sport." Distancing itself from hot rodding's earlier "outlaw" stigma, street rodding had come to represent a socially acceptable and family-oriented hobby within the American mainstream. Though STREET RODS come in a multitude of forms and styles, one common element is a vintage (generally pre-1949) body foundation. Differing from their true HOT ROD counterparts, STREET RODS tend to emphasize roadworthiness and comfort, often employing such amenities as sophisticated modern suspension systems, air conditioning, power windows, etc. Less constrained by tradition, STREET RODS have tended to evolve more freely, finding expression in modern trends like the HIGH-TECH and BILLET movements. STREET RODS are also more commonly constructed from entirely new, custom-fabricated components than are traditional HOT RODS. **2.** *n.* Early (generally 1950s and 1960s era) term relating to any vintage-bodied HOT ROD commonly and principally used in street-driving applications. In 1953, author Henry Gregor Felsen released a pulp novel entitled simply *STREET ROD*. The book's cover copy describes its content as, "An eye-opening novel about street-rodders—the ones who build and drive the stripped-down, souped-up bombs on wheels. They don't want to die—they just don't believe they can get killed!" Though obviously sensationalized, this early usage of the term STREET ROD exemplifies the difference between its connotations (and, indeed, denotations) from the 1950s and the period spanning the early 1970s to the present day. (Further, *HOT ROD* magazine's March 1961 issue included an article entitled "Sure Enough *STREET ROD*" describing the bob-fendered ROADSTER PICKUP as "the perfect HOT ROD." This interchangeable use of terms suggests that, at *that* time, *any* regularly street-driven HOT ROD might rightly be considered a *STREET ROD*.

**street rodder** *n.* Any individual involved in the building, driving, and/or showing of STREET RODS (Definition 1).

***Street Rodder*** *n.* Magazine that debuted in May 1972 and was originally published by RODDER Tom McMullen's successful McMullen Publishing, Inc. *STREET RODDER* played a strong role in the growth of the hobby and has remained a popular and consistent publication to the present day. *STREET RODDER* is currently published by Primedia Specialty Group, Inc.

**street-strip** *adj.* Relating to any automotive component or complete vehicle designed for both STREET and DRAGSTRIP usage.

**street sweeper** (also **street stomper**) *n.* Any exceptionally FAST or QUICK street-driven vehicle capable of winning or dominating STREET RACES.

**street Wedge** *n.* Any Chrysler Corporation 426-CID STREET WEDGE engine made available in Dodge and Plymouth automobiles during 1964 and 1965 model years as a more practical alternative to the radical 426-CID MAX WEDGE and race-only 426-CID HEMI motors. Featuring a WEDGE HEAD design, single FOUR-BARREL, cast-iron INTAKE, and hydraulic-lifter camshaft (see CAM), the STREET WEDGE maintained a respectable 365 BHP.

**strip**, see DRAGSTRIP

**strip car** *n.* Any vehicle created expressly for off-highway DRAG RACE competition. A DRAGSTRIP-only car.

**stripper** *n.* Any vehicle that has had all superfluous or unnecessary equipment removed. Term is most often applied to an OEM production vehicle equipped with high-performance running gear but entirely devoid of all appearance or comfort options to maximize its performance. From the 1950s through the mid-1970s PERFORMANCE and MUSCLE CAR eras, STRIPPERS were almost exclusively produced as SEDAN or POST models rather than the more upscale and expensive HARDTOPS.

**stripster** *n.* Alternative and early (generally 1950s era) expression for any purpose-built DRAGSTER. Name refers to the type's exclusive DRAGSTRIP usage.

**strobe stripes** *n.* Any of several graphic stripe treatments available on Plymouth or Dodge PERFORMANCE cars from the 1970 through 1974 model years. Although produced in a wide variety of styles, STROBE STRIPES all feature a series of generally vertically oriented rectangular marks arranged in such a way as to form a single continuous band or stripe.

**stroke** *n.* The distance a piston travels from its uppermost to lowermost positions on a given engine cycle. STROKE and BORE size (together with the number of cylinders) are the determining factors of an engine's displacement (see CID).

**stroked** *adj.* Relating to any crankshaft (see CRANK) or complete automotive engine that has been modified to include a longer STROKE, thereby increasing displacement (see CID) and boosting power levels.

**stroker 1.** (also **stroker crank**) *n.* Any crankshaft (see CRANK) modified or manufactured to increase an engine's STROKE over STOCK dimensions.

**2.** (also **stroker motor** or **stroker mill**) *n.* Any engine equipped with a STROKER crankshaft to increase its displacement.

**Stromie** (also **Strom**) (STRAWM-ee) *n.* Any Stromberg-brand TWO-BARREL carburetor (see CARB) as significantly popularized in 1930s-through 1960s-era multiple-carburetor hot rodding applications. Stromberg 97, 48, and 81 models were originally featured in single-CARB form on various 1930s- and 1940s-era production vehicles. While early FLATHEAD performance manifolds often featured a TWO-CARB configuration, as many as eight Strombergs were fitted to late-1950s competition INTAKES. The most popular Stromberg carburetor was the 97 model, so named for its .970 throttle bores.

**Stude** (also **Studie**) (STEW-dee) *n.* Any complete vehicle or vehicle component produced by the Studebaker Corporation. In hot rodding and CUSTOM CAR applications, the most recognized Studebakers are the unique BULLET-NOSE STUDES of the 1950–1951 period and the legendary SLIPPERY STUDES of 1953 through 1955. While these models achieved notoriety in various modified forms, Studebaker created a number of significant FACTORY PERFORMANCE cars as well. Standouts include: **a.** The 1956 Golden Hawk with a 275-BHP 352-CID V8 borrowed from Studebaker's sister corporation, Packard (Studebaker and Packard had merged in 1954); **b.** The Golden Hawks of 1957 and 1958, both with supercharged (see BLOWER) 289-CID STUDE V8s of 275 BHP; and **c.** The exotic fiberglass-bodied (see 'GLASS) Studebaker Avantis of 1963 and 1964. The stylish Raymond Loewy Associates-designed Avantis were made available with a host of PERFORMANCE options, including the R2 (289 CID with 289 BHP) and R3 (304.5 CID with an estimated 335 BHP) packages. Both the R2 and ultrarare R3 Avantis employed Paxton superchargers to boost their power output. Though never achieving the popularity of other manufacturers' engines, Studebaker V8s were sometimes SOUPED UP with AFTERMARKET speed equipment and/or swapped into 1950s and early-1960s era HOT RODS.

**Studillac** (STUDE-il-lack) *n.* Any Studebaker automobile modified by the inclusion of a Cadillac (see CADDY, Definition 2) engine. Term most commonly used during the 1950s when the contemporary large-displacement OHV Cadillac V8 engines were sometimes swapped into Studebaker vehicles for improved performance.

**stuffer**, see BLOWER

**stump puller** *n.* Any automotive engine, component, or complete vehicle possessing abundant torque. Term derived from the concept that such a TORQUEY vehicle or component could be used to easily pull tree stumps from the ground.

**stump-puller gears** *n.* Any exceptionally low (numerically high) final-drive ratio gear set (see REAREND). Traditionally, very low gear ratios have been used in commercial vehicles to multiply engine torque for low-speed, high-load work applications (ostensibly including pulling tree stumps from the ground). In DRAG racing, STUMP-PULLER GEARS work in conjunction with high-revving race engines to produce optimum quarter-mile acceleration.

**suds** *n.* Power. Horsepower or torque as produced by any engine.

**suede** *n.* Any low-sheen or matte automotive exterior finish, typically a primer. Historically, flat auto finishes were representative of nothing more than incomplete paint jobs, with primer undercoatings being a matter of function rather than styling. Over time, an appreciation developed for the "tough," "all-business" look of primered HOT RODS and STREET MACHINES. Flat-black primer (a.k.a. HOT ROD PRIMER), especially, was thought to provide a vehicle with a sinister or menacing character. During the 1990s and into the twenty-first century, matte finishes gained strongly in popularity as an element of the RETRO ROD and RAT ROD movements, and home-built RODS and CUSTOMS are commonly treated to easily applied yet distinctive low-sheen exterior finishes. Differing from earlier matte finishes, modern flat exterior treatments are produced in all conceivable colors, most often through the use of tintable primers. Matte clear coats sometimes serve to seal and protect vehicles while maintaining a desirable low-sheen look. The term SUEDE achieved its first widespread popularity during the 1990s.

**sugar donuts**, see WIDE WHITES

**suicide doors** *n.* Any vehicle side doors that open in a rearward rather than the more-conventional forward direction, providing the advantages of easier passenger-compartment entry and exit and a perceived elegance of style. SUICIDE DOORS were featured as original equipment on various early production cars (significantly including 1932 THREE-WINDOW and all 1933–1934 Ford COUPES), and their custom installation is relatively common in hot rodding and CUSTOM CAR applications. The type's name is derived from the potential danger of doors opening and/or being pulled backward in the windstream while the vehicle is in motion.

**suicide frontend** (also **suicide suspension**) *n.* Custom front suspension type featuring a transverse leaf spring set mounted in front of (as opposed to the more conventional position of directly below) a frame crossmember. A custom spring perch extends forward of and, significantly, *above* the crossmember, raising the position of the leafs and thereby lowering the vehicle's FRONTEND. The SUICIDE FRONTEND was an effective and popular alternative to a severely DROPPED AXLE in early (generally 1950s era) hot rodding applications.

**suicide knob** *n.* Small, independently rotating knob affixed to one point on the outside rim of a steering wheel (see also NECKER KNOB and SQUIRREL KNOB). To facilitate fast and one-handed steering, a driver grasps and spins the knob, in turn rotating the wheel. SUICIDE KNOBS were a popular accessory on early-vintage CUSTOM CARS and have returned to favor with the RETRO ROD and NOSTALGIA ROD movements of the 1990s and present day. The SUICIDE KNOB is traditionally referred to as a "steering-wheel spinner" in manufacturer advertising.

**sunken** *adj.* Molded and significantly recessed into a vehicle's exterior body panels as a custom styling element. Term may apply to any exterior trim piece, accessory, or component (oftentimes an antenna or license plate) whose mounting position has been moved into a custom-made body depression.

**supercar** *n.* General term for any ultra-high-performance MUSCLE CAR.

**supertrack**, see the COUNTY

surfer pedal

**surfer pedal** *n.* AFTERMARKET throttle pedal shaped as a stylized bare human foot. First popularized during the mid-1960s, the SURFER PEDAL is a chromed, diecast (some early versions were produced in polished aluminum) cover that is clamped over an existing automotive accelerator pedal. Serving no practical function, the SURFER PEDAL is employed solely for aesthetic purposes. A similar but significantly smaller four-toed headlight dimmer switch cover has also been traditionally available to complement the barefoot accelerator pedal.

**survivor** *n.* Any vintage HOT ROD, CUSTOM CAR, MUSCLE CAR, or DRAG racing vehicle that has survived in *unrestored* condition from a much earlier period. A historically significant vehicle whose history shows in its very appearance.

**swap** (SWOP) *n.* The practice of exchanging any major automotive component (engine, transmission, body, dashboard, etc.) for a type that was never originally available to the vehicle in an OEM FACTORY installation. SWAPS may be undertaken to improve vehicle performance, durability, and/or appearance.

**swap meet 1.** (also the **swaps**) *n.* Any organized gathering where automotive enthusiasts buy, sell, and trade (generally used) auto parts. Usually conducted outdoors, SWAP MEETS often feature an area where complete vehicles are also made available for sale and/or trade. **2.** *adj.* Acquired at a SWAP MEET. Example: "I scored some pretty decent SWAP MEET headlights for my '36."

**swap paint**, see TRADE PAINT

**swing**, see STROKE

**swinger rearend** (also **swing-axle rearend**), see WIGGLY REAREND

**swiss-cheese** *v.* To cut or drill holes in an automotive part or component for the purpose of performance-enhancing weight reduction, or sometimes solely to attain a traditional racy appearance. Expression was in use to describe DRAG racing components by the early 1950s.

**swiss-cheese Catalina** (also **swiss-cheese Cat**) *n.* Pontiac Catalina Sport COUPE model from 1963 that was FACTORY-produced expressly for DRAG RACE competition. SWISS-CHEESE CATALINAS featured a high-performance Super Duty 421-CID engine; aluminum front fenders, hood, bumpers, exhaust manifolds, and REAREND center section; Plexiglass windows; and more than 150 large lightening holes drilled in the vehicle's frame (the inspiration for the car's moniker). SWISS-CHEESE CATALINAS dominated the NHRA's B/FX class during the 1963 season.

**swoopy** *adj.* Possessing graceful, flowing curves. Term is often used to describe the aesthetically pleasing lines of an automobile's bodywork.

**swoopy** STREAMLINER

**Sy-Ty** *adj.* Relating to GMC's high-performance Syclone compact truck and/or Typhoon compact SUV models (see MUSCLE TRUCK).

# T

**T**, see T-bone

**T/A**
2002 WS6 Trans Am

**T/A** (pronounced as separate letters) *n.* Any Pontiac Firebird-based (see 'Bird) Trans Am pony car. Produced from 1969 through 2002, the Trans Am represented the most significant and longest-lived of all Firebird performance models. Like its Chevrolet Z-28 Camaro (see Z) cousin, the Trans Am was consistently equipped with handling and braking upgrades to complement its straight-line acceleration qualities. Trans Am performance standouts included the Ram Air-powered cars of 1969 and 1970; the 1971 and 1972 455-HO-engined models; the 455-SDs of 1973 and 1974; and the WS6-package equipped T/As of the 1990s and 2000s period. The Trans Am was retired, along with the entire Firebird line, following its 2002 production run. Indicative of a cultural era, the name "Macho T/A" was actually assigned to a series of customized Trans Ams during the 1976 through 1980 period. Macho T/As were modified for improved performance and a more distinctive appearance by DKM, Inc., of Arizona and sold by Pontiac dealerships throughout the United States.

**tach** (TACK) *n.* Any automotive tachometer, a gauge functioning to measure an engine's speed in RPM. Tachometers serve to notify drivers of accurate shift points in drag racing and other high-performance applications.

**tach out** (TACK) *v.* To rev an engine to its maximum practical RPM level (beyond which power levels decrease or mechanical failure may occur due to over-revving). Example: "I was already tached out when he blew past me in the lights."

**tach up** an engine (TACK) *v.* To increase an engine's speed as measured in RPM.

**taco tape** *n.* Derogatory term used by hot rodders to describe "prism tape," an opaque iridescent stick-on product used for decorative purposes. Taco tape experienced moderate popularity in automotive applications from the mid- to late 1970s when it was used on some race vehicles for exterior-body striping and lettering. Expression may suggest a moderate ethnic slur toward Mexican or Hispanic people, or may relate to something that is perceived as tasteless or tacky.

1960s-era **tail car** dragster

**tail car** *n.* Any slingshot dragster featuring a streamlined, fully enveloping tail section. Popular during the mid- to late 1960s, tail cars are distinguished by their highly stylish rear body treatments serving to completely enclose roll bar assemblies and partially surround drag chute packs. Tail car bodies were most often custom-fabricated from sheet aluminum to conform to individual chassis applications. Master craftsmen like Tom Hanna, Arnie Roberts, Bob Sorrell, and Wayne Ewing were responsible for the beautiful bodywork on a variety of 1960s-era DRAGSTER types.

**taildragger** *n.* CUSTOM CAR type or style featuring an overall low RIDE HEIGHT together with a slight rear-low STANCE (see NEGATIVE RAKE). Both the TAILDRAGGER term and style are most closely associated with the classic late-1940s through early-1950s CUSTOM CAR era.

1940 MERC **taildragger**

**tail job** *n.* Any early, open-wheeled STREAMLINER featuring a custom, pointed (circle-track sprint car style) tail section. Actual sprint cars were sometimes raced on the dry lakes during the 1940s and classified as STREAMLINERS as well.

**tall gears** (also **tall gearing**), see STEEP GEARS

**tall T** *n.* STREET ROD type based on any STOCK or near-STOCK-bodied Ford Model T (see T-BONE) closed car but most often a COUPE. With the TALL T style, no attempt is made to streamline or significantly change the inherently vertical, boxy lines of the Model T. Instead, the vehicle is appreciably restored and treated to full fenders and oftentimes many STOCK, OEM accessories. STREET ROD modifications come in the form of updated running gear, chassis, and suspension (including a lowered or RAKED STANCE), as well as custom wheels and interior. *HOT ROD* magazine's October 1960 issue showcased customizer Joe Cruces' FLATHEAD-powered 1921 T COUPE on its cover and in a feature article entitled "TALL T." The magazine feature served to perpetuate both a STREET ROD type as well as the term TALL T. The TALL T style achieved its greatest popularity during the 1960s.

1926 FORD **tall T** COUPE

**Tampa rake** (also **Tampa tilt** or **Tampa dump**) *n.* Engine-mounting position as sometimes applied to 1960s-era SLINGSHOT DRAGSTERS. Named for a style favored by renowned DRAG racer "Big Daddy" Don Garlits (originally of Tampa, Florida), the TAMPA RAKE located a DRAGSTER's engine with a decidedly nose-down attitude. When fitted with a TAMPA RAKE, a DRAGSTER performed as if having a longer WHEELBASE. Because more WEIGHT TRANSFER energy was necessary to lift the lowered weight in the nose of the engine, undesirable WHEELSTANDING tendencies were reduced.

**'Tang**, see 'STANG

**tank** (also **tanker**), see BELLY TANK

**tappet tickler** *n.* Any automotive engine's camshaft (see CAM). Name derived from the valve-actuating tappets or "lifters" that ride on a camshaft's lobes.

**taxi hubcaps** (also **taxicab hubcaps**) *n.* Any simple, inexpensive hubcaps as provided on bare-bones, functional "fleet" vehicles such as taxicabs (see POVERTY CAPS).

**taxiing aircraft** *n.* Derogatory term for any jet- or rocket-powered LAND-SPEED RACING vehicle (see JET). Thrust-motivated LSR vehicles are sometimes slighted by traditionalists who prefer internal-combustion engined, driven-wheel racers.

**T-Bird**
1956 FORD THUNDERBIRD

**T-Bird** *n.* Any Ford Thunderbird model as produced from 1955 to the present day. The Thunderbird has experienced a broad variety of permutations during its long history, with production being interrupted only once, during the 1998 through 2001 model years. Originally introduced to compete with Chevrolet's Corvette (see 'VETTE), the first T-BIRDS were mildly performance-oriented two-seat ROADSTERS. In subsequent decades, the Thunderbird evolved into to a large "personal-luxury vehicle," but for the 2002 model year, the 'BIRD came full-circle in a return to its sporty roots. Standout Thunderbird variations include: **a.** 1955 through 1957 first-generation models featuring an open two-passenger configuration, Y-BLOCK V8 power, and timeless, graceful styling; **b.** The radically redesigned four-passenger SQUAREBIRDS of the 1958 through 1960 period; **c.** The 1961 through 1963 futuristic BULLETBIRDS with available Sports ROADSTER option; **d.** The elegant and refined JETBIRDS produced from 1964 through 1966; **e.** The innovative Aerobirds of 1983 through 1988; and **f.** The sleek Thunderbirds of 2002 and 2003 that signal a return to a two-passenger open design and feature a highly modern interpretation of first-generation T-BIRD styling.

**T-bolt**, see THUNDERBOLT

**T-bone** *n.* Any Model T Ford as produced during the type's late-1908 through 1927 manufacture run. Although appreciably STOCK, Model Ts were commonly modified for improved performance during hot rodding's formative years (1910s through 1930s). By the 1940s, T chassis components and running gear were largely abandoned in favor of more modern alternatives. From the 1940s to the present day, lightweight and attractive Model T ROADSTER bodies have maintained a strong popularity when fitted to contemporary PERFORMANCE chassis. STOCK-bodied T closed cars have also experienced moderate popularity as STREET RODS, especially in the 1960s TALL T style.

**T-bucket** *n.* Any HOT ROD or STREET ROD featuring a Model T (see T-BONE) Ford ROADSTER body (generally 1923 through 1925 vintage or a fiberglass [see 'GLASS] facsimile thereof) on a custom-fabricated chassis. The T-BUCKET's elemental FENDERLESS style with diminutive, open, somewhat circular body shape (when viewed from above) inspires the type's BUCKET name.

**tear** (TARE), see HAUL

**teardrop hood** *n.* Unique, limited-edition hood type as produced by Ford Motor Company for its early- to mid-1960s LIGHTWEIGHT GALAXIE, THUNDERBOLT, A/FX Mustang, and A/FX Mercury Comet DRAG offerings. TEARDROP HOODS were constructed of fiberglass (see 'GLASS) and featured a large, teardrop-shaped bubble to provide clearance for Ford's powerful 427-CID HIGH RISER or CAMMER motors. Reproductions and variations of TEARDROP HOODS later became popular accessories in Ford STREET MACHINE applications.

teardrop hood ON
1963 1/2 GALAXIE

**teardrops 1.** (also **teardrop taillights**) *n.* Unique and stylish taillight type featured as original equipment on 1938 and 1939 model year Ford passenger cars. With their classic inverted teardrop shape, the highly popular Ford TEARDROP TAILLIGHTS have been adapted to a wide variety of HOT ROD, STREET ROD, and CUSTOM CAR applications. Because of their strong popularity, TEARDROPS have long been available in AFTERMARKET reproduction form. **2.** see TOMMY THE GREEK TEARDROPS

teardrops[1] ON
MODEL A ROADSTER

**teardrop skirts** *n.* Any of the teardrop-shaped FENDER SKIRTS commonly included on mid-1930s through early-1940s production era CUSTOM CARS. Name derived from smooth flowing, slightly convex teardrop shape. In OEM and AFTERMARKET forms, TEARDROP SKIRTS experienced strong popularity during the late-1930s to early-1950s CUSTOM CAR era.

**tech 1.** *n.* Any technical inspection, as performed on a DRAG racing vehicle prior to competition. Before being allowed to race, every vehicle is thoroughly checked to verify that it properly adheres to a race sanctioning body's safety standards and specific class regulations. **2.** *v.* To administer a pre-race technical inspection.

**tennies** (also **tennis shoes**) *n.* Any complete set of automotive wide-whitewall tires (see WIDE-WHITES) mounted on white-colored wheels. Term derived from the traditionally white color of tennis or athletic shoes.

**test and tune** (also **test 'n' tune**) *n.* Any open race course session allowing for participants to run practice and/or tuning PASSES. Most often held immediately prior to an actual race.

**test mule**, see MULE

**T-handle** (also **Tee-handle**) *n.* Unique shift handle introduced by various AFTERMARKET manufacturers during the mid-1960s, but significantly popularized when released by Hurst Performance Products in 1967. A T-HANDLE is a cylindrical, generally cast-aluminum handgrip serving to replace the more traditional spherical shift knob in manual-transmission floor-shift applications. (T-HANDLES have also been featured

HURST **T-handle**

**213**

on some PERFORMANCE automatic-transmission floor shifters.) The T-HANDLE's design provides a secure grip, reducing the possibility of missed shifts. The overall appearance of a vertical shift lever capped with a horizontally positioned handle accounts for the T-HANDLE's name. During the late 1960s and early 1970s MUSCLE CAR era, several manufacturers featured the Hurst T-HANDLE as original equipment on high-performance models.

**There's no substitute for cubic inches.** (also **There's no replacement for displacement.**) Traditional HOT ROD PERFORMANCE axiom positing that no amount of modification to a small-displacement engine can produce the level of torque and horsepower naturally inherent to a large-displacement motor.

MID-1950S **thingie**

**thingie** (also **thingy** or **thingey**) *n.* Early expression for any vehicle purpose-built or extensively modified to provide maximum DRAG racing performance. Term experienced its strongest popularity during organized DRAG racing's formative years (early to mid-1950s), and was later displaced by the expressions DRAGSTER, SLINGSHOT, RAIL, etc. Often appearing crude and ungainly, a THINGIE generally consisted of a narrowed automotive frame, the minimal vestiges of sheetmetal body panels, a centrally located single-seat driver configuration, and a maximum-performance drivetrain. While some THINGIES were adapted from more-established race-vehicle types (LAKES MODIFIEDS, sprint cars, etc.) many were constructed entirely from scratch.

**thrash 1.** *v.* To work in an intense or frenzied manner to effect major repairs or improvements on a DRAG racing vehicle between ROUNDS of competition. **2.** (also **thrash on**) *v.* To drive any vehicle in a highly aggressive or abusive manner.

**three deuces** *n.* Any high-performance induction system featuring three TWO-BARREL carburetors (see CARB). Popular expression was adopted by Chevrolet in print advertisements for its tri-CARBed 427-CID 1967 Corvette models (see 'VETTE), in which CHEVY proclaimed: "Deuces wild! Talk about a winning hand! THREE DEUCES to a FULL-HOUSE 427, the Turbo-Jet V8's got it, cold."

**three ducks** *n.* Early (generally 1940s and 1950s era) HOT RODDER's expression for any high-performance induction system featuring three TWO-BARREL carburetors (see CARB).

**three on the tree** *n.* Any three-speed manual transmission featuring a steering-column-mounted shifter. During the 1940s, American manufacturers transitioned from manual transmission floor-shift mechanisms to steering-column shifting. As this was perceived to be the modern TRICK SETUP, many upscale early-model HOT RODS were converted to column shifting during the late 1940s and early 1950s. Over time, the inherently awkward, indirect nature of the column shifter was perceived as a detriment to performance. From the late 1950s to the present day, the quick, positive attributes of the floor shifter have made it the favored SETUP in all high-performance applications.

**three-pedal** *adj.* Relating to any manual-transmission system/assembly or any complete manual-transmission-equipped vehicle. Example: "Yeah, I know that the automatics are quicker, but I guess I'm just a diehard THREE-PEDAL man."

**three twos**, see THREE DEUCES

**three-quarter cam** (also **three-quarter race cam** or **three-quarter race grind**) *n.* Traditional expression (most popular during and prior to the 1960s) for a camshaft (see CAM) GRIND with dimensions measuring approximately 75 percent of those of a FULL-RACE camshaft. A good STREET PERFORMANCE CAM.

**three-window** (also **three-window coupe** or **three-pane**) *n.* Any vintage COUPE model featuring three windows, not including its windshield. Term is most often used to describe COUPES of the 1930s era, a time when manufacturers commonly produced both THREE-WINDOW and FIVE-WINDOW models. THREE-WINDOW COUPES are generally perceived as more desirable than their FIVE-WINDOW counterparts due to their inherently cleaner styling and often rarer status. When first introduced, THREE-WINDOWS often represented the high-end, or "deluxe," model within a given manufacturer's line. The THREE-WINDOW COUPES produced by Ford Motor Company from 1932 through 1936 are among the most popular hot rodding foundations of all time.

**three-window**
1932 FORD COUPE HOT ROD

**throw in the label** *v.* To run a 100 percent NITRO FUEL load in a DRAG racing vehicle. Derived and extended from the traditional DRAG racing expression TIP THE CAN (which suggests a high percentage of NITRO fuel), THROW IN THE LABEL implies that *everything* must go into the racer's fuel tank, including the label from the can, to facilitate an all-out BANZAI RUN.

**throw out the anchor**, see HANG OUT THE LAUNDRY

**thumper 1.** (also **thumper cam**) *n.* Any radical, high-performance camshaft, producing a rough, "thumping" idle. **2.** *n.* Any loud and intensely powerful PERFORMANCE engine or vehicle (especially one with a radical, thumping idle).

**Thunderbolt** *n.* Intermediate Fairlane series-based DRAG racing vehicle produced by FoMoCo during the 1964 model year. Prior to the 1964 racing season, Ford had experienced consistent difficulties in keeping pace with its DRAGSTRIP competitors. Although Ford's motors were fundamentally capable, their full-size racers were just too heavy to win with any regularity. For 1964, FoMoCo addressed the problem head on by installing their maximum-performance engine types into mid-size Ford and compact Mercury products. Actual THUNDERBOLT PERFORMANCE modifications were subcontracted to Dearborn Steel Tubing, where Ford's powerful 427 HIGH RISER engines were fitted to the Fairlane SEDAN's chassis. Additional THUNDERBOLT modifications achieved severe weight reduction through the use of fiberglass (see 'GLASS) front fenders, TEARDROP HOOD, doors, and bumper. Lexan plastic windows (except the windshield) and the effective gutting of the Fairlane's interior completed the lightening treatment. Surpassing the NHRA minimum requirement of 100 cars produced, the THUNDERBOLTS were allowed to compete in the popular Super Stock class. With their favorable power-to-weight ratio finally achieved, THUNDERBOLTS proved highly competitive throughout the 1964 season, frequently recording ETs in the mid-11-second range.

**tight** *adj.* Relating to either an exceptionally high compression ratio or an engine featuring an exceptionally high compression ratio (see SQUEEZE).

tilt frontend ON
1950 AUSTIN GASSER

**tilt frontend** *n.* Any auto body FRONTEND (front fenders, hood, grill assembly, etc.) configured in such a way as to pivot or tilt forward as a complete unit, providing easy access to a vehicle's engine and/or chassis components. A TILT FRONTEND may be constructed from modified OEM sheetmetal panels but more often consists of a one-piece, lightweight (usually fiberglass [see 'GLASS]) AFTERMARKET unit. Although TILT FRONTENDS are sometimes fitted to STREET MACHINES, the type is most often featured on competition-only DRAG vehicles. TILT FRONTENDS initially gained popularity during the mid-1960s, with their period of strongest favor extending through the 1970s.

**time** *n.* Traditional HOT RODDER's reference to a racing vehicle's recorded *speed.* Expression is derived from the fact that (in both DRAG and LAND-SPEED RACING) a measured speed is calculated by the *time* that it takes for a vehicle to cover a prescribed distance. Example: "We were definitely off our normal pace today, with a best TIME of only 117 miles per hour."

**tin 1.** *n.* Any STOCK or custom-fabricated automotive sheetmetal panel. Term may apply to any sheet-steel or sheet-aluminum panel employed as a part of an external body surface, body substructure, or vehicle interior. **2.** *n.* Any complete steel automotive body, but especially referring to a body of early manufacture (see VINTAGE TIN). **3.** *n.* Early DRAG racer's expression for any trophies awarded to race winners.

**tin Indian** *n.* Any complete automobile or automotive component produced by the Pontiac division of General Motors. Term derived from the Native American portrayed on the division's emblems and logo from 1926 through 1955.

**tinworm**, see BODY ROT

**tip the can** (also **tip the jug** or **tip the bucket**) *v*. In a DRAG racing application, to run a very high percentage of nitromethane racing FUEL (see NITRO). Term most popular during the 1950s and 1960s. Example: "We're gonna really need to TIP THE CAN to make it through this next ROUND."

**tire fryer** *n*. Any high-performance HOT ROD or STREET MACHINE capable of BURNing RUBBER with ease.

**tits**, see BUMPER TITS

**TJ tuck 'n' roll** (also **Tijuana tuck** or **TJ tuck**) (TJ pronounced as separate letters) *n*. Any custom TUCK 'N' ROLL as installed by the auto upholstery shops of Tijuana, Mexico ("TJ" being a popular slang term for Tijuana). As a border town, Tijuana has always been reasonably accessible to California HOT RODDERS. Despite rumors of dubious workmanship and especially materials, the promise of inexpensive, negotiable pricing has lured many RODDERS south of the border for their upholstery work. The renowned TJ TUCK 'N' ROLL experienced its greatest popularity during the 1960s.

**Tommy the Greek teardrops** *n*. Distinctive pinstripe accent as popularized by the legendary Northern California striper Tom "Tommy the Greek" Hrones (1914–2002). Hrones' stylized TEARDROPS appear as a uniform series of very narrow, inverted teardrop-shaped stripes. Frequently, a set of parallel teardrops is diagonally canted and positioned near the end of a dashboard or exterior automotive body panel. Teardrop sets are also sometimes presented in a symmetrical grouping with a number of smaller stripes flanking a single central teardrop.

Tommy the Greek teardrops

**the ton** *n*. One hundred miles per hour. Example: "I finally ran the TON with my ol' FLATMOTOR."

**toolbox latches** *n*. Custom hood-latching system as often featured on vintage-bodied late-1940s through early-1950s era HOT RODS. Two-piece metal latches of the type commonly used on toolboxes were employed to join hood sides to a custom one-piece hood top.

**top chop** *n*. Any radical body modification that involves removing a horizontal cross-section from the GREENHOUSE area, followed by reattaching the roof to the vehicle (see also CHOPPED).

**top end 1.** *n*. The maximum speed attainable by a given vehicle. Example: "What's the TOP END after the gear change?" **2.** *n*. The uppermost part of any given engine's operational RPM range (as differentiated from BOTTOM END or MIDRANGE). **3.** (also **topside**) *n*. The upper components of any engine, most notably its cylinder-head (see HEADS) assemblies. **4.** see BIG END

**topender** (also **top-ender**) *n.* Any vehicle capable of very high TOP END speeds, sometimes at the expense of good all-around performance or DRIVEABILITY.

**Top Fuel 1.** *n.* Ultimate-performance DRAG racing class consisting of purpose-built DRAGSTERS burning nitromethane (see NITRO) for FUEL. Since their 1950s introduction, FUEL DRAGSTERS have consistently been DRAG racing's top-performing vehicles. **2.** (also **Top Fueler**) *n.* Any individual DRAGSTER competing in a TOP FUEL racing class.

**toploader** (also **top loader**) **1.** *n.* Ford high-performance, four-speed manual transmission featuring a distinctive top-loading configuration. With the TOPLOADER design, internal transmission components are accessed or "loaded" through an opening in the top of the case rather than the more common side-loading method (when in operation, the TOPLOADER's case opening is covered by a removable plate). Ford's TOPLOADER configuration offers the advantage of a stronger, more rigid overall case structure and eliminates the problem of side-mounted access covers working loose through shift-linkage action. The exceptionally durable TOPLOADER was commonly featured in OEM Ford high-performance and MUSCLE CAR applications from 1964 through 1973. As a testament to the original FoMoCo design, NASCAR's modern Jerico-brand four-speeds are directly evolved from production Ford TOPLOADER transmissions. **2.** *n.* Any manual transmission featuring a top-loading configuration.

**Topo** (TOE-poe) *n.* Any Fiat Topolino (Italian for "little mouse") compact automobile as originally produced for the 1936 through 1948 model years. (Simca of France concurrently produced a version of the Italian Topolino, introduced in 1936 as the Simca Cinq.) Topolino/Simca COUPE bodies were commonly employed in late-1950s through 1960s-era gas and FUEL ALTERED DRAG racing applications, where they were strongly favored for their small size and light weight. During the mid-1950s, racer Jim "Jazzy" Nelson significantly popularized the Fiat body's usage with the exceptional performance of his FLATHEAD MERC-powered Topolino COUPE. Early 1960s TOPO DRAG cars featured OEM steel bodies teamed with purpose-built tube chassis, but by the mid-1960s fiberglass (see 'GLASS) replica bodies generally replaced the heavier STOCK units. Though still in occasional competition usage, Topolino bodies were largely supplanted by ROADSTER (generally Model T Ford [see T-BONE]) replica bodies during the 1970s. Note: When contemplating the DRAG racing permutations of the Topolino, with horsepower levels often measured in the four-figure range, it is interesting to consider that in STOCK configuration the TOPO was motivated by a 569cc four-cylinder engine producing all of 13 BHP.

the **top of** a given gear *n*. The maximum practical or effective engine RPM in any specified gear. Example: "I caught him at the TOP OF third and had him by a length IN THE LIGHTS."

**torch** *n*. Any competition vehicle (see JET or JETSTER) propelled solely by the thrust of a jet or rocket engine. The first recognized use of jet power in a hot rodding application came on the night of January 4, 1947, when a group of Southern California RODDERS tested an experimental jet-propelled race car on ROSAMOND dry lake. The rudimentary vehicle consisted of a bare and appreciably STOCK early automotive chassis with a 15-foot, liquid-propane-fueled tube affixed as a power source. The vehicle's driver, Bob Yeakel, wore a full asbestos suit but was still slightly burned by the power unit while underway. The car "idled" across the lake bed at approximately 35 miles per hour during its two trial passes.

**torch job**, see FLAME JOB

**torpedoes** (also **torpedo headlights**) *n*. Any of the exotic, teardrop-shaped headlights produced by the Edmunds & Jones Corporation of Detroit, Michigan, during the 1920s. Officially designated E&J Type 20 headlights, TORPEDOES were offered in AFTERMARKET form and as original equipment on several fashionable production models (significantly including the Kissel Gold Bug Speedster and the Jordan Playboy ROADSTER). Original E&J HEADLIGHTS featured a cast-aluminum three-piece body, black enamel finish (with nickel-plated rim), and a triangular brass identification tag. The most recognized instance of E&J HEADLIGHTS in an early rodding application came in 1953 with the renowned Frank Mack ROADSTER. Mack's FENDERLESS, track-nosed 1927 Ford featured genuine 1927 Jordan TORPEDOES for lighting. While experiencing moderate favor during the 1950s, the E&J HEADLIGHTS' greatest popularity has come when fitted to RETRO RODS and NOSTALGIA RODS of the early twenty-first century. Modern demand is such that several versions are currently being offered in reproduction form.

**torpedo** HEADLIGHT

**torque monster** *n*. Any engine producing exceptionally high levels of torque. Example: "With those big inches, the new motor's gotta be a real TORQUE MONSTER."

**torquey** (TORK-ee) *adj*. Possessing abundant torque. Term may be used to describe a complete engine or specific engine component.

**track nose** *n*. Custom, streamlined replacement for the STOCK GRILL SHELL assembly of an early-model automobile. Employed for improved aerodynamics and/or appearance, TRACK NOSES feature a smooth, rounded style and, typically, a well-integrated oval grill opening and insert. While originally popularized on early TRACK ROADSTERS, TRACK

**track nose** ON
1934 FORD COUPE

NOSES were commonly fitted to DRAG and LAND-SPEED RACING vehicles as well as some street driven HOT RODS during the 1940s and 1950s.

**track roadster** (also **track job**) **1.** *n.* Type of custom fabricated circle-track racing vehicle featuring a STOCK-based racing chassis and early-model (usually pre-1935) FENDERLESS ROADSTER body. Typically elemental and often relatively crudely constructed, TRACK ROADSTERS were treated to an engine HOP UP, protective NERF BARS, and sometimes a streamlined custom TRACK NOSE in place of a STOCK GRILL SHELL. TRACK ROADSTERS experienced outstanding popularity on America's dirt ovals during the late 1940s and early 1950s, after which public interest generally shifted toward organized, late-model STOCK CAR racing. **2.** *n.* Any modern HOT ROD or STREET ROD constructed with the look or style of an original TRACK ROADSTER.

**track T** *n.* Any TRACK ROADSTER featuring a Model T Ford (see T-BONE) body.

**trade paint** *v.* During the course of aggressive racing action, for one auto body to contact or rub against another, resulting in an exchange of body paint between vehicles. Term generally applies to full-bodied STOCK CARS in circle-track or ROUNDY-ROUND competition.

**trailer** someone, see PUT someone ON THE TRAILER

**trailer queen** *n.* Derogatory term for any HOT ROD, STREET ROD, or CUSTOM CAR that is not driven to rodding events, but is rather transported by trailer. Term generally refers to a vehicle that is street-legal and fully functional but is so pristine in nature that its owner is reluctant to expose it to the hazards of everyday road use.

**tranny** (also **trannie** or **trans**) *n.* Any automotive transmission.

**tranny drop**, see NEUTRAL DROP

the **traps** *n.* On any DRAGSTRIP, the area in which the top speed of the competing vehicles is measured. In order to calculate speed, two measurements must be taken by separate timing devices near the track's finish line. The first timer is typically positioned 66 feet before the actual finish line and the second exactly at the finish line. The area between the two timers is known as the TRAPS.

**tree 1.** see CHRISTMAS TREE **2.** *n.* Any vehicle's steering column.

**tree chopping** *n.* The occurrence of a DRAG racing vehicle accidentally running into a track's CHRISTMAS TREE starting system. High-powered DRAG cars sometimes lose control at the immediate outset of a race, veer toward the track's centerline, and come in contact with the CHRISTMAS TREE. While potentially dangerous, TREE CHOPPING is also troublesome, since an event's racing may be postponed or curtailed by damage to the equipment.

**tribal flames** *n.* Custom paint treatment (see FLAMES) featuring sharp reversed hooks or barbs in conjunction with traditional sinuous rearward LICKS. TRIBAL FLAMES have experienced moderate popularity in STREET ROD and, oftentimes, SPORT TRUCK applications during the late 1990s and into the twenty-first century.

tribal flames ON
HIGHBOY ROADSTER

**tri-carb** *adj.* Relating to any high-performance induction system featuring three TWO-BARREL carburetors (see CARB).

**trick** *adj.* Relating to any vehicle or vehicle component that is custom, unique, or one-off in nature, as well as exceptionally well engineered and constructed. Example: "My buddy machined me this TRICK dash insert from BILLET."

**trick out** *v.* To extensively modify any vehicle or vehicle system in a custom or exotic fashion. Expression carries with it a slight bias toward aesthetics or appearance rather than engineering and practical function. Example: "As soon as I get the cash together, I'm gonna TRICK OUT the interior with a CHOPPED WHEEL, full TUCK 'N' ROLL, pinstriped dash, and bullet knobs."

**tri-five Chevy** (also **tri-Chevy** or **tri-year Chevy**) *n.* Any Chevrolet passenger car produced during the three model years of 1955 through 1957. Though entirely new for 1955, CHEVY's passenger cars were moderately "facelifted" for 1956 and 1957, leaving strong similarities between the three model years. TRI-FIVE CHEVYS have maintained exceptional and perennial favor among hot rodders and DRAG racers from their introduction to the present day due to the type's classic styling, overall availability, inherent simplicity, and status as the first model years offering the SMALL-BLOCK Chevrolet V8 engine (see MOUSE). The tri-five's three-year status ("tri") combined with its 1950s-era of manufacture ("five") accounts for its popular name.

tri-five Chevy
1957 CHEVROLET NOMAD
STREET MACHINE

**trim job** *n.* Any automotive interior upholstery, but most often referring to a custom, one-off interior as applied to a HOT ROD or CUSTOM CAR.

**triple-black** *adj.* Relating to any MUSCLE CAR or STREET MACHINE featuring a black exterior paint scheme, black interior upholstery, and a black passenger compartment top (either a convertible soft top or fixed, decorative vinyl top). Note: While other colors may substitute as a part of this phrase (e.g., triple-white, triple-red, etc.), TRIPLE-BLACK is the most common usage.

**triple manifold** (also **triple intake**, **triple**, or **triplet**) *n.* Any high-performance intake manifold configured for three carburetors (see

CARB). Term most often refers to a triple TWO-BARREL carburetor induction system from hot rodding's early FLATHEAD era. Sharp Speed Equipment advertised its high-performance, three-CARB manifold as a TRIPLET during the late 1940s.

**tri-pot** (also **tri-pots**), see THREE DEUCES

**tri-power** *n.* Any high-performance induction system featuring three TWO-BARREL carburetors (see CARB).

**Tri-Power** *n.* Pontiac trade name for its FACTORY-produced induction systems featuring three TWO-BARREL carburetors (see CARB) and offered for the 1957 through 1966 model years.

**trombones** *n.* Traditional East Coast expression for any custom or AFTERMARKET hairpin-style radius rods (see HAIRPINS). Type's name is derived from its similarity in appearance to an actual trombone's slide.

**tromp on it** *v.* To aggressively and fully depress a vehicle's accelerator pedal.

**trucker** *n.* Any customized-van owner, builder, or driver participating in the 1970s-era VAN CRAZE. Term was oftentimes preferred over "vanner" within the 1970s VAN CRAZE culture.

**truck-in** *n.* Any large-scale outdoor gathering of customized vans occurring during the 1970s VAN CRAZE. TRUCK-INS were generally presented over a period of several days and offered such informal activities as VAN PULLS, VANKHANAS, Frisbee tosses, beer-chugging contests, VAN CRAMS, and volleyball tournaments.

**Truck-Ins** *n.* An annual series of immense, national van events presented in various central U.S. locations beginning in 1973.

**tub** *n.* Any PHAETON model automobile. Name is derived from the type's likeness to a bathtub when top is lowered or removed altogether.

**tubbed** *adj.* Modified by the installation of WHEEL TUBS.

**tube axle** *n.* Any front automotive axle made of tubular steel. TUBE AXLES are often preferred in rodding and DRAG racing applications for their cleaner appearance and lighter weight as compared with similar BEAM AXLES. The first TUBE AXLES commonly used on HOT RODS were those originally found on 1937 through 1940 Ford V8-60-model production vehicles. The V8-60 axle featured the shallow contour common to STOCK axles of its manufacture era, but differed from BEAM AXLES in that it could not be easily dropped through a heating and bending process. HOT RODS incorporating the V8-60 TUBE AXLE necessarily used different means to achieve the lowered FRONTEND preferred in the HOT ROD look, oftentimes incorporating a SUICIDE FRONTEND. Beginning in the 1960s and continuing to the present day, AFTERMARKET-produced TUBE AXLES have been made abundantly available with appropriate sizes, shapes, and drops integrated during original manufacture.

**tube grill** *n.* Custom automotive grill type featuring uniform horizontal rows of small-diameter brightmetal tubing. TUBE GRILLS have experienced moderate popularity in a variety of CUSTOM CAR and STREET MACHINE applications from the 1950s to the present day.

tube grill ON
1956 FORD CUSTOM

**tubs**, see WHEEL TUBS

**tuck 'n' roll** (also **tuck and roll**) *n.* Type of custom auto upholstery featuring a simple, most often parallel, rolled and pleated pattern. The style experienced its strongest popularity during the 1950s and 1960s but has returned to favor with the RETRO ROD and NOSTALGIA ROD movements of the 1990s and early twenty-first century.

tuck 'n' roll UPHOLSTERY

**Tudor** *n.* Ford Motor Company's traditional designation for its two-door SEDAN models. The stately name was introduced by Ford in 1915 along with the first Model T (see T-BONE) two-door SEDAN. Early-model Ford TUDOR SEDANS have experienced moderate to high popularity as foundations for HOT ROD, competition, and STREET ROD modification. While Ford used the similar Fordor name to describe its contemporary four-door SEDANS, the models never achieved significant favor in PERFORMANCE or hot rodding applications.

1932 FORD **Tudor** DRAG CAR

**tunes** *n.* Any vehicle's stereo or sound system, as distinguished from the more common usage referring to actual songs.

**tunneled** *adj.* Relating to any component that has been very deeply recessed into a "tunnel-like" cavity in a vehicle's exterior body panels. As a custom styling element, tunneling is most often applied to headlights or multiple antennas.

tunneled ANTENNAS

**tunnel ram** *n.* Any high-performance V8 intake manifold employing exceptionally tall, vertical intake runners. The TUNNEL RAM design is noted for its ability to produce maximum, high-RPM horsepower in NATURALLY ASPIRATED race engines. TUNNEL RAMS have also experienced moderate favor in STREET MACHINE and STREET ROD applications exclusively for their racy appearance. Though sometimes equipped with a single FOUR-BARREL CARB or fuel-injection unit, TUNNEL RAMS most often accommodate DUAL QUADS. The Ram Chargers' *High & Mighty* Plymouth coupe (see JACKED-UP) is generally accepted as having introduced the dual-QUAD, TUNNEL RAM concept. Constructed in the late 1950s, the car's crude-but-effective INTAKE featured a custom-fabricated sheetmetal plenum and long rubber hoses acting as intake runners. An

**223**

early "production" TUNNEL RAM-type manifold was created by Pontiac in 1963 and used in the division's various racing programs. Pontiac's aluminum "bathtub" INTAKE (so-named for its large bathtub-shaped plenum chamber) mounted dual Carter AFB carburetors and featured a two-piece design with relatively long and tall runners. In 1968, AFTERMARKET manufacturer Edelbrock introduced a tall vertical PERFORMANCE manifold, significantly naming its product "Tunnel Ram." While other manufacturers would produce similar manifolds, each with its own trade name, Edelbrock's designation came to be universally applied by RODDERS and remains generic to the type.

**tupperware** *n.* Derogatory term for any fiberglass (see 'GLASS) automotive body or body component. Name derived from the popular brand of plastic household products.

**turbo** *n.* Any automotive turbocharger. While, in principle, a turbocharger works in much the same manner as a supercharger (forcing air/fuel mixture into a running engine to increase its efficiency and produce greater power levels), the two types differ significantly by their drive modes. The term "supercharger" generally relates to a unit that is mechanically driven by an engine's crankshaft. A turbocharger is powered, rather, by the flow of spent gasses as they pass through an engine's exhaust system.

**turn a wrench** *v.* To perform automotive mechanics on a very basic and fundamental level. Example: "Truth is, he's really not all that much of a mechanic, but when we need an extra hand he can get in there and TURN A WRENCH with the rest of the crew."

**turn-key 1.** *adj.* Relating to any vehicle that is absolutely complete, roadworthy, and ready to be driven. Term generally describes a custom-fabricated vehicle, distinguishing it from an unfinished or incomplete product. Example: "I don't want to have to finish up someone else's project. The next time I buy something it'll be TURN-KEY." **2.** *n.* Any vehicle that is absolutely complete, roadworthy, and ready to be driven. [Rare]

**turnpike cruisers**, see CRUISER SKIRTS

**turtle deck** *n.* Distinctive trunk type as featured on various early passenger cars, but especially relating to the trunks of mid-1920s and earlier Model T Fords (see T-BONE). Affixed to the rear of an automobile's main body structure, the diminutive TURTLE DECK'S sweeping lines remotely resemble those of an actual turtle shell. TURTLE DECKS are sometimes featured on the popular T-BUCKET-type HOT RODS as well as T-bodied DRAG RACE vehicles.

**turtle deck** ON MODEL T DRAG ROADSTER

**T-V8** (pronounced as separate letters) *n.* Any Model T Ford (see T-BONE) modified by the installation of a V8 engine. (Model T's were factory-produced with FLATHEAD four-cylinders exclusively.) Term was most often used from the 1930s through the 1950s to describe an original T-chassis vehicle with a FLATHEAD Ford V8 swapped in, or a 1930s-vintage chassis equipped with FLATHEAD engine and earlier Model T body. The term T-V8 is seldom used in reference to more modern T-BUCKET-type HOT RODS.

**twelve-port** *n.* Any high-performance Chevrolet or GMC six-cylinder HEAD featuring a custom TWELVE-PORT design (see HORNING and WAYNE).

**twice pipes** *n.* Any automotive dual exhaust system, but most often relating to a dual system servicing a high-performance six-cylinder engine.

**twin 1.** *n.* Any DRAGSTER equipped with two engines in either an inline or side-by-side configuration, a design most commonly employed by gasoline-burning SLINGSHOTS from 1959 through the early 1970s. The famed Bean Bandits HOT ROD club is generally credited with the creation of the first TWIN DRAGSTER in 1951. Their relatively primitive RAIL featured inline Ford FLATHEAD V8 motors in front of a narrowed and shortened ROADSTER body. Interestingly, the car could be quickly converted to run in a different class by the addition of a one-piece, FULL-FENDERED Model A (see A-BONE) SEDAN body. Throughout the 1960s, a series of BLOWN SMALL-BLOCK CHEVY-powered TWINS were campaigned by racer John Peters, with all post-1963 versions being dubbed *Freight Train* (an early-1970s *Train* iteration was retrofitted with twin Chrysler HEMIS). Peters' *Freight Train*s achieved the greatest and most consistent success of any dual-engined DRAGSTERS. **2.** *n.* Any LAND-SPEED RACING vehicle (typically of a STREAMLINER type) powered by two engines.

THE *FREIGHT TRAIN* **twin**[1]

**twin pots** *n.* Any induction system featuring two carburetors (see CARB) but most often describing a high-performance 1940s- through 1950s-era FLATHEAD Ford V8 twin TWO-BARREL SETUP.

**twin quads,** see DUAL QUADS

**twin spots** *n.* Any two spotlights (see SPOTS) mounted to a single vehicle, one affixed to each A-PILLAR. In the interest of aesthetic balance, most CUSTOM CARS feature twin spotlights rather than a single driver's-side unit.

**twin-stick** *adj.* Traditional expression relating to any double-overhead camshaft (see CAM) engine configuration.

**twin-throat** (also **twin-throat carb**), see TWO-BARREL

**twist** *n.* Torque, as produced by any engine.

**twisted hemi** *n.* Any Boss 429 high-performance engine produced by Ford Motor Company during the 1969 and 1970 model years (see Boss). The type's name is derived from its modified-HEMI configuration resulting in peculiar valve angles.

**two-barrel** (also **two-barrel carb**) *n.* Any carburetor (see CARB) featuring a two-venturi configuration. In high-performance applications, TWO-BARRELS are most often used as a part of a multiple-carburetor induction system.

**two club**, see 200 MPH CLUB

**two fours**, see DUAL QUADS

**typewriter** (also **typewriter drive**), see BUTTONS

# U

**uncorked** *adj.* Relating to the running of an engine in an "open-exhaust" condition, with exhaust gasses released to the atmosphere immediately after exiting exhaust manifolds or HEADERS. Term is most often used to describe a vehicle equipped with a full, muffled exhaust system, but which is running nonetheless in an open configuration expressly to enhance race performance. A full exhaust system may be UNCORKED through the use of built-in exhaust CUTOUTS (DUMPS, LAKES PLUGS, etc.) or simply by detaching its exhaust head pipes from its HEADER collectors.

**undersquare** *adj.* Relating to any engine with a STROKE length longer than the diameter of its cylinder BORE, a configuration noted for producing abundant LOW END torque. Although rarely manufactured in modern V8 form, UNDERSQUARE engines are nonetheless occasionally used in high-performance applications. Pontiac's 455-CID, Oldsmobile's 455-CID, and Cadillac's 500-CID production engines all feature an UNDERSQUARE design.

**unwind 1.** *v.* To aggressively and fully exploit an engine to its absolute maximum performance level. Term relates the actualization of engine power to the discharge of energy when a tightly wound spring is released. **2.** *v.* To drive any vehicle to its highest possible TOP END speed, pressing for absolute maximum performance. Example: "I'll never forget taking that brand-new CHEVY out to the Great Highway and really letting it UNWIND."

**urge** *n.* Power. Horsepower or torque as produced by any engine.

**urged**, see STOKED

**ute** (YUTE) **1.** *n.* Any Australian passenger car/pickup truck hybrid model as produced from 1934 to the present. Term may be derived from the type's first officially designated name (COUPE Utility), to "utility truck," or simply to "utility." Substantially differing from the conventional pickup trucks of their time, the early automobile-based UTES foreshadowed the American Ranchero (see 'CHERO) and El Camino (see CAMINO) models introduced in the late 1950s. Beginning during the 1930s and 1940s, UTES were produced in Australia by a wide variety of manufacturers, significantly including Ford, Chevrolet, and Dodge. These vintage UTES have long been a popular part of Australia's substantial hot rodding and street rodding scenes and, more recently, have gained moderate favor in American street rodding applications. Unlike their now-defunct American counterparts, UTES still maintain a strong niche in the Australian new-car marketplace. Currently available high-performance models include Ford's Boss 290 V8-powered FPV Pursuit and General Motors' Holden SS with standard independent rear suspension and high-output 5.7-liter fuel-injected V8. Interestingly, a number of Australian manufacturers actually produced open or "ROADSTER" UTE versions during the 1930s, similar in concept and yet distinctly different from early-model American ROADSTER PICKUP trucks. **2.** *n.* Any modern American sport utility vehicle (SUV) customized in a STREET MACHINE fashion.

1946 CHEVROLET **ute**[1]
STREET ROD

# V

**V6** (also **V-6**) *n.* Any six-cylinder automotive engine featuring two separate banks of three cylinders and configured in the overall shape of the letter "V." While never achieving the immense popularity of larger-displacement V8 engines, V6s have nonetheless experienced moderate success in a number of PERFORMANCE and rodding applications. Based on the rear-drive Regal SEDAN, Buick's turbocharged (see TURBO) V6-powered Grand National models were the top-performing American MUSCLE CARS of the 1980s. The type culminated in the rare GNX of 1987, with its turbocharged and intercooled engine providing 276 BHP and mid-13-second quarter-mile times. During the early 1990s, V6-powered GMC Syclone and Typhoon light trucks (see MUSCLE TRUCK) delivered similar performance numbers. From the late 1970s to the present day, compact and relatively efficient V6 engines have been commonly adapted to mild-mannered STREET RODS as well.

**V8** (also **V-8**) *n.* Any eight-cylinder automotive engine featuring two separate banks of four cylinders and configured in the overall shape of the letter "V." The V8 has been the dominant engine design in virtually all American hot rodding, street rodding, and DRAG racing applications from the late 1940s to the present day.

**V8-60** *n.* Unique, scaled-down FLATHEAD Ford V8 engine created as an economy-minded alternative to Ford's concurrently produced full-size FLATHEAD offerings. Produced in America from the 1937 through 1940 model years, the V8-60 featured a diminutive 136-CID, 17-stud head (see HEADS) layout and the 60-BHP rating that inspired its name. In rodding applications, the V8-60 is best known for its successes in late-1940s midget circle-track racing. Running on nitromethane (see NITRO), speed merchant Vic Edelbrock's V8-60-powered midgets proved highly competitive, breaking the Offenhauser racing engine's midget-car dynasty.

**V8-60 axle** *n.* Any of the unique tubular axles featured as standard equipment on Ford's 1937 through 1940 V8-60-equipped vehicles (see TUBE AXLE).

**V8 Vega**
1971 BALDWIN-MOTION
"PHASE III"

**V8 Vega** *n.* Any Chevrolet Vega four-cylinder compact model as produced from the 1971 through 1977 model years and featuring a swapped-in Chevrolet SMALL-BLOCK or BIG-BLOCK V8 engine. Beginning in the 1970s, a number of AFTERMARKET manufacturers offered comprehensive V8 conversion kits for the Vega, making for a popular and common STREET MACHINE type. The Vega's original running gear suffered from notoriously poor engineering, most notably a sleeveless aluminum cylinder block (see BLOCK) that was prone to excessive and premature wear. Even before the end of the model's production run, Vega body SHELLS were already becoming cheap and plentiful, making the lightweight car a logical and practical choice for PERFORMANCE modification. During the early 1970s, the renowned Motion Performance speed emporium extensively modified a number of Vegas to include potent V8 power. The resulting Motion "Phase III" V8 VEGAS were sold to the general public through the PERFORMANCE-oriented Baldwin Chevrolet dealership of Long Island, New York.

**valve-in-block** *adj.* Relating to any FLATHEAD-type engine.

**van cram** (also **van kram** or **van stuff**) *n.* Contest to determine how many adult bodies could be "crammed" into a standard-sized van within a 45-second period. VAN CRAMS were a popular activity at TRUCK-IN type events during the 1970s VAN CRAZE, and a VAN CRAM record of 50 people was set at the 1976 National Street Van Association (NSVA) TRUCK-IN, with winners awarded halter tops as prizes.

the **van craze** *n.* Movement or trend consisting of an incomparable level of popularity for customized vans and van-related activities (most notably, car/van shows and TRUCK-IN or VAN-IN social gatherings). Gaining its initial momentum during the early 1970s, the VAN CRAZE lasted with varying intensity throughout the remainder of the decade. Customized vans of the era were most often based on American-made, full-sized vehicles as manufactured during the 1960s and 1970s. Common exterior modifications included: **a.** Flamboyant custom paint schemes, including multicolored GRAPHICS, lettered names, and elaborate MURALS; **b.** Round PORTHOLE or custom-shaped windows; **c.** BOLT-ON fiberglass (see 'GLASS) FENDER FLARES and roof and CHIN SPOILERS; **d.** Chrome SIDE PIPES; and **e.** Custom wheels and tires. Interior spaces were outfitted with: **a.** Overall shag carpeting; **b.** Pivoting captain's chairs; **c.** CB radios; **d.** Stereo sound systems; **e.** Wall and ceiling mirrors; **f.** Draperies; **g.** Chandeliers; **h.** Built-in beds; and **i.** Refrigerators, bars, and television sets. By 1976, major American manufacturers attempted to capitalize on the trend by FACTORY-producing vans with similar features. Dodge claimed that its "Street Van" was "the first van that comes FACTORY-customized," while Ford maintained its "Cruising Van" was "the industry's first FACTORY-built completely customized van!" In addition to innumerable local van clubs, several national van organizations also flourished during the craze, among them the NSVA (National Street Van Association), the NAVA (North American Van Association), and the NAVO (National Association of Van Owners). During the VAN CRAZE's 1976 peak, *HOT ROD* magazine actually dedicated a monthly department exclusively to van-related topics. Titled "Van Stand," the feature included a regular comic strip, "Dan Man and His Van," about a TRUCKER and his many van-related adventures. Since falling from favor during the early 1980s, the customized vans of the 1970s have generally been perceived as being in poor taste by HOT RODDERS and CUSTOMIZERS, as well as the general public.

**van craze**
MID-1970S ERA CUSTOMIZED
FORD VAN

**van-in**, see TRUCK-IN

**vankhana** (van-KAH-nah) *n.* Popular event as practiced during the TRUCK-IN type gatherings of the 1970s-era VAN CRAZE. Consisting of a timed contest over a prescribed course, a VANKHANA tested van performance and driver skill with elements of slalom, backing, and parking. Term is adapted from the expression "gymkhana," which typically describes games on horseback involving intense skill, quickness, and agility over a very tight, closed course. (Gymkhana may also relate to similar games as practiced with motorcycles or automobiles.)

**van pull** *n.* A tug-of-war contest between two competing vans, with the vehicles chained together back-to-back and pulling in opposite directions for a period of 30 seconds. Held on either dirt or pavement (where rear tires would typically be destroyed by excessive rubber burning), VAN PULLS were a popular activity at 1970s-era TRUCK-IN events.

**V'd spreader bar** (also **Vee'd spreader bar**) *n.* Custom SPREADER BAR featuring a subtle, point-forward "V" shape. Have experienced moderate popularity on FENDERLESS HOT RODS from the 1940s to the present day.

**velocity stacks** *n.* Any custom, high-performance venturis functioning to increase the speed or "velocity" of air prior to its being introduced into a running engine's carburetors (see CARB) or fuel-injection unit.

**ventilated** (also **vented**), see LOUVERED

**'vert**, *n.* Any convertible model automobile.

**vertical-valve Buick**, see NAILHEAD

1969 BIG-BLOCK STINGRAY **'Vette**

**'Vette** *n.* Any Chevrolet Corvette model as produced from 1953 to the present day. The most commercially successful sports car in history, CHEVY's Corvette has experienced myriad significant styling and performance variations throughout its long production run. Though continually evolving, the Corvette's sporty two-seat configuration, fiberglass (see 'GLASS) body construction, and overall commitment to PERFORMANCE have remained constants. Significant and milestone Corvettes include: **a.** The limited-production first-year 1953 model, powered by a 150-BHP triple-CARBed STRAIGHT SIX (CHEVY's SMALL-BLOCK V8 [see MOUSE] would not arrive until 1955); **b.** The innovative 1957 model, featuring the performance breakthroughs of an optional four-speed manual TRANNY and mechanical fuel injection (see FUELIE, Definition 1); **c.** The 1963 introductory Sting Ray model with its one-year-only SPLIT WINDOW (Definition 1) COUPE design; **d.** The legendary BIG-BLOCK-powered Stingrays (shortened from "Sting Ray" beginning in 1969) of 1965 through 1974; **e.** The twin-turbocharged (see TURBO) "Callaway" 'VETTES specially prepared for CHEVY from 1987 to 1991; **f.** The 1990 through 1995 ZR1 models with 4-CAM, all-aluminum V8 power; and **g.** The sophisticated and powerful 2001 through 2003 Z06 Corvettes with the single-CAM LS6 V8 producing up to 405 NET HORSEPOWER. With their greater initial purchase price, significant STOCK PERFORMANCE options, and inherently exotic styling, Corvettes are less frequently modified by RODDERS than other contemporary models. 'VETTES nevertheless have long experienced moderate favor as the foundations for personalized STREET MACHINES and CUSTOM CARS. While interest in the customizing of Corvettes dates to the 1950s, the popularity of 'VETTE RESTYLING peaked during the 1970s. Integrating all of the STREET MACHINE and STREET FREAK trends of the period, 1970s-era STREET and show 'VETTES were commonly treated to FENDER FLARES, crushed-velvet interiors, and flamboyant paint schemes.

**'Vette Vega**, see V8 VEGA

**Vicky** (also **Vickie**, **Vick**, or **Vic**) **1.** *n.* Any Victoria model passenger car as produced by the Ford Motor Company during the 1930 through 1934 model years. The Victoria was configured as an intermediary between contemporary COUPE and SEDAN models and featured a full-width front bench seat and abbreviated rear seating to accommodate "occasional" passengers. The relatively rare VICKYS have long experienced moderate favor in hot rodding and especially street rodding applications. **2.** *n.* Any early-vintage, non-Ford passenger car designated as a Victoria model.

1932 FORD **Vicky**[1]
STREET ROD

**vintage tin 1.** *n.* Any original, vintage automobile body or auto body panel (as distinguished from a modern reproduction of any type). **2.** *n.* Any complete, early-vintage automobile or group of early autos. Term is most often used to describe vehicles modified in a STREET ROD style.

**Volksrod** *n.* Unique adaptation of the popular FAD-T STREET ROD type, featuring a traditional air-cooled "flat-four" Volkswagen engine in place of the more conventional American V8. As with most FAD-Ts, the typical kit-based VOLKSROD employed a fiberglass (see 'GLASS) reproduction 1923 Model-T (see T-BONE) ROADSTER BUCKET as its main body structure. The VOLKSROD differed, however, by a specially designed replica pickup bed serving to cover its rear-mounted engine. A custom sheetmetal hood was also unique, enclosing the forward space normally occupied by the standard T-BUCKET's engine and offering a desirable closed storage area not available to most T-BUCKET models. VOLKSRODS (or alternately V-RODS) experienced moderate popularity during the late 1960s and early 1970s, when they were touted for their reliability, economy, and practicality.

EARLY-1970S **Volksrod**

**Von Dutch 1.** *n.* Celebrated artist and cultural icon Kenneth Howard, the self-proclaimed "originator of modern pinstriping." The son of a sign painter, Howard was raised in the Los Angeles suburb of Maywood. While working as a motorcycle mechanic during the mid-1950s, VON DUTCH (his newly acquired alias) began experimenting with highly elaborate and innovative freeform pinstripe motifs. His exciting new work created a sensation, establishing a style that continues to the present day. In addition to his legendary striping, VON DUTCH was well respected for his talents as a fabricator, gunsmith, and custom knife-maker. VON DUTCH died in 1992. **2.** *n.* Any pinstriping executed in the style of Kenneth "VON DUTCH" Howard. **3.** *v.* To render or create VON DUTCH-style pinstriping. Example: "I'm really gettin' the itch to VON DUTCH the DECK LID."

**Von Dutch**[2] STRIPING

**V-rod**, see VOLKSROD

# W

**waffle head**, see LUMPY HEAD

**wail**, see HAUL

**walk** someone *v.* To defeat an opponent in a DRAG RACE by pulling steadily and consistently ahead. To "walk away" from a slower vehicle.

**walk into** the throttle (also **walk on** the throttle) *v.* While DRAG racing, to fully depress a vehicle's accelerator pedal but to do so in a slow, measured fashion in hopes of avoiding excessive wheelspin and thus recording a lower ET.

THE NHRA's **Wally** TROPHY

**Wally** *n.* The National Hot Rod Association's (see NHRA) official winner's trophy, as first awarded in 1969. Formally designated "Man and Wheel," the WALLY's bronze-finished sculpture represents a fire-suited race driver standing beside a DRAG SLICK-shod wheel. Actual DRAGSTER driver Jack Jones was recruited to model for NHRA photographer Leslie Lovett, with the resulting images worked into a final design by Chicago's American DRAGWAY Trophy Company. In the tradition of nicknaming significant awards with an individual given name (Oscar, Tony, Emmy, etc.), the "Man and Wheel" trophy has come to be called the WALLY after renowned motorsports personality Wally Parks (born 1913). Parks has contributed immensely to both hot rodding and DRAG racing as one of the SCTA's original 1937 organizers, first POSTWAR SCTA president, chief organizer of the first HOT ROD BONNEVILLE speed trials in 1949, *HOT ROD* magazine's first editor, and founder and first president of the NHRA in 1951. An avid racer as well, Wally Parks drove the second (rear-engined) Burke/Francisco BELLY TANK from 1947 through 1949 and in 1957 established a NASCAR experimental-class speed record while piloting the *Hot Rod Magazine Special* Plymouth Savoy HARDTOP across the sands of Daytona Beach, Florida.

**Wayne** (also **Wayne twelve-port**) **1.** *n.* High-performance cylinder head (see HEADS) designed and initially produced by Wayne F. Horning as an AFTERMARKET complement to the inline Chevrolet six-cylinder engine. Unlike the STOCK CHEVY SIX's HEAD, which featured an inefficient SIAMESED port design, the WAYNE HEAD included one intake and one exhaust port per cylinder, or a true TWELVE-PORT configuration. The WAYNE HEAD also incorporated a "cross-flow" design with intake ports on its left side and exhaust ports on its right side (STOCK engines crowded both on the left). The WAYNE HEAD was introduced during the late 1940s, making the venerable STOVEBOLT SIX a formidable PERFORMANCE alternative to the more common FLATHEAD Ford V8 and achieving a high level of popularity in a variety of racing applications during the early 1950s. **2.** *n.* Any complete high-performance Chevrolet engine equipped with a WAYNE TWELVE-PORT HEAD.

**W-block**, see LUMPY HEAD

**Wedge** (also **Wedge motor**) **1.** *n.* Any of Chrysler Corporation's BIG-BLOCK B and RB Series V8 engines as produced during the 1958 through 1978 period. (Note: Although the 426 HEMI is based on an RB BLOCK, it is not considered a WEDGE MOTOR by virtue of its distinctly different HEAD design.) The B and RB engines' WEDGE name describes its combustion chamber shape and has been popularized, in part, to differentiate it from the concurrently produced Chrysler HEMI. MOPAR released WEDGE MOTORS in CID variations of 350, 361, 383, 400, 413, 426, and 440. **2.** *n.* Any engine featuring wedge-shaped combustion chambers.

**wedge channel** *n.* Any channel body modification (see CHANNELED) performed in such a way as to lower a vehicle's body in an uneven or slanted manner (most often dropped more deeply over the front of the vehicle's frame). A WEDGE CHANNEL typically serves to accentuate a vehicle's RAKE.

**wedge chop** *n.* Any chop body modification (see CHOPPED) performed in such a way as to lower a vehicle's roofline in an uneven or slanted manner (either sloping forward toward the front or backward toward the rear of a vehicle).

wedge chop ON
1967 CADILLAC HEARSE

**weedburners** (also **weedcutters** or **weedsweepers**) *n.* Exhaust system consisting of separate individual tubes extending downward and generally rearward from each engine exhaust port. Name is inspired by the fact that exhaust is released to a vehicle's side and relatively close to ground level. Commonly used in late-1950s through early-1960s DRAGSTER applications, WEEDBURNERS were effectively replaced by ZOOMIES during the mid-1960s.

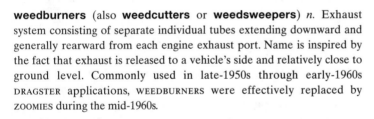
LATE-1950S ERA
**weedburners**

**weekend warrior** *n.* An amateur or hobbyist DRAG RACER. Term derived from the open GRUDGE RACES and BRACKET RACING programs commonly held at sanctioned DRAGSTRIPS on weekends.

**weenie roaster** *n.* Any jet or rocket-powered DRAG (see JETSTER) or LAND-SPEED RACING (see JET) vehicle.

**weight transfer** *n.* Any DRAG racing vehicle's rearward shift of "sprung" weight during hard acceleration. In a rear-wheel-drive vehicle (the traditional DRAG racing configuration), the natural transfer of weight under acceleration can work to great advantage; with more effective weight on the driven wheels, a vehicle's traction properties, and thereby DRAG performance, are strongly enhanced.

**weirdo** (also **weirdo character**) *n.* Any highly stylized and grotesque "monster" caricature, usually relating to youth-oriented culture (hot rodding, surfing, skateboarding, etc.) and significantly popularized during the 1960s. Artist, HOT ROD builder, showman, and cultural icon Ed "Big Daddy" Roth

**weirdo**
1963's MR. GASSER™

(1932–2001) is generally credited with initiating the WEIRDO/monster phenomenon. During the late 1950s, Roth began airbrushing gruesome and bizarre figures on T-shirts and sweatshirts, selling his products at fairs, car shows, and via mail order. As his business grew during the early 1960s, WEIRDO iron-on "decals" and silkscreened shirts replaced Roth's hand-painted designs. By the mid-1960s, a multitude of Roth characters were mass-produced in Revell-brand model kit, T-shirt, collector card, decal, beach towel, and even record album forms. A partial list of Roth's colorful WEIRDO CHARACTERS includes: DRAG NUT, Surfink, Mother's Worry, Angel Fink, Mr. GASSER, Chicken Shift, Superfink, and Scuz Fink, as well as his most popular and enduring creation, RAT FINK. Roth's substantial success naturally inspired others to enter the WEIRDO market. During the early 1960s, MONSTER/WEIRDO SHIRTS were made available from a number of sources, significantly including CUSTOMIZER and painter Dean Jeffries, pop-artist Stanley Mouse, and cartoonist Pete Millar. In 1962, even Barris KUSTOM City offered "krazy" and "wayoutsville" dye-screened monster sweatshirts at $3.50 each. Similarly, the Aurora, Monogram, Lindberg, and Hawk plastic-model companies each produced variations on the theme (Hawk's "Weird-Ohs" series characters were described as "car-icky-tures" and inspired their own Mercury-label record album released in 1964). Popularized in large part by children and teenagers, 1960s-era WEIRDO CHARACTERS were decidedly and deliberately irreverent but seldom overtly vulgar.

**weirdo shirt** *n.* Any T-shirt or sweatshirt adorned with a WEIRDO caricature and produced from the late 1950s through the1960s. Though WEIRDO-type shirts have been sporadically available to present, the WEIRDO SHIRT term has not been commonly applied since the 1960s.

**Westergard style**
1936 FORD COUPE

**Westergard style** *n.* Early and important CUSTOM CAR style as originated by renowned Sacramento, California, bodyman Harry Westergard. A highly skilled tradesman, Westergard developed a unique mixture of customizing elements that some argue gave birth to the LEAD SLED era. The WESTERGARD STYLE was most often applied to 1936 Ford COUPE or ROADSTER models and typically included: CHOPPED top, Packard or LaSalle grill, replacement hood sides (either solid, custom-LOUVERED, or including 1934 Pontiac vents), DeSoto RIBBED BUMPERS, FENDER SKIRTS, and 1940 Chevrolet headlights molded into the front fenders (STOCK 1936 Ford headlights were mounted separately above the fenders). Originating during the late 1930s, the WESTERGARD STYLE experienced its greatest popularity throughout the 1940s. Westergard directly and significantly influenced a number of younger Sacramento-area CUSTOMIZERS who strived to imitate his style and craftsmanship. Among them was a young George Barris, who apprenticed with Westergard during the early 1940s. Westergard died in an automobile accident in the mid-1950s.

**whacked**, see CHOPPED

**whale** (also **whale motor**) *n.* Any Chrysler Corporation-manufactured EARLY HEMI engine as produced for the 1951 through 1958 model years. The type's considerable size and weight accounts for the WHALE nickname.

**wheel** *v.* To drive any race car in competition. Term most often used in reference to circle-track racing. Example: "The revered Kurtis Kraft midgets were WHEELEd to many victories in the POSTWAR period."

**wheelbase** (also **wheel base**) *n.* In any motor vehicle, the measured distance between the precise center of the hub on a front wheel and the center of the hub on the same-side rear wheel.

**wheelie** (also **wheeley** or **wheely**) *n.* Less formal and highly popular version of the term WHEELSTAND.

**wheelie bars** *n.* Custom devices (traditionally two separate metallic bar assemblies) extending backward from the rear portion of a DRAG racing vehicle and employing one or more small casters close to the track's surface. WHEELIE BARS function to keep the front of a DRAG vehicle on or near to the track surface during extreme WEIGHT TRANSFER.

**wheels**, see SET OF WHEELS

**wheelstand** *n.* The occurrence of a DRAG racing vehicle's front wheels lifting clear of the track surface due to extreme WEIGHT TRANSFER. Generally occurs from a standing start at the outset of a race.

**wheelstander** *n.* Any DRAG racing vehicle purpose-built to produce extreme and prolonged WHEELSTANDS, sometimes lasting the entire quarter-mile length of a race course. WHEELSTANDERS are typically not competitive, class-based racers, but rather exhibition vehicles performing sideshows between legitimate racing ROUNDS. The type was introduced during the mid-1960s by popular vehicles like the *Hurst Hemi Under Glass* BUBBLE-BACK BARRACUDA and *Little Red Wagon* Dodge A-100 compact pickup truck.

wheelstander
THE *LITTLE RED WAGON*

**wheels up** *adj.* Relating to a DRAG racing WHEELSTAND. Example: "If we lower the tire pressure any more, we'll be asking for a seriously WHEELS UP LAUNCH."

**wheel tubs** *n.* Custom cylindrical sheetmetal (generally aluminum) housings serving to surround exceptionally large rear tires. WHEEL TUBS are featured in place of STOCK panels when tire/wheel mass encroaches into the interior space of a vehicle. The use of WHEEL TUBS is closely tied to the PRO STREET movement of the 1980s.

**wheelwell headers**, see FENDERWELL HEADERS

**wheezer**, see BLOWER

**When you snooze you loose.** Generally 1960s-era expression emphasizing the importance of a good REACTION TIME at the outset of a DRAG RACE. If a driver is CAUGHT NAPPING (snoozing) at the light, his or her chances of winning the race are dramatically reduced.

**whitewall slicks** *n.* Any early DRAG racing SLICKS featuring a pie-crust design and white sidewalls. Experienced strong popularity in DRAG RACE, show car, and, sometimes, HOT ROD applications during the late 1950s and early 1960s.

**wide whites** *n.* Any whitewall tires featuring an especially wide sidewall color band.

**wiggly rearend** *n.* Any automotive independent REAREND assembly. Term is derived from the type's "flexible" or non-rigid mode of operation. An independent REAREND isolates each rear wheel's suspension action with an elaborate system of half-shafts and universal joints. Advantages of the independent REAREND over a conventional solid axle include improved handling and ride. Independent REARENDS are also favored solely for their distinctive, exotic appearance (when adapted to HOT RODS, components are often chrome-plated and/or highly polished to reflect and scatter light while in operation). Standard equipment on all Chevrolet Corvettes (see 'VETTE) from 1963 to the present day, WIGGLY REARENDS experienced strong popularity in street rodding applications during the 1970s and have maintained moderate favor since.

**wind** (also **wind** an engine **tight** or **wind** an engine **up tight**) (WINED) *v.* To REV an engine to an exceptionally high RPM level.

**winder** *n.* Any high-performance engine producing its maximum horsepower at an unusually high RPM level.

**'winder,** see SIDEWINDER

**windmill,** see BLOWER

**wind out** (WINED) *v.* To REV an engine to its maximum practical RPM level, beyond which power levels decrease or mechanical failure may occur due to over-revving.

**window mags** *n.* General expression for any AFTERMARKET MAG WHEELS produced with "windows" or slots in their surfaces. Windows may be provided for lightening, brake cooling, and/or appearance enhancement.

**window the block** *v.* To significantly damage an engine's cylinder block (see BLOCK) as a result of a major BOTTOM END mechanical failure. A BLOCK is said to be "windowed" when one or more of its connecting rods (see RODS) break through its external surface, creating holes or "windows." Windowed production-type BLOCKS are generally discarded, but expensive AFTERMARKET racing BLOCKS are often repaired when possible. Some racing BLOCKS incorporate removable side panels that may be completely replaced if damaged in use.

**wind the piss out of** an engine (WINED), see PISS WIND

**wing** an engine *n.* Any automotive GROUND EFFECTS SPOILER, but most often referring to a horizontal rear DECK SPOILER mounted on vertical pedestals.

**wing** *v.* In a racing application, to "free-rev" an engine as the result of a missed shift, broken driveline component, etc. If normal load (i.e., vehicle propulsion) is instantaneously removed from an engine while in a full-throttle condition, the motor's internal components are often seriously stressed and/or damaged as a result.

**winged warrior** *n.* Any 1969 Dodge Charger Daytona or 1970 Plymouth Superbird (see 'BIRD) AERO WARRIOR PERFORMANCE car. MOPAR's WINGED WARRIORS were named for the exotic 25-inch-tall rear airfoils that each carried above its rear DECK lid.

**win going away** *v.* In any DRAG RACE, for a competitor to defeat his opponent by steadily extending a lead through the finish line.

**wires** *n.* Any automotive wire wheels. Various forms of STOCK and AFTERMARKET WIRES were virtually standard equipment on the HOPS UPS and GOW JOBS of the PREWAR period. Solid steel wheels (see STEELIES) came into PERFORMANCE vogue in the late 1940s, effectively replacing the earlier WIRES in lakes (see the LAKES) and hot rodding applications. On the DRAGSTRIP, purpose-built RAILS commonly employed exceptionally narrow front WIRES (often adapted from motorcycle usage) from the late 1950s through the mid-1980s. From the mid-1970s through the mid-1980s, chromed AFTERMARKET wire wheels (most notably of the Tru-Spoke brand) experienced strong popularity on contemporary STREET RODS. In CUSTOM CAR applications, the Kelsey-Hayes WIRES (see KELSEYS) FACTORY-available on select 1950s- and 1960-era domestic models have since been adapted to a variety of STREET and SHOW CUSTOMS, while AFTERMARKET wire wheels have long been popular ROLLING STOCK on LOWRIDERS. Traditionally, a small-diameter wheel (oftentimes 13-inch) has been favored with LOWS, but during the early twenty-first century, large-diameter (typically 20- to 22-inch) WIRES have gained in popularity. Modern LOWRIDER WIRES are commonly finished in chrome or gold plating, or sometimes a combination of both.

**wishbones** *n.* Any automotive radius-rod assembly with suspended locating points affixed near axle ends and at a single, centrally mounted chassis locating point. The component's "V" shape consequently resembles a chicken's breastbone, or wishbone. WISHBONES were featured as FACTORY equipment on the early Ford passenger vehicles so commonly modified in a HOT ROD or STREET ROD style.

**W-motor**, see LUMPY HEAD

**woody** (also **woodie**) **1.** (also **woody wagon** or **woodie wagon**) *n.* Any vintage station wagon model automobile featuring a primarily wooden body structure. While somewhat similar in overall configuration to early SEDAN models (long roof extending to the rear of the vehicle), WOODIES differ substantially by their construction and intended function. Typically,

1947 FORD **woody** WAGON

**237**

the wagons manufactured before and during the late 1940s featured fully wooden body SHELLS, with only ancillary components (floor pans, bracketry, cowl sections, FRONTENDS, etc.) being produced in steel. The presence of rear-access tailgates as well as spartan interior layouts reflect the type's intended purpose of hauling light freight and passengers. Since the 1950s, WOODY station wagons have been closely associated with California surfing culture, with many STOCK and often somewhat dilapidated vehicles being used for transporting surfers and their equipment. During the 1960s, WOODIES (most desirably 1929 through 1948 Fords) were commonly modified in a STREET ROD style, representing a blending of the then closely associated surf and HOT ROD cultures. WOODY STREET RODS maintained moderate popularity throughout the 1970s and 1980s followed by a strong resurgence of favor during the late 1990s and early twenty-first century. Note: The term "station wagon" was originally coined in reference to the type's frequent use for hauling passengers and baggage to and from train stations. **2.** *n.* Any automobile featuring wooden exterior panels or cladding for aesthetic enhancement.

**Woody car**
LATE-1960s WOODY DRAGSTER

**Woody car** (also **Woody dragster**) *n.* Any DRAGSTER chassis as fabricated by Gar Wood "Woody" Gilmore. Prominent and influential from the mid-1960s through the mid-1970s, WOODY CARS were known for their innovation and strong performance. Gilmore's revolutionary components and features included ZOOMIE-type exhaust HEADERS, saddled chassis uprights, and extreme frame flex (see FLEXI-FLYER). Along with Don Long-built DRAGSTERS, WOODY CARS were further distinguished by their extended-WHEELBASE design during the late 1960s. By the early 1970s Gilmore had begun adapting his talents to the construction of cutting-edge FUNNY CARS.

**worked** (also **worked over**) *adj.* Modified for improved performance. Term may relate to virtually any automotive component or system, but is most often used in reference to a high-performance engine.

**wrench** *n.* Any automotive mechanic.

**wrench on** *v.* To perform mechanical work on any vehicle or automotive component. Example: "I really need to get out and WRENCH ON the CHEVY if I'm gonna be ready for next Sunday's GRUDGES."

**wrinklewalls** (also **wrinklewall slicks**) *n.* Any DRAG racing SLICKS featuring exceptionally pliable sidewalls and employing very low air-pressure levels. During a DRAG LAUNCH, the type's sidewalls tend to severely deform or "wrinkle" to maximize their traction. Variations have been the standard design in all-out DRAG competition from the late 1960s to the present.

# X

**X** *n.* Any Plymouth GTX model. Introduced for the 1967 model year, the GTX was an upscale, luxurious PERFORMANCE car based on Plymouth's intermediate Belvedere line. Throughout its production, the GTX featured a high-performance 440-CID engine as standard equipment, as well as the optionally available 426-CID HEMI. (By mid-1969, buyers could also choose a SIX-BARREL version of the 440.) Although the GTX name was later carried on as a subseries of the Plymouth Road Runner model (see BIRD), production of true GTXs ceased after the 1971 model year.

**X-body** *n.* Official corporate designation for any of several small-car models produced by General Motors during the 1960 through 1970s MUSCLE CAR era. Although the 1970s-era Pontiac Ventura, Oldsmobile Omega, and Buick Apollo were each based on the common GM X-BODY platform, in a PERFORMANCE context the X-BODY term is most often used to describe Chevrolet's Chevy II/Nova models (see DEUCE, Definition 2).

# Y

**yank the frontend** (also **yank the front wheels**) *v.* In any vehicle, to perform or experience a WHEELSTAND.

**Y-block 1.** *n.* Overhead-valve V8 engine type as produced by Ford Motor Company for the 1954 through 1964 model years (Ford's Lincoln division offered a slightly different Y-BLOCK from 1952 through 1957). Name is derived from the engine's lowered block skirts extending well below the crankshaft's (see CRANK) centerline. When viewed from the end, the BLOCK's shape appears more as a "Y" than as a "V." Interestingly, Ford actually referred to its Y-BLOCK engine as a "Y-8" rather than the more conventional V8 in mid-1950s advertising. Although the Y-BLOCK design is generally not considered viable in high-performance applications (due to its heavy weight and relative inefficiency), Ford did create several PERFORMANCE versions during its production run. Standouts include a 312-CID dual-QUAD variation FACTORY-rated at 270 BHP, and a Paxton-supercharged (see BLOWER) 312 rated at 300 BHP (both for 1957). **2.** *n.* Any V8 engine with lowered block skirts.

**'Years** *n.* Any tires produced by Goodyear (Goodyear Tire and Rubber Company).

# Z

**Z** (also **Z-car**) *n.* Any Camaro Z-28 high-performance PONY CAR model. Introduced in 1967, the Z-28 subseries was originally released to HOMOLOGATE an SCCA Trans-Am racing package. (True to its road-racing origins, the Z-28 has consistently represented a well-balanced PERFORMANCE machine, emphasizing handling and braking as well as straight-line acceleration.) In pre-production, the name "Cheetah" was considered for the new PERFORMANCE-oriented Camaro, but Chevrolet eventually settled on their in-house option number, RPO (Regular Production Option) Z-28. The Z-28 experienced a long and distinguished run as the premier all-around PERFORMANCE Camaro, until ultimately being retired, along with the rest of the Camaro line, after the 2002 model year. Z-28 production was interrupted twice during its lengthy history: at the height of the 1970s emissions era (1975 to early 1977) and during the late 1980s when the Z-28 name was briefly suspended and Chevrolet's hottest PONY CARS were referred to as IROC Camaros (after the popular International Race of Champions series).

**Z'd** (also **Zee'd** or **Z-notched**) *adj.* Relating to any automotive frame that has been altered with "kick-up" at one end so that the modified segment in profile view resembles the letter "Z." The process serves to raise that portion of the frame above the front or rear suspension components, thereby lowering the body and chassis of the vehicle.

**zing**, see WING

**Zingers 1.** *n.* Series of scale-model car kits produced by MPC (Model Products Corporation) during the early 1970s. ZINGERS featured reasonably accurate scale representations of actual car bodies teamed with ridiculously out-of-proportion engines and tire/wheel combinations (bodies were scaled at 1/43, while engines were featured in 1/20 scale). ZINGERS inspired show promoter Bob Larivee to contract for larger interpretations to be displayed on his International Championship Auto Shows circuit featuring full-scale, actual automotive engines and ROLLING STOCK combined with approximately half-scale auto bodies. **2.** *n.* As a byproduct of the popular model series and SHOW RODS, the term ZINGER is sometimes used to describe an actual vehicle bearing the exaggerated, outrageous character of the original ZINGERS.

*SUPER VOLKS* SHOW **Zinger**

**zoomies** *n.* Highly popular DRAG RACE exhaust system consisting of short, separate tubes sweeping rearward and upward from each engine exhaust port. In DRAGSTER applications (where positioned immediately forward of rears tires), ZOOMIES provide traction-enhancing downforce and rear-tire debris cleaning. Before the mid- to late-1960s developments of slipper clutches and improved tire technology, ZOOMIES were also favored for their ability to dissipate excessive tire smoke, allowing for better driver visibility. ZOOMIES have remained the dominant exhaust design in most supercharged (see BLOWER) racing applications to the present.

MID-1960S ERA **zoomies**

# Numbers

**'09** (oh-nine) *n*. Any Chevrolet 409-CID, W Series (see LUMPY HEAD) V8 engine. Produced beginning in 1961 and replaced by the 396-CID RAT MOTOR during the 1965 model year, the 409 achieved significant PERFORMANCE success despite its inherent handicaps of poor breathing and inefficient combustion-chamber design. FACTORY 409 development peaked during the 1963 and 1964 model years, with the high-compression, solid-CAM and dual-QUAD-equipped BIG-BLOCKS producing an advertised 425 BHP. The popular Beach Boys surf-rock band immortalized CHEVY's '09 with their mid-1962 recording titled simply "409" (see HOT ROD MUSIC). The song's lyrics pay homage to a "four-speed, dual-QUAD, Positraction (see POSI) 409," a clear reference to the ultimate-performance 409-BHP version of the 409 as produced for the 1962 model year.

**1320** (thirteen-twenty) *n*. A general reference to any DRAGSTRIP, the most common length of such a course being one-quarter mile or 1,320 feet. Example: "Can't wait to see what it'll do in the ol' 1320."

**2 Club**, see 200 MPH CLUB

**2+2** (two-plus-two) *n*. Model designation for any of several 1960s-era PERFORMANCE cars featuring front BUCKET SEATS along with rear seating for two additional passengers. Significant examples of the type include the Ford Mustang 2+2 FASTBACK COUPES (see 'STANG) of 1965 and 1966 and the Pontiac Catalina-based 2+2 (see CAT) of 1964 through 1967. As was the case with Pontiac's highly successful GTO (see GOAT), Pontiac "borrowed" the generic and uncopyrighted 2+2 name from Ferrari. The Italian manufacturer first used the designation with its Pininfarina-designed 250 model in 1960 and continued to distinguish its four-seat models as such throughout the American MUSCLE CAR decade.

**21-stud** *n*. Early Ford FLATHEAD V8 engine, produced for the 1932 through 1938 model years. Name derived from the 21 studs securing each HEAD to its cylinder block (see BLOCK). Though sometimes used in 1930s- and 1940s-era PERFORMANCE applications, the 21-STUD was largely overshadowed by the improved Ford and MERC 24-STUD FLATHEAD.

**24-stud** *n*. Late Ford and Mercury FLATHEAD V8 engine, produced for the 1939 through 1953 model years. Name derived from the 24 studs (or, after 1948, bolts) securing each head (see HEADS) to its cylinder block (see BLOCK). The 24-STUD was a significant improvement over the earlier 21-STUD engine and is consequently the preferred base in PERFORMANCE applications.

**200 MPH Club** (also **two club** or **2 club**) *n*. The BONNEVILLE 200 MPH CLUB, originally founded with five members in 1953 as the *HOP UP* Magazine 200 MPH CLUB (after the organization's first sponsor).

Through the years, the club has grown steadily and now even includes a 300 MPH chapter. To qualify for membership, a competitor must break an existing speed record of more than 200 miles per hour or an established class minimum speed over 200 miles per hour.

**³/₈ x ³/₈ flathead** *n.* Popular FLATHEAD Ford V8 engine type, featuring an increased displacement for improved PERFORMANCE. By stroking a STOCK, 4-inch Mercury crankshaft (see CRANK) by ¹/₈ inch, the resulting STROKE is ³/₈ inch longer than that of a STOCK Ford CRANK. When the STROKED MERC CRANK is installed in a 239-CID Ford BLOCK and the BLOCK is, in turn, BORED ³/₁₆ inch to 3³/₈ inches, the resulting engine yields a large, by FLATHEAD standards, 296 CID.

**3-window** (also **3W**), see THREE-WINDOW

**350/350** (three-fifty, three-fifty) *n.* Any 350-CID, SMALL-BLOCK Chevrolet V8 engine mated to a GM Turbohydramatic 350, three-speed automatic transmission. The 350/350 combination has long been favored in street rodding applications for its low cost and practical function.

**440-6** (also **440+6**) (four-forty-six or four-forty plus six) **1.** *n.* Any high-performance 440-CID engine produced by the Chrysler Corporation and FACTORY-equipped with an induction system comprising three TWO-BARREL carburetors (see CARB). Chrysler produced this ultimate iteration of its venerable 440 for the 1969 through 1971 model years. Known alternately as the 440 SIX PACK (Dodge) or SIX-BARREL (Plymouth), the 440-6 peaked at 390 BHP with 490 ft-lb of torque, making for an excellent STREET performer and a practical alternative to the more expensive and temperamental STREET HEMI. **2.** *n.* Any complete automobile produced by Chrysler Corporation and featuring a 440-6 engine.

**5-window** (also **5W**), see FIVE-WINDOW

**'59 Cadillac bullets**, see BULLETS (Definition 1)

**'92** (ninety-two) *n.* Any 392-CID HEMI engine as produced by the Chrysler or Dodge truck divisions of the greater Chrysler Corporation. Initially released for the 1957 and 1958 model years, the 392 represented the final and most powerful iteration of MOPAR's EARLY HEMI V8 line. When powering the revered Chrysler 300 luxury/PERFORMANCE cars (see LETTER CAR), the massive 392 produced as much as 390 BHP in pure STOCK trim. While the engine's FACTORY performance was impressive for its day, it was in modified form that the 392 achieved its legend status. From the late 1950s through to the early 1970s, the efficient and durable 392 was strongly favored in maximum-performance, nitromethane-fueled (see NITRO) DRAG racing applications.

**97s** (ninety-sevens) *n.* Any Stromberg (see STROMIE) Model 97 TWO-BARREL carburetors (see CARB).

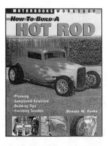